THE WINGS OF PEGASUS

THE WINGS OF PEGASUS

THE BATTERY PRESS
NASHVILLE

First U.S. Edition 1982 by
The Battery Press, Inc.
P.O. Box 3107, Uptown Station
Nashville, Tennessee 37219 U.S.A.
Fourteenth in the Airborne Series
Originally published in Great Britain by
MacDonald and Co. (Publishers) Ltd.

ISBN: 0-89839-060-5

PRINTED AND BOUND IN THE U.S.A.

FOREWORD

It is entirely fitting that this book, the story of the Glider Pilot Regiment, should be written by the man who created and commanded the Regiment during the last war. It tells of the birth pangs and later the achievements of a unit which consisted of soldiers trained to fly by the Royal Air Force, who were destined to pilot their comrades of the Army into battle, and then to join them in the fighting on the ground. This dual rôle required the highest standard in the individual, the ability to work with and thoroughly understand the technique, training and language of two Services, and to be acceptable and integrated with both.

The fact that the raising and training of the Regiment was achieved in so short a time was largely due to the imagination, the foresight, and the inter-Service knowledge of the Commanding Officer.

The author, Brigadier George Chatterton, had the advantage—which he sets out in the early chapters—of being trained as a Naval cadet at Pangbourne, then to become a fighter pilot of great ability, and finally to gain experience in the Army when commanding a Company in an old and distinguished Regiment of the Line. Because of this background he was ideally suited to undertake the task of creating a Regiment which was to play a vital part in the organisation of Britain's first airborne forces.

To anyone like myself, intimately concerned with the creative period and its fulfilment, the story is of absorbing interest, but the same should hold good for all those readers, and there will be many, who read this history of the Glider Pilot Regiment, and so come to learn of its early days of frustration owing to lack of aircraft, the difficulties it overcame, and the formidable success achieved. Seldom has any unit of any arm or Service attained such a peak of efficiency and made such a name for itself as the Glider Pilot Regiment in its all too short life.

It is good to know that the standards of the Regiment, and its esprit de corps, will be carried on by the Army Air Corps, and its traditions perpetuated in the Flying Arm of the Army of to-day.

F. A. M. BROWNING.

MAY, 1962.

AUTHOR'S NOTE

DURING the year 1941 the German Army committed their Airborne Forces, including a small glider force, to the assault on the island of Crete. After this, the German Airborne Army was never used in strength again, owing to the huge casualties it sustained.

A little later in that year two British Horsa Gliders were towed over Norway, to attack the German Atomic Plant there. The glider pilots and the military load were never seen or heard of again. Hardly a promising baptism for British Airborne Forces.

In 1942, however, the Glider Pilot Regiment was established by the War Office, perhaps the most unique military organization conceived. The personnel were all qualified pilots—yet fully organized, trained and equipped to fight in all and every capacity on the ground.

This is the story of the Glider Pilot Regiment. It contains my own adventures in building it up and leading it, based on my own diary and notes and accounts contributed by a number of individuals who took part.

My grateful thanks are due to Messrs. Gollancz for permission to quote material from *Lion With Blue Wings* and to Mr. Ronald Seth, the author of that book. Also to the many gallant glider pilots who contributed their own individual accounts of the actions in which they were involved. I must add to this my sincere thanks to the editor of the *Eagle*, the Regimental Magazine, for permission to reproduce material from its pages.

CONTENTS

LIST OF PLATES

1

THE ROYAL AIR FORCE . . .
AND THE ARMY, 1930-39

THERE were four of us in the railway carriage: Zulu Morris, a South African, Tubby Mermagen, myself, and one other whose name I have now forgotten. We sat in the four corners of the carriage looking out of the windows and surveying the flat, drabness of the scene outside. We were on our way to a school to learn the first rudiments of flying.

There were forty of us on the train, all between the ages of nineteen and twenty-five, some of us still green from school, some of us sporting our senior years of twenty-three or four with a solemn air of knowing the lot—particularly about women.

In our suitcases and trunks were our brand new uniforms: tunics, trousers, breeches, puttees, white shirts with stiff and soft collars, Service caps and, above all, our mess kits comprising monkey jackets and overalls, with short Wellington boots, stiff shirts and collars. Secretly, we could scarcely wait to wear them!

The train began to slow down and Tubby Mermagen, glancing at his watch, said: "This is it; we've arrived." An officer in uniform greeted us on the platform—Sleaford, I think it was—and ushered us into three lorries. I remember that well for they were cold and uncomfortable and the only view was from the back, but at last we arrived at the hutted camp, and as we jumped down we saw in the fading gloom the dark shapes of hangars, within which stood the aircraft we hoped to fly on the morrow.

Next morning was bitterly cold as we taxied out to take off, and in the aircraft I sat tense with excitement, never taking my eyes off the back of the instructor's head. He seemed to me to be a god and the machine a Leviathan. And what a machine! The Avro 504. Today, it is almost impossible to think that this aircraft was ever meant to fly. A biplane, a left-over from the 1914-18 war, it was still the basic training aircraft of the Royal Air Force in 1930. It was all wires, wood and fabric and sported a radial engine, yet no aviator could have been more excited than I. (I don't believe excite-

1

ment ever changes in a man, it is only conditions that change.) The pilot turned into the wind, looked left and right and opened up. With a hollow bumping and the noise of the engine revving up we sped across the grass, lifted once, and then rose into the air, I was flying! No moment of my life has, or will ever be, the same as it was at that moment, except, perhaps, when I eventually flew solo.

In the year that we were there, 1930, the school taught us to live. The flying was everything, but with it went mess life and all that it entailed. It was one of the customs—to encourage comradeship—for the Senior Course to try to throw the Junior Course out of the ante-room. It was a battle royal watched by the instructors, and I do not think anything brought us more together than that first night brawl.

We lived on £4 5s. a week, which saw us through everything, including our mess bill, which was never less than £2 10s. a week, leaving us 35s. to play with—and play we did!

Of course, everything revolved around the flying. We did six months on the Avro, then six months on Service types, as they were then known. It is incredible to think that as late as 1930 these Service types were still to be seen: such aircraft as the Bristol Fighter, used in 1917, thirteen years before, and the twins Vinny and Virginia—also antiques. Yet nothing will compare with those wonderful old aeroplanes, rolling and bumping their way across the airfields. The beauty of them to us was unsurpassable, and I remember one of my friends, Ned Harman, saying: "You know, George, when I first flew solo in a Bristol Fighter I was so overjoyed and thrilled that I felt that I should be paying the Air Force for the privilege of flying rather than that they should be paying me."

And that put the views of all of us in a nutshell.

Quite a few killed themselves, and their belongings were auctioned in the billiards room. We were quite callous about it. I remember one brilliant pupil who crashed and was killed. He had gone solo in six and a half hours—a unique effort—and promised a brilliant future, but he succumbed to the over-confidence that is never far away from the flyer. Perhaps, one day when he was feeling over-exhilarated, he started to dive and aerobat, showing off to people on the ground, until, eventually, the machine flew too low, hit the ground and burst into flames. I mention this because there was an unwritten "warning" in the Air Force that there were three danger points in flying: the first twenty-five hours, the first hundred hours and, finally, the first five hundred hours. Each of these was recognized as a danger point at which a man could kill himself through over-confidence and the belief that he knew all the answers. In fact, *all* the answers can never be found in flying.

All that I learned at the flying school was to stand me in good stead some thirteen years later in an entirely different environment. At Digby I was taught to fly in a fashion second to none. I was taught the discipline required, the importance of always keeping my eyes open, particularly around the airfield, and I was taught personal discipline, for we were paraded every day with rifle and bayonet and were drilled ruthlessly. Even though I was taught to fly on an outmoded aircraft, I maintain that I and my friends had to fly all the better because of it, for we had few instruments—no radio or contact with the ground—and so learned to be entirely reliant on eye, brain, and quickness of thought.

As I emerged from that year I had, in my 200 hours flying, flown all the old dead and finished aircraft, and I count myself lucky, for I had behind me all the experience of my predecessors; I knew exactly what they had gone through in defeating the German Air Force in 1914-18. I also emerged with my wings. I emerged a man, disciplined on the ground and in the air and, strangely enough, completely trained for the rôle I was to take over in 1943, for the air training required one to land with the throttle back and to glide in, and he who opened up was laughed at, for he had "rumbled"—always a source of embarrassment. Looking back, the training I received had been tailor-made for my future, thought neither I nor those who trained me could have appreciated this.

From the elementary school of flying I was sent to the Central Flying School to be trained on fighter aircraft. This was, at the time, the Mecca of flying, for here the instructors were taught to *instruct* and the finest aviators in the world were on the staff.

How well I remember Tubby Mermagen and I arriving at Wittering, and our intense excitement. I can still taste the superb food in the mess, the complete sense of relaxation, and the almost astounding nonchalance of the staff and the pupil instructors. The Commandant of the Central Flying School at that time was the great "Mary" Coningham who made such a name for himself later in the Second World War.

At Wittering, perhaps the most remarkable part of the day was between 1 p.m. and 2 p.m., when the Air Ministry waived all rules and limits. In that hour I saw breathtaking aerobatics that I shall never see again: aircraft inverted, upside-down flying, dives which knocked the petals off the rose trees in front of the mess, slow rolls terminating at heights less than fifty feet from the ground, all exhilarating and exciting. The weeks I spent there have left an indelible impression on my mind. Even the local pubs such as the Haycock, just outside Stamford, still spell romance to me, especially the frolics with the girls in the pubs.

And so we passed from training to squadron life. Tubby and I were both posted to R.A.F., Tangmere, Tubby to No. 43 Squadron and I to No. 1 Squadron. Side by side, there we were, still fast friends. I was to live in the mess at R.A.F., Tangmere, for some years, and it was here that all I had learnt about flying was to be developed.

The two squadrons consisted of four flights of four aircraft with an establishment of some fifteen pilots in each squadron. For most of the time I was there we were equipped with single-seater Hawker Furies—superb aircraft. We were classified as interceptors, and each week the Battle Flights were permanently at the ready, fuelled and armed, and patrolled the South Coast at 30,000 feet.

There were three R.A.F. squadrons equipped with Hawker Furies, and a fierce rivalry raged between them. They were No. 43, No. 25, and No. 1, in which I served. No. 25 was stationed at R.A.F., Hawkinge, in Kent. In all aspects of life this rivalry was apparent. Although we were outwardly friendly, inwardly the antagonism never left us, which, of course, encouraged intense competition and raised the standard of flying to great heights.

I remember a memorable occasion when I was a Flight Commander. I was selected to represent my Squadron in the R.A.F. Champion Battle Flight Competition, which entailed a number of operations such as camera-gun shooting or intercepted aircraft, rapid rearming of guns and refuelling. It also included turnout of men, machines, tools and armament. Each squadron was represented by a flight, and the three squadrons were running neck and neck, everything depending on the tools inspection. My flight gained success and the Championship Cup, mainly because the Flight-Sergeant had sat up all night polishing the tips of every tool in the equipment.

At about this time another incident created fierce rivalry. It was during the waiting period while squadrons were being allotted the parts they were to play in the R.A.F. Display at Hendon. No. 25 Squadron had made a great name for itself the year before—when they were equipped with Armstrong Siskins, a cumbersome fighter —by performing a squadron loop, that is, the three flights looped in squadron formation. We were all wondering if this same exhibition would win them the laurels in the forthcoming display.

One beautiful day, when we were lounging outside the mess at about 12.30 p.m., there was a sound of aircraft overhead and, as always, our heads turned skywards. "My god, look at this. It's a flight from 25 Squadron," cried an indignant voice. As we gazed into the clear blue sky three silver Furies, with the markings of 25 Squadron on them, approached in a slight dive and then, to our amazement, lifted their noses slightly, went up and rolled right over —an aerobatic we had never seen before. We stood transfixed as they repeated the performance, and then, looping twice, turned and sped off home in the most impertinent fashion. There was a continual buzz of indignation at lunch, and that afternoon the sky was filled with aircraft in flights of three attempting the aerobatics they had seen performed by 25 squadron! I was eventually to become an expert in this type of flying, and I cannot forget those early attempts, for we were far too proud to go over to Hawkinge to find out how to do it. The laugh was finally on 25 Squadron, for they were left out of Hendon that year and we were chosen to represent the aerobatics. The *pièce de résistance* was the flight roll which they had invented. How they must have cursed the three "show-offs" who had come over to see us at lunchtime that day.

I was selected to do the individual aerobatics, performed in unison with another pilot, Sergeant Wroath. But later I was given a much more exciting job—to visit Canada and tour the major cities there in flying demonstrations. This flight consisted of four pilots and was under the charge of Wing-Commander George Pirie, who later became an Air Chief Marshal. We went out by boat with our aircraft in crates, landed at Montreal, where we were stationed at St. Hubert Airport, and where our Hawker Furies were put together before we started our tour of Canada.

Flying in 1934 was in the doldrums, as Canada had been severely hit by the 1929 slump. At St. Hubert there was an old station mast of the ill-fated airship R101, and the airfield hangars and offices were in tatters, grass growing from the roofs, and rust everywhere.

B

We lived under canvas and really had the most delightful stay.

Of course we were a great draw to the Canadians, whose heart and spirit, in aviation, had been laid low. In those days the U.S.A. had few aircraft to compare with ours, and we had the fastest level-flight aircraft in the world. We could climb to 32,000 feet in eight minutes and cruise at over 200 m.p.h., which in 1934 was no mean feat.

By now the four of us had become completely expert in formation and individual aerobatics and there was little that we could not do either in a flight or singly. We looped, rolled, rolled off the top— that is, a half loop and then a roll off the top, never attempted before. We dived line astern, then the leader lifted up in a great climb, the two behind climbed higher on either side of him and all three completed the loop in line abreast.

Perhaps one of the most exciting experiences of all this tour was demonstrating, with Flying Officer Willie Donaldson, an exhibition of individual aerobatics. This was performed in front of a huge audience at Quebec. The scene was set in front of the famous Heights of Abraham, some 300 feet above the St. Lawrence. We dived right down into the valley and demonstrated our rolls and loops on the level of the audience, probably a unique bit of flying, and, as Willie said afterwards: "I bet that shook them rigid!" Which I am quite sure it did.

It was all a wonderful experience that contributed towards building up progress and efficiency as a pilot. For some six months we rolled and looped round Canada and then returned home to continue our duties as interceptors of the Royal Air Force.

It was about this time that my destiny was re-directed. It came about through the culmination of a series of accidents. One morning my Flight Commander and I decided to make a practice interception. This entailed climbing to some 30,000 feet, seeking a single aircraft and attacking it. I remember climbing into the cloudless sky and watching the target aircraft, which had flown up with us, break away at 25,000 feet. We were then over Guildford. We reached our decided height and began looking for the target aircraft, but although we searched endlessly we could not find him and decided to return to base. Some time later we heard the sound of an aircraft and there was our target machine making a circuit of the airfield. Landing, he walked over to us (I remember his name was Sergeant Wragg) and said: "At what height and at what place and time did I leave you, Sir?"

I answered: "At 09.45 hours, at 25,000 feet over Guildford."

His face was pale, and with an anxious air he said: "Well, all I can tell you is that I blacked out and came to over Littlehampton at 5,000 feet and that was at 10.20 hours by my watch."

We looked at him incredulously, walked over to his machine and examined the oxygen equipment. There seemed to be nothing wrong with it, though we examined and tested it carefully. Later that day another pilot took up Wragg's machine. Some time afterwards we heard the ominous scream of an engine in a power dive, and in the distance saw him diving straight for the earth. It was all over in a second. There was a great crash and a cloud of black smoke, and then nothing.

When the retrieving squadron eventually arrived at the aircraft its nose was twenty feet in the ground and the pilot—well, he had just disintegrated. It was finally decided that probably a washer had become loose and that his oxygen had leaked just enough for him to become unconscious, as Wragg had done, but unluckily for him the aircraft had dived straight to earth.

As a result of this accident I had to make a test to see just how far one could go before becoming unconscious. I climbed to 22,000 feet before I realized that I was being affected, and then trimmed the aircraft so that it would fly itself. I then proceeded to lose my full senses and dived the aircraft until I regained them. I found it was like being very drunk, a feeling I had experienced once or twice in the mess 22,000 feet below! It least we were pioneering, and something was learnt from this experience.

It was a few days later that the accident which was to affect the whole of my life occurred. It was on a morning when the sky was filled with great white clouds, and we took off as a flight of three to practise aerobatics and general flying. It was an intoxicating day for flying and I can remember, as we climbed up thousands and thousands of feet, the clouds, superlative and spotless, towering above us as the sun shone from a blue sky beyond them.

We flew in and out of the clouds for some time until the leader gave us the signal to fly line astern. This we did, each stepped down one below the other. My place as second in command was beneath the leader, and young Anderson, a Pilot Officer, behind me.

We flew on and eventually we were led into a great cloud. I lost position, and as I could not see the leader I broke away and climbed up over the clouds. From there I spotted Anderson, who was streaking after the leader, and I joined in, taking the last place, rather reluctantly, I remember. Then we proceeded to fly on, the leader quite unaware of the goings-on behind him.

Climbing again we were confronted by a huge black cloud, and as we approached this, Anderson broke away to the left and I to the right. I climbed again and noticed that my height was about 8,000 feet. Then, beneath me, at something like 5,000 feet, I saw the leader. I could not see Anderson anywhere, so I decided to dive down and take up formation in my original position behind the leader. I remember the air speed mounting as I descended—200, 220, 250, 280, 300 m.p.h.—and was drawing closer, trying to catch up. Suddenly there was a loud twang, a rending of fabric, and I received a sickening blow on the head. Anderson and I had collided. I can remember little, except that it seemed the earth was where the sky ought to be and vice versa. I crossed my arms and released my straps but at first I was unable to get out. Only by kicking and struggling did I eventually succeed in falling out of the cockpit and into the air below, my parachute opening and leaving me dangling in the harness. Looking down I could see that it was over Lancing College with the River Arun and the sea far away to the left. What I could also see were some high tension wires, towards which I seemed to be drifting. Panicking, I pulled at the parachute strings but I only seemed to side-slip nearer to the wires, so I snatched at the other side and swung away. Now I was swinging just as a child might on his garden swing. Slowly I descended to earth, but at the last moment my parachute swung in the air and collapsed, and I hit the ground and lost consciousness. When I came to I had the most agonizing headache and a pain in my back, but I managed to get up and walk up the side of the downs. Climbing the steep chalk path, I found the two crashed aircraft deep in the ground. Alas, Anderson hadn't managed to get out and was killed instantly. Indeed I was very lucky to be there at all for I was told that we had been locked together for thousands of feet, and only at a lower height had the aircraft parted and enabled me to fling myself out to safety.

This accident had a most depressing effect on me for, at the enquiry, one of the examining officers suggested that it might have been my flying back into position that had caused Anderson to make a mistake. I was completely exonerated of this, but the doubt had its effect on me, and I became haunted by the possibility that I should have waited. My headaches increased and I became a prey to insomnia. Although I was X-rayed, nothing showed on the plates, so I continued to fly.

One evening I went out for a jaunt with some friends and we drank rather a large quantity of beer. Without warning I became like a man possessed—with a sense of revulsion for everything and everybody. The next thing I remember was standing on the wall of Little-hampton Harbour with an intense desire to jump into the darkness and the waiting sea below, but at the moment when the urge became unbearable I was heaved backwards, and I can still hear a voice shouting: "What the hell do you think you're trying to do?"

The next day I was stopped flying, ordered to see the Medical Officer and informed that I should be required to have a medical examination. This I did, and I was ordered to the R.A.F. Hospital, Uxbridge, with what was termed "delayed concussion". One of the officers in the medical ward was Douglas Bader who was there after having had his legs amputated as the result of an accident some months before mine. We knew each other, having been in Fighter Command together.

Later, when the hospital seemed satisfied that I was convalescent, they allowed Douglas Bader and me to go out together. He had just received his legs (tin ones, officers for the use of) and wanted someone to accompany him on a jaunt outside the camp.

We visited a café called Pantowers, where subsequently he met his wife, but my recollection was Douglas's insistence on playing clock golf. It is hard to imagine a man with greater courage than Douglas Bader, for here he was out on two tin legs for the first time, and immediately wanting to play a game. He did it, and to this day I can still see the sweat of pain and effort pouring down his face as, without any sure contact with the ground, he balanced himself and putted round the course—and he beat me into the bargain!

Later we both went to the movies. I remember so well sitting in the front row of the dress circle. Suddenly Douglas put one leg up in the air like the mast of a ship to adjust the nut at the knee, which kept it stiff. After a while the lady behind said rather irritably: "Do you mind moving your leg, sir, I can't see properly."

And so the time passed, with headaches and insomnia and terrible depression. I finally saw a remarkable doctor who sat me down in his consulting room and said: "Look here, you see this sheet of paper. Well, I am going to divide it into two and I shall shade one side. That shaded side is your subconscious mind. Now, I am going to make a dot—like this." And he made a dot in the shading.

"This," he continued, "is something you do not like or want to think about; and the longer it is there and the more it is sat on the larger it grows, until it comes over into the clear half of your conscious mind—and all hell is let loose!"

He looked at me and said: "Now I suggest this dot is in you, in this crash, so for three days a week I shall talk to you, and you to me, of nothing else but the crash. Question and answer. Do you see? And then suddenly you will be freed."

We did—and I was.

Looking back on those years I feel that I was very fortunate to have had such a wonderful experience. I had the privilege of growing up with many splendid "types", who were to prove of immense worth in the coming years. Small as the Air Force then was, it was second to none, and its standard was remarkable, both in aircraft and men, but few realized how little money was expended on it.

At that time Sir Philip Sassoon, an immensely rich man, was the Under-Secretary of State for Air. It was said that the entire budget for the Air Force was equivalent to Sir Philip's fortune of fifteen million. And how much we owed to this man, strange as he was. It was his foresight in encouraging the Royal Auxiliary Air Force that finally enabled it to fulfil its purpose in the Battle of Britain. Sir Philip entertained lavishly and owned three magnificent houses: one at Lympne, near Hythe, one in London (25, Park Lane), and a beautiful house called Trent Park. I stayed at all these houses and they were packed with treasures of all kinds. He only entertained officers—no ladies—and to refuse to accept his invitation was to incur his wrath. I am convinced, now, that in those weekends he was taking stock of the material of which the Air Force was made. In some way I think he knew what was to come, the frightful challenge that was appearing on the other side of the Channel, the building up and recovery of the German Air Force.

In this conviction I am left with a clear memory of two significant factors in the R.A.F. story. The first was the realization that by 1934 Germany not only had parity with the Royal Air Force but had already passed it in total number of aircraft; and that they had already begun to stock-pile, in large numbers, all and every necessary spare part. This information had been in the hands of the Government for some time but had been held back for some inexplicable reason. It burst upon the British public like a bomb, exploded, in fact, by Mr. Baldwin in the House of Commons.

The second significant factor was the review of the Royal Air Force by George V in 1935. It is said that up to that time he had not shown much favour to the Royal Air Force, but one Sunday, as he was passing Bircham Newton, an R.A.F. station, on his way to Sandringham, Her Majesty Queen Mary persuaded him to go and look around. The station was caught by surprise, for nearly all the personnel were on week-end leave. Neither the guard commander nor the orderly officer would believe the equerry when he announced that the King was at the gate. However, they were persuaded that George V was there and hurriedly arranged a conducted tour of the station. The aircraft on this station were pretty antiquated, and it is said that this visit inspired the King to demand a Royal Review of the Air Force—the first of its kind.

I should think that must have made a horrid impact on the then rulers of this country. I took part in this Royal flight, and the fact that the entire Air Force was able to fit on to one airfield—Mildenhall—showed up our appalling weakness as an air power. Perhaps even more significant was the fact that the bombers who led the Air Force in the fly past had a top speed of ninety miles an hour. This in 1935! However, mercifully, the Air Force received a rejuvenating injection and was able to expand at a rapid rate.

Shortly afterwards I came to the end of my time in the Air Force. It was the training I received during this period and the high standard of flying on which the Service insisted, that later enabled me to assume command of the Glider Pilot Regiment.

I was retired to the Reserve of Air Force Officers. The years passed. At the time of Munich I was recalled—but with a difference; I was informed that I had been put in category C—ground duties. Dreading this, I asked if I could be transferred to the Army, as I felt I could be more active there than that of Administrative Officer on the ground, which, to me, was abhorrent. Thus, I found myself transferred to the 5th Battalion of the Queen's Royal Regiment—the Royal West Surreys—and gazetted as a Lieutenant to an infantry battalion, which was to be the third stage of the experiences which prepared me for what lay ahead. When I say third stage, this was in fact, my third taste of Service life, for I had been, before my service in the Royal Air Force, a Naval Cadet at the

Nautical College, Pangbourne! I mention this because it held a true significance for me.

The Nautical College at Pangbourne had originally been founded by Devitt and Moore—a shipping company—to boost the ever-increasing demand for officers in the Merchant Navy, also the Royal Navy. It had a full charter from the Admiralty of Royal Naval Reserve, and the cadets were patterned accordingly. I joined this college in 1925 and endured the full rigours of the Naval Cadets life. I slept in a hammock in a dormitory with thirty-five other boys, and I learnt how to lash up and stow my hammock in the most seamanlike manner. I paraded nine times a day and we lived in "terms" of thirty-five cadets, commanded by a Cadet Captain. Each House had a Chief Cadet Captain and over all was the Chief Cadet Captain of the College.

It is true to say that in this environment I learned the essentials of man management, and eventually I became Chief Cadet Captain of the College and King's Cadet.

Thus I had behind me basic training in severe discipline from the age of thirteen, and had added to it the discipline of flying. Now I was called upon to satisfy the demands made on both Platoon Commander and Company Commander in the British Army. The experience was to prove of prime importance.

The Queen's Royal Regiment had great traditions. Founded in 1661, it was originally the bodyguard of the Queen to Charles II, and had a long tradition of fame and service all over the world. It had a distinctive background in that it was one of the last regiments of the line to serve in ships, to be superseded by the Royal Marines, and it still shows the Naval Crown in its badge. This was to suggest something to me later, as will be seen.

It is said that one of the finest commands in the world is that of the Platoon Commander, for he is responsible for human beings, and each of the men is in some way his personal property. If the young officer obtains the confidence and respect of his platoon, he becomes, in effect, their father, and if he is to get the best out of them he must seek out everything that will encourage that respect, and thus produce the perfect fighting machine. Discipline and military training are not enough—not wholly anyway. It is imperative to know the men backwards, their temperaments, their loves and hates, their family life, and their misfortunes and inspirations. I learnt this thoroughly, and I was not to regret it.

In those early days at the end of the peace and the beginning of the conflict of 1939, our military knowledge and training were antiquated, being based on the First World War. Equipment was sparse, and what there was of it was sorely needed by the regular battalions, who must be the first in the line of battle. Mine was a Territorial battalion, manned by enthusiasts of every walk in life, and we quickly learned by our mistakes.

Some time before the outbreak of war my company was concentrated in the Farncombe drill hall, and we all thought that the Germans were on the move and might be in the Isle of Wight at any moment. But that excitement died down as the days drew on towards a formal and "polite" declaration of war. At once we expected massive air attack—and gas at that.

The entire 5th Battalion was housed in a country mansion at Nutfield, owned by a wealthy man who had never reckoned on 600 men living in his house. I slept in a room with fifteen officers and each room from top to bottom had an average of thirty men in it. The damage was formidable, but hardly surprising, for no door in a house is designed to be opened and shut at least ten times a minute or the stairs to suffer 1,200 hobnail boots endlessly tramping up and down them. Later we moved to Sherborne School, where we were dispersed among the Houses, and we remained there training for some time. It was from here that I made my first abortive visit to France as a member of the British Expeditionary Force.

Without warning I found myself posted overseas, and I arrived at Cherbourg on a very, very cold morning in 1939. On arrival I was informed that I had been attached to the 3rd Battalion, The Grenadier Guards, on the Belgian frontier. The winter was intensely cold, and when I arrived at the headquarters of the battalion in a small chateau, I felt that I was back in 1914-18. The atmosphere was incredibly the same. The battalion was one of a Guards Brigade, not far from Lille, and it was dispersed round some new fortifications facing Belgium. These represented an utter waste of time, for they were to be over-run in a matter of hours when the Germans advanced into Belgium and France in 1940.

It was significant that the battlefields of 1914-18 were all around us and the old scars could still be seen. The walls of the cottage in which I was billeted still bore the marks of the old Prussian Guard. These circumstances influenced the attitude of northern Frenchmen to the whole aspect of the later conflict, which the following incident illustrates.

The headquarters of the Grenadiers was in a small chateau, as I have said, and the owner had been squeezed into one of the wings. One Sunday morning the Commanding Officer invited the Frenchman in for a glass of sherry before lunch. The man—I remember he had a greying beard—had a bitter, hard and despairing expression. I must say that the Colonel was not gifted with tact, and his remarks made me blush with shame.

"Well, monsieur," he said, " I see from the markings on the wall of the chateau that you had the old Prussian Guard here, and now you have the British Grenadier Guards. How do you like it?" The Frenchman raised the glass to his lips, answered: "Monsieur Colonel, I see no difference!" and walked out. He certainly left an indelible impression on me, if not on the Colonel.

This was during the "phoney" war of 1939—and phoney it was. It was difficult to believe that there was really a war on and that it was not a vast training exercise. Once there was a false alarm and we began to enter Belgium—only to beat a hasty retreat when we learned it was a mistake in the signal and that we were in grave danger of infringing Belgian neutrality. If there was ever a farce it was this "phoney" war.

I returned to England after a few weeks but shortly was back again in France with my own battalion, this time Second in Command of a company, which gave me considerable experience in the feeding of soldiers and the general background of man-management and administration.

When we landed at Cherbourg we were immediately informed that we were to take part in a march of 150 miles in four days, apparently with the object of trying to draw the Germans into Belgium. I had never marched more than about twenty miles in my life, so I found it quite an experience, both marching forty miles a day in full battle-order and in keeping up the morale of the men, few of whom had ever marched any distance at all.

One of the rules in the Queen's Royal Regiment was that the men came before everything. On Major route marches, at the end of each day no officer was permitted to unbuckle a button on his equipment or to read or to lie down or sit until all his men had been fed, their feet inspected, and they had been bedded down for the night. I was to make use of this rule later, when I had the task of forming a regiment.

I had hardly been with my battalion more than a week when, once again, I was sent back to England, this time to attend a course at the R.A.F., Old Sarum, with the object of becoming an Air Liaison Officer because of my Air Force background. The appointment, however, fell through, and instead I was posted to the depot of the Queen's at Guildford where I learned the importance (and impotence) of depot life. The situation was unusual in that the depot was completely unarmed and had to borrow rifles from the armoury of the Charterhouse School O.T.C. But as least I learned the immense value of *esprit de corps,* for the C.O. was a martinet and did wonderful work in maintaining all the major traditions of the depot.

I was eventually posted to the 2nd/7th Battalion, the Queen's Royal Regiment, at Faversham in Kent. This was a typical Cockney battalion, most of the men having been recruited from the East End of London. The battalion was completely unequipped at this time, which was 1940, and when the men stood-to at night to resist invasion, it was necessary to borrow rifles from the Home Guard in order to man the posts fully. After "stand down" at dawn the rifles were handed back to the Home Guard!

Later we were posted to the beaches, and here our arms were even more ludicrous. It was a blessed miracle that the Germans did not know the deplorable state of the British Army, for they would have had little difficulty in getting ashore.

In my company I had two guns, 6-pounder calibre, mounted on Austin-10 chassis. The guns had come from the tanks of the war of 1914-18. My rightful platoon was in the Dymchurch Redoubt, well known to holiday-makers. I also had another platoon farther down the beaches. One day I was informed that a gun would be placed in the Redoubt, and along the road came a building contractor's lorry carrying the gun. It was a huge naval gun, which had been dug up from the grave in which it had been interred after the Disarmament Convention of 1922. It fired solid shell as well as solid shot, and we mounted it, as ordered, on the Dymchurch Redoubt. As I visited the posts at night, walking in between the minefields, I often looked out to sea and thought to myself: Just how long can we last? Was it all a farce or a fearful dream? We were not ready to meet a full-scale attack because of our defeat and loss of arms at

Dunkirk, and because of the neglect of our forces between the wars. Luckily, the invasion never came and we were spared the humiliation we might have experienced—thanks to the men of the Battle of Britain, who "dissuaded" the Germans from attacking us.

A few months later my battalion was moved to the Eastern Counties before going overseas, and it was now that fate really took a hand. I was, at this time, not very happy in the battalion, and was frustrated and bored with infantry life. One evening, bending down to the waste-paper basket for a piece of paper to light my pipe, and finding a piece, I opened it. My eye happened to catch an advertisement which read: "Volunteers for the rôle of Glider Pilot." I read further, and with deepening interest, and found that I was eligible to volunteer as a pilot, and possibly to become second in command of the new battalion of the Glider Pilot Regiment. I immediately rang up the Adjutant and asked if it was too late to volunteer. The answer was: "Today is the last day. You can just get your application in."

That action was to change completely the whole of my life in the Army. Here I was, a fully-fledged pilot, with considerable experience of soldiering in the practical sense and in the field. And here was something new, to be formed and developed into a really worthwhile command, which required just this combination of qualities. I was on the threshold of a new career and I could feel it in my very bones.

2

BIRTH OF THE GLIDER PILOT REGIMENT

IT WAS exceedingly cold and snow lay everywhere. My train pulled into Salisbury Station at 8.35, and as I stepped on to the freezing platform I was full of anticipation and excitement. Jumping into a jeep that had been sent to collect me I turned up the collar of my greatcoat and sat back waiting for the cold drive ahead—and indeed it was cold. The wind blew through the jeep, making my eyes run, and the set expression of the driver, who was obviously frozen too, warmed me that conversation was not to be encouraged.

We drove out on to Salisbury Plain along the Amesbury Road, where, in the distance, I saw Old Sarum and reflected on my last visit there and how I had failed to become an Air Liaison Officer I fell to wondering what this next adventure might hold. Driving on through the lanes, we came to the edge of a snow-covered airfield—Royal Air Force, Netheravon—then turned down a lane to enter the drive of a small Georgian house. This was the headquarters of the newly-formed Airborne Division and the seat of command of Major-General "Boy" Browning.

I jumped down from the jeep and entered the house. It was charming, old-fashioned, and had panelled walls. It had been denuded of furniture, which had been replaced by the fittings customary in all houses taken under military command. On the floor was the usual coconut matting, and odd chairs and tables were everywhere. Yet there was a distinct and exciting atmosphere—something new?

I reported to the G.S.O.1, Colonel Walch, who motioned me to a chair. "Please sit down. The General will see you in a moment."

I looked at the door and wondered what sort of man sat in that room, how he would receive me, and if he would accept me as one of his officers. After a pause the bell on the Colonel's desk rang and he got up and disappeared. There was the usual silence, punctuated by the beating of my heart, and I wondered if the staff officer was describing me and my appearance. Indeed, I had taken

17

a great deal of trouble in the early morning to make myself look smart. Soon the door opened and he came out and, without so much as a glance in my direction, sat down again and went on with his work. My nervousness increased and I began to feel awkward and ill at ease. Again the bell rang, and again he went to the door, my eyes followed him as he disappeared inside the office. A few minutes later he came out and said curtly: "Major Chatterton, General Browning will see you now," his steel-blue eyes catching mine. "Will you step this way."

I marched into the room and moved up to the desk. Saluting in my best barrack-square fashion I stood stiffly to attention, my blood pounding in my ears. Looking down at the man in front of me, I saw a thin face with darkish hair brushed backwards; a well-trimmed moustache lined the top lip. The lips were firm, the body slight but athletic. I noticed that his uniform was beautifully cut and that his regimentals were those of the Grenadier Guards. The Sam Browne sparkled and shone, and a thin gold chain hung from the upper pocket. A row of medals lined the breast, and I espied the D.S.O. leading. The desk was spotless and neat, and two delicate and well-manicured hands lay on the pad in front of him.

"How do y'do. Take a chair and for God's sake relax, I'm not going to eat you," I heard him say. "Thank you, sir," I replied, and drew up the chair beside where I stood.

"Well, what do you want to join the Airborne Division for?" he asked, looking keenly at me.

"Sir, in the first place I have been a pilot," I replied, "and as a result it attracts me enormously."

"I see you have R.A.F. wings. When were you with them?" he asked.

"I joined in 1930, sir."

"Oh! Quite a long time ago," he said, looking a little surprised. "Did you have much experience?"

I told him of my life as an R.A.F. pilot and all that lay behind me, and he listened intently. I told him that I felt that I was equipped for this "unknown" job and that this was because I had had the good fortune to wear both uniforms, that of the R.A.F. and of the Army, which I felt gave me a dual capacity.

He listened and then said: "I have already selected a Second-in-Command and he has gone up to Derby to learn to fly, with the Commanding Officer, Colonel Rock."

My heart sank, for by now I felt I could not bear life unless I was able to become an officer in the Glider Pilot Regiment.

"However, I do think you have very good reasons for me to consider you in some capacity. I will give it my consideration. Come and have a drink in the mess."

Thus I met "Boy" Browning for the first time, and fell under his spell as everyone did. Just how closely we should be linked in building up the Airborne Forces, I could not then know.

As I was sitting fumbling with my hat and gloves in front of the General commanding the 1st Airborne Division, the fate of the German effort in this form of warfare was, in fact, being settled, and it is incredible to think now that we, the British, were only about to begin building up an airborne army, while the Germans had reached the point where, unknown to us, they were abandoning theirs because of the heavy casualties in Crete and the resultant drain on their crack troops.

A few weeks after the interview with General Browning, I received a telegram informing me that I had been selected Second-in-Command to Lieutenant-Colonel Rock, 1st Battalion, The Glider Pilot Regiment, and that I was to report to Salisbury Plain where I would take over the new depot, Tilshead, which was to be the Training Depot of the regiment. I arrived there on a bitterly cold afternoon, with Alec Gaul, my batman. The camp was situated near Devizes on an old artillery range and was no more than a cluster of wooden huts of early vintage.

Standing in the empty hut which was to be my orderly room, I felt cold and nervous. It was most uninviting, and I could not imagine how this empty wilderness could ever act as an inspiration to one of the most unusual regiments that the Army had ever conceived. The passages rang with the sound of my footsteps, and I felt that the ghosts of many military figures were lurking in the shadows, resentful of my presence. The wind howled outside and the naked electric-light bulbs cast a hard glare on the dismal scene. Yet I experienced a strange feeling of hope. Here, perhaps, was the chance of a lifetime, despite all the external evidence to the contrary.

All round Netheravon the various units of the new Airborne Division were gradually collecting: Parachute Brigades, one Heavy Glider Brigade, and the 1st Air-landing Brigade. It was this last-named brigade, and supporting arms, which we hoped to carry in the gliders that we were to pilot. The main airfield was that of

R.A.F., Netheravon, which embodied the headquarters of No. 38 Wing, Royal Air Force, and was a famous landmark in R.A.F. history.

I was informed that the first force of 300 glider pilots would arrive in three weeks and that, in the meantime, I would receive a skeleton staff to assist me. It was then that I sat down to think out what I was going to do with these men, and what approach would be best to give them inspiration. I thought deep and long, visualizing, by calling on my past experience, the rôle each man would have to play in an invasion and the problems he would have to meet, not only to survive but also to become an effective unit in a fighting force. First, I assumed that flying a glider on tow must impose a severe strain on the pilot, a strain that would in no way be alleviated by the knowledge that on landing in the battlefield there would be no prospect of an immediate return.

Now, I knew that on landing, after flying a power aircraft for a long time, there is an overwhelming desire to relax completely and to sleep. Such facilities are available for pilots landing at an air station; but, I asked myself, what would happen to the pilot who landed in the middle of a battle? In addition to being a first-class pilot he would need to be possessed of a deep sense of responsibility since the lives of the fully-armed troops transported in his glider would be dependent on his skill, determination and courage. On top of this, on making a landing on the target, in the twinkling of an eye he would have to transport himself from a highly-trained pilot to an equally highly-trained and courageous soldier. Were we, was I, expecting the impossible? I thought not, but I had no illusions as to the complexity of the task ahead.

I came to the conclusion that I must fall back on experiences of the past: what I had learned in my days at Pangbourne as a Naval Cadet; the basic training necessary to make a pilot in the early stages of flying; my more recent experiences as a Company Commander in The Queen's, which convinced me that I would be wise to tackle the whole scheme on the lines of the depot at Guildford, where I had been an instructor.

As soon as I had arranged for the usual domestic details of the camp to start, I asked for an interview with General Browning, to explain my views. The interview being granted, I pointed out that since, in the glider pilot, we would be trying to create a very special dual character—a highly-trained soldier as well as a skilful and

No. 1 Fighter Squadron R.A.F.

The Prime Minister talking to Major-General F. A. M. Browning, Commanding
Airborne Division.

resourceful pilot—such men could only evolve from a regiment possessed with a strong sense of *esprit de corps*. "And," I added, "to achieve this goal, sir, I feel that I must have the very best N.C.O.'s as instructors; if possible from the Brigade of Guards, for I feel that this should be the basis of our inspiration."

The General looked at me and said without hesitation: "You will most certainly need the very best that can be got and I will deal with it at once."

And so Company-Sergeant-Major Briodey of the Irish Guards and Company-Sergeant-Major Cowlie of the Coldstream Guards arrived at my camp at Tilshead. As I write now, I can still visualize the scene, and feel the excitement of it. I can hear the stamp of these two young men as they marched into my cold office. Briodey— tall, thin and erect; Cowlie—huge, dark and handsome.

"Good morning," I said to them in greeting.

"Good morning, sir," they answered in unison, after the magnificence of their salute. The Guards had arrived—irrevocably. That morning I told them of my plan to create the Total Soldier—the complete man, in the military sense and in the sense of a pilot.

"You see, I have had the good fortune to be both pilot and infantry soldier, and I am quite certain that to fulfil this job we must create in the men a basic discipline which they can fall back on once they have left the aircraft. I am sure that this originates on the parade ground and in the barrack hut. Therefore, once the man has mastered the knack of being smart in himself, proud of his regiment in bearing and turnout, the rest will follow. I am asking you to instil into them all what you have learnt in your own regiments, the Irish and the Coldstream Guards. It will not be easy for you or for me, and neither of us will be popular, for the volunteers will have come from all and every unit, with varying points of view as to the application of discipline. They will also have volunteered to fly and will regard square-bashing as thoroughly ridiculous. *But,* I think otherwise.

"As soon as the first batch of men arrive," I continued, "I want you to make it clear that only the highest standard of bearing and discipline will be tolerated in this camp. It is an appalling place, where morale can easily slip. Let us make it into something worth while and really try to inspire the men."

The warrant officers looked at me seriously and I knew that my words had not fallen on deaf ears.

C

The following morning the first batch of officers and men arrived. They were, indeed, a very mixed lot, from every regiment in the British Army, with experience of every kind of discipline. How the Army could have tolerated such varied forms of dress I don't know, and many were not even clean, physically or otherwise, let alone their uniforms. The phoney war and Dunkirk had certainly taken their toll, for one could see the signs of deterioration which always follow in the track of boredom and lack of inspiration.

It was an amazing experience, for confronting me was a potted history of the British Army. The Cheshire Regiment, the Irish Guards, the Queen's, the East Surreys, the Royal Artillery, the Royal Engineers, the Hampshires and the Sussex Regiments. In fact, nearly every unit of the Army ever conceived. With them came the good, the bad, and the indifferent. Good-tempered, Bolshie, rude, casual and kind—and all adventurous, even if a great many were only looking for a change. Nevertheless, they were just the material for this remarkable experiment—the making of the Total Soldier.

As soon as Briodey and Cowlie had sorted them out I told them to gather the men in the N.A.A.F.I. In the meantime I had a large map of the world prepared, and on it I marked the various parts of the world we had lost up to that time, but it also showed how we had developed the British Empire.

I got up on the stage and addressed them as follows: "You have all come here as volunteers—not quite clear what you have volunteered for, but at least it has the tang of adventure in it.

"You also are the first to form the Glider Pilot Regiment, a regiment without history or tradition, and at a time when we have experienced a series of bad defeats all over the world." And at this point I pointed to the map.

"This being the situation in the moment of defeat, we will forge this regiment as a weapon of attack, but in order to do so we will have to find inspiration. Now we consider ourselves to be unique in that not only will we be trained into pilots but also we will have to fight on the ground. Therefore we must be *total*—in all and everything. We shall fly, master all infantry weapons, drive tanks, jeeps and trucks. We shall learn to command and obey, use wireless sets, to receive and send. In fact there is nothing we will not train ourselves to do.

"But in order to do this we must instil in ourselves the highest form of discipline and *esprit de corps*. We will therefore look to the example of our ancestors. I make no apology for asking you to remember men like Raleigh and Drake. I think it appropriate at this grim moment, to remind you of the achievements of the Cromwellian Ironsides, who, in a short time, came to be regarded as the finest soldiers in Europe, of the Army of the Peninsula's victory over Napoleon, and the remarkable quality of the Contemptible Little Army whose 100,000 men held up a million. This is the tradition which you inherit, and which is represented in the various cap badges that you wear.

"In the matter of discipline we will take the lead from Sergeant-Majors Briodey and Cowlie of the Brigade of Guards, and this shall be our pattern of behaviour. Remember that it is by the self-discipline which we learn now that we shall stand or fall in the future. Of this I am sure.

"Let me repeat that I make no apology for talking to you like this. May I add that I shall be quite ruthless. Only the best will be tolerated in loyalty and discipline, apart from anything else. If you do not like it then go back whence you came—it would be far better."

I do not even apologize now, for after all that has happened I know that I was right, notwithstanding much criticism.

Briodey and Cowlie set the highest standards. Many fell by the wayside and could not, or would not "take it." Many grumbled. The R.A.F. laughed and criticized, but I refused to alter my views. I was even railed at by politicians, and called a Fascist; and an investigation was started. I was informed that one man who had failed to make the grade had complained to his M.P. who, in turn, asked a question in the House of Commons.

One day I was told that an officer from the War Office was coming down to investigate. At that time I had over 600 men in the camp, so I paraded the lot. When he arrived I took him on the parade, but I made him inspect the parade from the rear to the front, for in the rear were the recent arrivals.

At the end he asked me: "How long have these men in the front rank been here?"

I said: "Four to six weeks."

He looked at the parade and said: "I have never seen anything like it. Do you mean to say that such a change can come over men in such a short time?"

"Yes," I answered, "if they are made of the right stuff. The man who made the complaint obviously was not, but then no man can be accepted here who is average. He must have the highest aspirations and ideals, for we have an immensely difficult task to achieve. Because of this the men change—as you have seen."

I heard no more, and we continued our job in peace.

During the first stages, Lieutenant-Colonel John Rock was learning to fly at the Elementary Flying School at Derby and I decided to fly up there and have a word with him. Now, I had not flown for quite a long time and before flying up to Derby I had to have an R.A.F. Medical Board, so this was arranged for me at R.A.F., Cardington.

I was somewhat apprehensive, for this was where I had previously been before medical boards, when I was in the R.A.F. and an R.A.F. pilot, and I wondered if I was going to be recognized.

I went through all the routine: eye tests, blood tests, chest tests, and all the paraphernalia of the Medical Board. It was a wonder that my blood test was not suspect because of my fear that they would ask me if I had ever been examined before. However, I was finally sent for by the Chairman of the Medical Board who said:

"Well, Major Chatterton, I am very pleased to tell you that we find you fit in all departments and that we pass you fit for full flying duties as air crew and on operations."

He did not know or hear the sigh of relief that I gave, for he was obviously not aware that I was really Flying-Officer George Chatterton, passed fit only for ground duties. I wonder where that record it. Perhaps it was destroyed.

Now to fly again. I took the car up to Netheravon Airfield and made friends with the Flight Commander of the Communication Flight, and we finally obtained permission to have a test. I shall remember that flight for two reasons. One, because I was in the air again, the thrill of it all, and the knowledge that my hand was still in, when the pilot handed over to me. The other was the inescapable signs of things military on the ground, for, having served down there with soldiers, so much more familiar to me than before, such as formations of men marching, types of transport, artillery, and such like, and of course I realized how immensely important all this was.

It took only ten minutes for me to go solo, and this, including five minutes dual in a Hotspur Glider, was the only dual practice I had in the whole period of my service in the Glider Pilot Regiment. I mention this for I feel it needs to be emphasized how wonderful the basic training of the R.A.F. was, and is; also, how once flying is instilled in his blood, it never leaves the pilot. This factor will play an immense part in the story to come.

The next day I took the Tiger Moth and flew up to Derby, where I lost myself in the industrial haze, and had to land in a field and ask my way. I had only a few pints of petrol left when I landed.

At Derby I met John Rock for the first time, a serious and studious soldier who made me wonder how long he and I would last together, as quite obviously his point of view was entirely different from mine. What amazed me was the fact that the Command should have been given to a man who knew little or nothing about flying, and who was, indeed, a pupil now. This was just one of the amazing and extraordinary situations that had arisen from conception of the Glider Pilot Regiment. I could also see that the other members of the course had very strong views about how things should be run. They did not know that I viewed them with a professional airman's eye, and that I could already see the danger signs in their conversation—the confidence that is always apparent in flying pupils at the twenty to thirty-hour stage. In fact, Rock was already talking to me in this way, and I could see there was going to be trouble ahead.

As I flew back I pondered over the problem, for I knew that he and this course of pilots would be returning in six months' time, when all the friction caused by differences of opinion would introduce problems.

About this time there arrived in the regiment two officers who were to have a great influence on the whole course of events. One day I found a message on my table in the office informing me that Captain Alistair Cooper had been posted as my Adjutant by the War Office and would arrive at Amesbury Station. I met the 4.30 p.m. train from London, and while I waited for it to arrive I paced the platform wondering what he would be like, for the Adjutant is of great importance in building up morale in a battalion. His influence could make or mar everything.

The train drew in and down the platform came a small, dapper figure. As he came nearer, his face became clearer and then familiar, and suddenly I knew who he was. By some strange stroke of fate, he had been in my term at Pangbourne and I remembered him well.

He was one of those boys who had the misfortune not to grow quickly, and therefore was handicapped by his height and weight. For courage and guts, however, there was never his equal.

"Good afternoon, sir," he said, as he saluted smartly. "I wondered if it might be you."

If ever a Commanding Officer had a perfect Adjutant, I had him in Alistair Cooper. A regular officer of the Cheshire Regiment, he was all that an officer should be, for he supplied the inspiration that was needed. The story of Alistair Cooper, an epic of courage and determination, will be told later, but I can record here his unlimited patience, for he was to see officers, less worthy than he, promoted over his head, without grumbling or complaining. He served on faithfully and loyally.

The situation in these first days of the regiment was decidedly out of the ordinary. The headquarters of the 1st Airborne Division was developing alongside the headquarters of No. 38 Wing, R.A.F., commanded by an enthusiast, Sir Nigel Norman, who held the rank of Wing-Commander, and if the Airborne Division was ever to be lifted into the air it would have to rely on No. 38 Wing, which was being developed for the purpose. At that time, however, it was equipped with a collection of antiquated aircraft, the chief of which was the twin-engined Whitley, now obsolescent so far as the R.A.F. was concerned, but which was supposed to act as a parachute aircraft and glider tug. Also in the Wing was a series of aircraft, Hawker Hind, a biplane, and the Miles Master, for towing the lighter gliders.

There is little doubt that both Sir Nigel Norman and General Browning were encountering difficulties, for neither the 1st Airborne Division nor 38 Wing, R.A.F., could have been very popular with the Air Ministry or the War Office. This was, perhaps, natural, for both Ministries were weighed down with the formidable task of turning defeat into victory, and disasters were still hanging over them heavily every day.

I came to know General "Boy", as he was affectionately called, well, for he asked me to teach him to fly—and one certainly comes to know a person under those circumstances. In so doing I soon got to know the true state of affairs. There was little doubt that his requests for the special equipment necessary for airborne divisions were not warmly received. The Glider Regiment introduced a new conception of war and with it new ideas and requirements. Transport had to be light, instead of solid and heavy; guns and equipment had to be viewed differently; clothing, helmets, and a thousand and one things, had to be of a new design. Many difficulties accompanied their creation. The Ministries were conservative of mind, and it was obvious that General "Boy" was becoming frustrated by their attitude.

Learning to fly, therefore, was a relief to him; and for me it was a great experience—teaching a General of over forty-six to fly was no easy matter, particularly this one, for he was a very determined person, and highly inflammable! Nevertheless, he was amazingly good, and quickly learned the technique of flying an aeroplane. He went solo in eight and a half hours, which is the average for a young man of twenty-one, and very creditable to General Browning. I have never been quite sure whether it was a wise thing to do, for once one is off the ground and has a taste of flying—the flying bug —it can have serious consequences.

About this time, the two Services were very suspicious of each other, and the R.A.F. had a very definite attitude to the Army, whom they called "Pongos" or "Khaki Jobs" or "Brown Jobs", and the Army were very well aware of their weaker position, particularly after the Battle of Britain. Between the wars the R.A.F. had been "sat on" and neglected, but when the expansion came, and after the success of the Battle of Britain, from the Chief of Air Staff downwards there was a "never again" attitude, particularly towards the Army. Since my time a completely new and much larger Air Force had come into being. In fact, a completely new outlook and language was apparent also, and words and names had appeared which were never used in my time. Spit and polish and "bull" were ridiculed in the Air Force, and this was fully understandable, but it was quite extraordinary the gulf that it opened up everywhere. As for the Army, they too had their attitudes, and in some way it shocked them to see the R.A.F. walking around in the way they did. Also, they were being brought into contact with the new element—the air—not as airmen, but in an unnatural way. The Royal Air Force was also very aware of this, and dealing with the problems that arose was a matter of life and death to me in my Command, for I had to watch the developments most carefully in the early training.

As I have already explained, my view was that if the pilot of the glider had to get out and fight at the other end of the flight he must have what amounted to a dual personality; first, the flexibility of the pilot for his long tow to the target; secondly the *esprit* and discipline and all that went with it in order that he should stand up to the rigours of battle at the end of his journey. Already, because of the discipline and drill and barrack-room pride, the R.A.F. Elementary Flying Schools were reacting, for the first stage of the glider pilot's flying training was a three-months' course on light aircraft. The pupils were arriving with the attitude Briodey and Cowlie had instilled in them, and the R.A.F. saw it as a lot of nonsense. But, I argued, all they could see was the turning out of the pilot, not what he had to face on stepping from the glider.

One of my answers to the R.A.F. attitude was to dress myself up in top boots, Sam Browne belt, gloves and stick, and then to borrow a Tiger Moth and fly around the Stations of the R.A.F. where the glider pilots were training. Here I would land in the most "split arse" manner and show that I could do this despite the fact that I was dressed up with all the "bull" of the soldier. I feel sure that it was through the comradeship I managed to create and build up with the Station Commanders, most of them my contemporaries, plus my wings and the background which I represented, that confidence was regained and the Glider Pilot Regiment was able to thrive.

Thus, the scene began to develop, and slowly the regiment took shape and the pilots grew in number. As the first course began to finish its training on powered aircraft, so the Royal Air Force opened up their Glider Training Units. Up to this time the gliders were of two kinds: the Hotspur, manufactured by General Aircraft, and the Horsa, designed and manufactured by Airspeed Limited. Both types were made of wood and glue, and very little metal appeared anywhere. The Hotspur had beautiful lines and carried two pilots, one behind the other. Its total load was in the region of one ton, or eight fully-equipped soldiers. It was used entirely for training, and the glider pilots transferred direct from the Tiger Moth to the Hotspur. At this time the tug for the Hotspur was a vintage aircraft, the Hawker Hector. Later, the Miles Master replaced this old biplane and did some wonderful work in training many hundreds of glider pilots.

One of the things that always astonished me was the calmness of these trainee glider pilots when anything went wrong. Most of them at some time during training escaped catastrophe by the skin of their teeth, yet, if anything, it spurred them on rather than discouraged them. Here is the account of a somewhat unhappy, yet satisfying afternoon in the life of one of them, Lieutenant-Colonel John Place, told in his own words:

I had only three flights to do to complete my course. On the day in question the weather was heavily overcast with thick cloud and mist down to about 1,000 feet or less. However, low-tow glider flying was in full swing. I was duly authorized to take up a fully-ballasted Hostpur glider, and having signed the Form 700 and the Flight Authorization Book, and having given instructions to the tug pilot for a low-tow, off we went.

We had just become airborne and had not yet reached the boundary fence when the cockpit lid of the Hotspur—which I had taken particular care to see was correctly latched—flew open. I instinctively jammed my left elbow into the perspex just above the lower framework of the cockpit lid and tried to slam the cover shut; but the wind pressure was much too strong for me, and after two or three frantic attempts, the wind was definitely not only coming into the cockpit, but was going through me—vertically.

I couldn't communicate with the tug, and as we were not far off the ground I decided to try to sit tight with my left elbow still jammed in the left side of the lid, and hoped that I could stay there long enough to gain some height before either the lid got the better of me and blew away, or I could attract the tug pilot's attention by one or other of the accepted signals. We had, however, barely cleared the aerodrome boundary when the tug pilot turned fairly smartly on a left-hand circuit, and I barely managed to follow him, as the pressure of the cockpit was forcing me into the right-hand corner, and I was getting more tired every second—especially as I began to feel that the trim of the glider was all wrong and was much too nose-heavy. By this time we were turning on the downwind leg of the field, some considerable distance out; then lots of things crossed my mind in a hurry. I realized I would have to fly with my knees when I wished to release the rope—the release plug was, of course, on the left side of the cockpit and out of reach of my already very occupied left hand and arm. I also realized that I shouldn't be able to use the flaps either—the lever being well down on the left-hand side, level with my knees—nor could I trim the glider, which was already nose-heavy and would be considerably more so after release.

In my agitation I was not keeping very good station behind the tug. The next thing I knew was I was in an almost vertical bank to the right and not more than a hundred feet above a pretty considerable wood. What was more startling was the fact that I couldn't see the tug—not even the rope was visible! And for a second or two I couldn't realize what had happened as I was still travelling at cruising sped. I did everything I knew to get back on an even keel. The glider just wouldn't budge from a vertical bank, and I was losing height fast. I could practically pick out every leaf on every tree as we whipped past. Then suddenly, for no apparent reason and certainly not because of anything I did, I found myself right way up again and looked frantically round for the tug which was not in front of me—in fact was nowhere in sight through an arc of 180 degrees to the front; nor could I see the rope.

My left elbow was still rammed rigidly into the cockpit lid and my arm by this time was quite paralysed; then I saw the tug. We were formating practically wing-tip to wing-tip at a distance of a few feet. I was on the starboard side of the tug, and as I looked across I could see the astonished face of the tug pilot, and I have no doubt *my* expression of incredulous horror was even more obvious to him. By the grace of God he kept straight on, and I managed to fish-tail back into position behind him; then as we gently turned across wind, I let go the stick with my right hand, reached across, and yanked the rope release lever, and the rope fell away.

I eased the stick back—nothing happened. I sat back and hauled as hard as I could—still nothing happened; then the nose dropped. I took a quick glance at the air-speed indicator, which registered 105 m.p.h. and was going up steadily. I had an instant's impression of skimming some tall green things, which later turned out to be trees, and my eyes focused a tug-aircraft which was approaching to land at its usual 85 to 90 m.p.h., and I was passing him fast, while the grass was coming up at a most unnatural angle. With one final haul on the stick I managed to decrease the angle of descent, but I hit the ground with an appalling bump which jarred every bone in my body, and probably every joint in the Hotspur—with its full load of sandbags. As I hit the ground I saw that my air-speed was over 110 m.p.h.

We crossed the whole length of the Croughton airfield with my nose rammed well into the ground, the control tower bearing down on me at an astonishing rate! I kicked my right foot and pushed the rudder over as far as it would go, then with screaming tyres and everything shaking and vibrating, we shot round in a colossal ground loop, ending up back on the tow line, having done a complete circuit of Croughton airfield—on the ground!

Having come to rest, I let go my left elbow which felt as though it was almost permanently fixed at right angles to my body; but at least the cockpit cover was still on the glider.

I went over and reported what had happened to the Tow Master and asked if I could finish off the other two flights which I had to do, as the weather hadn't got any worse. I got into another Hotspur for another low-tow, and away we went. We had scarcely cleared the end of the airfield when, for apparently no reason whatever, the tug pilot climbed straight into the low overcast. Before I knew what had happened, we were in thick cloud and I couldn't see the tug. I thought the best thing to do was to stay on tow as long as possible in case anybody else below was taking off. However, flying by the angle of the rope, I held on; and then, with a little more than 1,000 feet on the clock—when it should have been 200 or 300 feet— I decided that the only thing to do was to pull off and see if I could get down somewhere without bending myself or the aircraft too much. So I "pulled off" and got my speed down to 65 m.p.h. on a course which I judged to be approximately across wind. Suddenly I broke cloud about a mile from a village which I recognized as being about a good four miles from the aerodrome, and I had 1,000 feet on my altimeter! On take-off I had noticed that the wind was reasonably strong so that I thought with luck I might just scrape back to the airfield; and more by luck than by good judgment I quite literally scraped through the top twigs in the boundary hedge on the up-wind side of the airfield and a little to one side of the take-off path. We were gliding so slowly by this time that the poor old Hotspur actually flopped on to the grass and barely moved thirty yards.

I still had one more flight to do to complete my quota before the C.F.I.'s test, and I only hoped that the third and last flight would not be like the previous two. I was more than relieved when it ended up a perfectly uneventful low-tow.

About this time I took part in an extrordinary demonstration in front of Winston Churchill, as he then was. I had flown up to R.A.F., Kidlington, had one circuit dual on the Hotspur, and found it an amusing glider to fly. I remember I joined in with a series of other glider pilots carrying out what they call the dive approach. It was most exhilarating. The pilot was towed to 1,000 feet at one end of the airfield, and then, putting the glider's nose down, he dived straight at the ground, flying along, without engines, at some fifty feet above the ground, turning left by the hangars, and then landing just over the hedge with a bump. It was an amazing sight to see the gliders release up wind of the airfield, somewhere in the region of a thousand feet, dive sharply, and watch their speed gathering as they went.

For the demonstration which was to be given in front of Churchill, the Prime Minister had demanded a display by a full Airborne Division. It was not a very successful effort, for there was a very limited number of tug aircraft and parachute aircraft, and all that could be produced were a few Whitleys for the parachutists, about thirty in number, and nine Hectors towing nine Hotspur gliders, one of which I flew.

The parachutists dropped in a field, which did not impress Winston, owing to the small number, and the nine Hotspurs which were released at 10,000 feet came in to land in front of the gathered V.I.P.'s. The first glider overshot and nearly ran the Prime Minister down, two landed correctly, and then I followed the leader of the next three. The leader turned in to land, hit the top of the trees edging the field and took his wing off—I can still see the splinters as it cartwheeled in front of me. I landed with my heart in my mouth and only just stopped in time in front of the Prime Minister. It is the only time I have had a close up of this famous man. It is amazing to relate that no one was seriously injured that afternoon, and I understand that Winston was furious at the poverty of the numbers with which we had tried to impress him. I also believe that fireworks from Downing Street resulted.

A curious situation was arising with regard to the Horsa gliders. Many were coming from the factories, hundreds in fact, and they were parked all around R.A.F., Netheravon, but there were hardly any tugs that could be spared to tow them into the sky.

The Horsa was truly a remarkable aircraft. The pilots sat side by side in a cockpit which was not unlike a conservatory, with an almost 360 degree view. There were two control columns of the spade-grip type. On the panel were a height and air speed indicator and a compass, and beside the pilot were the flap controls and the brakes; otherwise there were no other instruments to worry about. Designed as a high-winged monoplane, it had a detachable undercarriage and a nose wheel. Two sliding doors gave access to the large cabin, which had seating capacity for over thirty men. A bifurcated hemp rope was attached to the leading edges of the wings, with a special fitting for quick release, the main rope being 150 feet long and attached to the tail unit of the tug-bomber.

One afternoon I flew the first of the Horsa deliveries. It was an extraordinary experience. The procedure is for the tug and glider to move into position with the ground crew waiting by the glider.

Silence is noticeable, as compared with the noise of the engines of ordinary aircraft. The crew by the bomber signal her forward until the rope is taut along the runway, then the thumbs-up signal is given to the glider ground crew, who, in turn, give it to the glider pilot in charge of the glider. He sits on the left, or port, side of the glider cockpit.

Interwound in the hemp rope is the intercommunication wire between the tug pilot and the glider pilot. There is a crackling sound in the earphones of the glider pilot, and a conversation, somewhat like the following, takes place:

"Tug Y 66117 calling. Tug Y 66117 calling. Hullo, Matchbox, are you receiving me? Are you receiving me?" "Over to you. Over."

"Glider K 661 answering. Glider K 661 answering. Yes, loud and clear. Yes, loud and clear. Are you receiving me? Over."

"O.K., Glider. Tug calling. Loud and clear. O.K. Loud and clear. Are you ready for take off? Are you ready for take off?"

"O.K., Tug. Ready for take off. Ready for take off. Over to you. Over."

"O.K., Glider. I shall now take up the slack. I will climb to 2,000 feet and steer at 75 degrees."

"O.K., Tug. O.K., Tug."

"O.K., Glider. O.K., Glider. Closing down now. Off."

Thus the conversation goes and the tug engines gradually rev up. The tug moves slowly forward and the glider pilot holds the brakes on until the rope is fully taut, when, gradually, the glider moves forward behind the tug. It is a thrilling and strange sensation. The dust flies up from behind the tug and the speed increases —fifty miles, sixty miles, seventy-five miles an hour. The glider pilot eases back the control column, the nose wheel comes off the runway, and into the air the glider jumps. The tug-aircraft still rumbles along the runway and the glider at the end of the rope flies above it. The only sound is the rush of the slipstream—a clear roar of rushing air. The handling is rough, for there is no finesse in glider construction. Soon the tug leaves the ground, the runway drops below, and the whole combination is airborne. The ground below slowly recedes and both aircraft climb into the sky. It is a delightful sensation and one that can never be produced by other means.

At 2,000 feet the tug levels out and flies on a course. At this height the glider pilot, who is flying above the tug, drops into the low-tow position below the tug. In lowering the glider he slides through the slipstream of the tug, and flies below the tug to keep the rope just above the cockpit. There are only two positions, high and low. The latter is used for bad weather flying, for by flying in the position of the "V" of the rope, the glider can keep roughly in position. From above, it is almost impossible to keep position if in cloud or fog.

At the end of the exercise the tug flies back to the airfield on receiving a radio signal from the ground that the glider may land. The glider pilot reaches forward and pulls the tow-rope release handle, the rope snapping away out of its sockets in the wings. There is a slight jolt, then a feeling of exaltation as the tug rushes away. The glider becomes incredibly smooth and a strange silence comes over the cockpit. On my first flight in a Horsa I felt that I never wanted to come down again, but just to drift on up there for ever. The height indicator, however, does not permit this; eyes must be kept on the airfield lest the glider get too far away and unable to get back to the runway.

It was borne in on me, as I flew this great bird of wood and glue and bits of tin, that the training in flying a conventional aircraft was suited also to flying gliders. We never "rumbled in" in powered aircraft, we always throttled back and ticked over into a glider landing. I found myself using the same technique for judging and assessing height as before.

As the pilot turns into the final run he pulls the flap lever to half flap and with a great hiss from the air bottles, and from the wings, two flaps or air brakes come down into position. The glider checks and the nose is pushed down. At the right moment the full flap is pulled on and the glider takes on an ever steeper angle. The ground rushes up, the control column is eased back and the glider lands safely and gently and runs forward only a few yards in doing so.

But Horsas, like Hotspurs, or for that matter any glider, horse or human being, react according to the way they are handled and to the burden they carry. There is an amusing story told by Major T. D. B. McMillen, M.C. that illustrates this. This story has a sequel, about which the reader will hear later. Here it is:

> The Horsa gliders had been loaded and lined up for take-off under supervision of the Battalion Air Loading Officer. We had already been briefed as to which glider each of us was to fly to Hurn and, as soon as we arrived at Netheravon, we went to check our own gliders.

The Air Landing Battalion had not enplaned, but when I peered into the inside of my own particular Horsa I was horrified to see what they had seen fit to cram into it. It was obviously the Battalion H.Q. glider because, besides a jeep and trailer and three motorcycles, most of the battalion orderly room equipment had been piled into it. By this time my passengers had arrived and it was too late to do anything except to protest feebly against the gross maltreatment of a poor Horsa, not to mention its slightly reluctant pilot.

"The senior passenger introduced himself as Colonel Jones, Commanding the battalion, and we all climbed aboard, strapped ourselves in and prepared for the worst. At least, I did, for I knew roughly what to expect, but my passengers were mercifully ignorant of the behaviour of an overloaded Horsa on take-off.

For those who do not know Netheravon Aerodrome I must stop to describe this prototype of all aerodromes. Most prototypes bear little relation to the glossy up-to-date model and Netheravon was no exception. It was a grass aerodrome which, in my jaundiced view, seemed to be built on two hills. Our gliders were marshalled on one hill and we were due to take off towards the other. To make matters worse, our towing aircraft was to be a slow, under-powered Whitley.

When our turn for take-off came, the tow rope tightened and we started trundling forward. The normal procedure was that the Horsa, being the lighter of the combination, should take off before the towing aircraft and should keep above its slipstream all the time. Not so in our case; the assorted ironmongery in my poor glider kept us anchored firmly to the ground long after the panting Whitley was airborne. We eventually became unstuck, but long before we could gain any altitude the second of Netheravon's two hills was upon us and once more we felt our wheels tumbling and bouncing along on the turf. At last, with a herculean effort, our gallant tug yanked us off the ground and we started to climb. It was then that the tricky part began. I was well below the slipstream and had to climb through it to gain my correct position. This, at the best of times, was not a pleasant operation, and to do it before one had gained a proper flying speed and in an overloaded glider is not to be recommended.

We staggered up through the turbulent air, alternately wallowing and corkscrewing, and eventually won through to smoother air above the Whitley. It had been a few moments of great tenseness, and I was not really in a frame of mind to observe the niceties of protocol when the somewhat grey-faced Colonel poked his head through the intercom door to ask if everything was all right. The rest of the flight went smoothly and by the time we reached Hurn, both physical and mental equilibrium had been restored, though Col. Jones's parting words made it quite clear that his opinion of military gliding was not of the highest!

I was to meet Col. Jones less than four months later and the recognition was mutual.

This wase an amazing period of my life, for I seemed to be all and everything—depot commander, disciplinarian, confidant of the R.A.F., adviser to the Army and general "dogsbody". The parachute force was building up in strength and was becoming very demanding. The Air Landing Brigade was also at full strength but handicapped by little or no flying because there were few tugs for the mass of gliders already crowding the park round Netheravon. By now some 600 glider pilots were in training and the first course was on its way to the depot at Tilshead—it was as if the head were meeting the tail.   As I had foreseen, there was undoubtedly an "atmosphere" between those who had been on the flying courses and those who had not.

Lieutenant-Colonel Rock was obviously a brilliant officer, studious and courageous, who had been one of the first parachutists and the original protagonist for the airborne operations at the War Office. In fact he was the pioneer. However, his outlook was different from mine. I could see that he did not approve of my spit-and-polish methods, and he insisted that I slacken them off. I, of course, argued with him, but he was determined and I think he had decided already that I was not of his school. However, events settled the question of our differences in outlook.

The first event was that the 2nd Battalion, The Glider Pilot Regiment, was created, and I was selected to be its Commander. This, of course, parted us and we could follow our own ideals and ideas despite the fact that we were both in the same camp.

The second event, however, was more tragic. Colonel Rock was a brave man and felt that he must show an example to his Command. Night flying was one of the important features of glider training and he was determined to encourage and improve training methods. I remember warning him, in conversation, to respect the fact that he had little or no knowledge of night flying, and to obtain as much dual as possible before he started experimenting. However, one night he decided to take a night flight with a second pilot who had just recently returned from the Glider Pilot School. They were towed

Glider Pilot in flying kit.   Note crash helmet and head phones.

Glider pilot equipped for ground fighting.

off by a Hector tug, and unfortunately as they were taking off the rope parted from the tug. In trying to make a landing in the dark the pilot hit an obstacle, the sandbag load in the back of the glider broke through the bulwark, and both Colonel Rock and the pilot were badly crushed. Rock was so badly hurt that although he lingered for a day or so he died of his injuries.

Part of an obituary, clearly written by a colleague, which appeared in the *Sunday Express* read:

"Lieutenant-Colonel John Frank Rock, pioneer of British para-troops and airborne forces, has given his life for his work. After surviving a number of narrow escapes in experimental parachute jumping and glider work he died in a military hospital from injuries received in a glider crash.

"He always tested the risk himself before asking his men to do it, and such was the force of his example that we gladly followed where he had led."

Rock's death brought about immediate changes. I was transferred from the Command of the 2nd Battalion to the Command of the 1st Battalion, something I did not relish since the officers of this battalion were naturally loyal to Rock and likely to take badly to me.

The Command of the 2nd Battalion was handed over to Lieut.-Colonel Iain Murray, whose story is an interesting one in that originally he had been in the Auxiliary Air Force and had, therefore, considerable experience as a pilot. However, he had left the R.A.F. to join the Grenadier Guards, and had arrived at General Browning's headquarters as a possible A.D.C. The General, however, had referred him to me, and so Ian Murray had joined the regiment with enthusiasm. He helped me enormously in the whole build-up of the Glider Pilot Regiment and, finally, went off on a full course of flying. In so doing he had risen from Lieutenant to Lieutenant-Colonel in the amazingly short time of a year. As things turned out he was more than eminently suited to be one of our leaders.

The regiment had taken shape now and one battalion had been through the flying schools and was back in the depot. The 2nd Battalion was about to be formed.

This was the situation when the 1st Airborne Division was posted overseas—to battle. For the Glider Pilot Regiment this was astonishing, for they were a regiment of pilots whose only experience of flying was in the schools, and they had had practically no operational flying or training whatsoever.

D

This being the case I visited G.S.O.1 with Group-Captain Tom Cooper, D.F.C., and I recited the facts. We both spoke as pilots of experience, and we argued that to send overseas 200 to 300 pilots who had had, in all, little over eight hours' glider flying over the last six months, and who were, therefore, totally unfit for operations, was a mistake. I suggested that the pilots should be left behind and given a concentrated course of flying, both by day and night, and then flown out to join the Airborne Division in Africa.

However, I was not heeded and it was decided that the pilots should go out in the same way as the rest of the division.

The die was cast, and there was nothing I could do about it, but I was becoming somewhat mystified about the set-up of Airborne Divisional Headquarters. General Browning seemed to have been changed from Divisional Commander and had become known as Major-General Airborne Forces. He, in turn, was relieved by Brigadier Hopkinson, the original Commander of the 1st Air Landing Brigade, who was an unusual little man with a little knowledge of the air, in that he had flown as an amateur in peacetime, and had made his name by being a founder of the Phantom Force, a communications group.

It was an interesting situation, for up to this time there had been strong rivalry between the parachute side of affairs and the air landing troops, or so it seemed to me. The main reason was that aircraft had been very difficult to obtain and therefore rivalry arose as to who should have such aircraft as they became available for practising operations. The Airborne Division had been desperately trying to put itself across, and although we had built up an extremely strong *esprit de corps*, our requirements were quite often ignored because the Air Force were reluctant to part with bombers other for the purpose of towing gliders or dropping parachute troops.

On one occasion, a party of M.P.s came down to see the airborne forces and we put on a demonstration to show them the state of readiness of the Airborne Division. I was in a glider which carried thirty of the M.P.s and General Browning. Owing to lack of practice both the pilots crashed the gliders and their loads were battered and shaken. In my glider was Miss Ellen Wilkinson, who broke an ankle. A question was subsequently asked in the House of Commons: "Was your journey really necessary?" However, it did bring to the notice of the authorities that the airborne forces were in a pretty poor state.

3

NORTH AFRICA ADVENTURE

UP TO THIS TIME—late 1942—two major airborne operations had been undertaken. One had been used as a morale builder. It was a night drop by a parachute company, led by Major John Frost, upon a radar station on the coast of France at Bruneval, and then a withdrawal by sea. It was very effective propaganda. A certain amount of useful lessons were learned—not least the importance of *esprit de corps* and discipline, characteristics which were, I think, rather lacking in this company. John Frost agreed with me on this point when we discussed the operation afterwards.

The second was the dropping of a parachute brigade in North Africa, ahead of the advancing 1st Army. In this operation the force was dropped too far in front of the main army and, therefore, was placed in a perilous position.

However, the valour and fighting ability of the parachute brigade was proved beyond doubt. So much so that they were used as frontline infantry although this was really a waste of valuable and specially trained men; nevertheless the parachute brigade earned great distinction because of its courage and dash on this occasion.

Thus, with only these two minor operations as a guide, the 1st Airborne Division embarked—for destinations unknown. I had been informed that I was to detail two companies of glider pilots to stand by; the rest of the battalion was to follow. I detailed this force to be commanded by my Second-in-Command, Major Maurice Willoughby, but General Hopkinson insisted that I myself should command the first group and go out with the 1st Airborne Division to Africa.

It was a strange experience, and I was full of foreboding. I knew that headquarters had no idea what they were driving up to as far as the Glider Pilot Regiment was concerned, but no effort of mine succeeded in bringing even a glimmer of light into their darkness. There was, indeed a great gulf between those in authority and myself as to our proper rôle in battle.

39

The majority of the pilots in my force had had little flying at all, other than that in the training schools, owing to lack of tug-aircraft. I calculated that in something like six months they would have been lucky to have got in even eight hours; I had already mentioned this to the Staff. It was very little to have to face an operation with. I simply could not get any information about how and where they were to obtain flying practice in Africa when they arrived, and as a result I was deeply depressed with the whole arrangement. I was accused, quite often, of worrying too much, but after all I was an aviator, and I knew what this quite casual treatment could do to the aspirations of my pilots. I was, also, not unaware of the signs of envy and even jealousy—the unspoken hope that we might be brought down a peg or two, whether we liked it or not.

Our first sight of North Africa was the port of Oran, where we disembarked at night. We boarded some American transport, driven by Negroes I remember, and were carried in an endless convoy throughout the night, arriving the following morning at a temporary prisoner-of-war camp, where we were given American pup tents. The camp was near a place called Tizi on the Mascara Plain, a rather beautiful part of North Africa, and those who were with me won't forget that camp in a hurry! It was an inappropriate place for an airborne assault force to end up in.

We had been there only a few days when I was sent for and told to fly to Algiers, where I was to meet Colonel Dunne, the Commander of the United States Wing that was to train and tow us to whatever target would be needed. After some time we were moved out of the camp and on to another part of the Mascara Plain, where the Americans were attempting to clear several airstrips. My whole concern was to get the pilots on to the airstrips and into the air, as I wanted them in a flying environment as quickly as possible.

I still could not find out if there were any gliders, and this distressed me, for I was becoming really concerned about the morals of my aircrews. No one could tell me what arrangements had been made and there had been no sign of General Hopkinson, the Divisional Commander, for weeks!

General Browning had also lost him. I found out afterwards that Browning had waited in North Africa for as long as he was allowed, in order to discuss the impending operation with General Hopkinson, but the latter had kept out of General Browning's way.

At last I was sent for and told to report to General Hopkinson in

Algiers, where I met him as arranged. He was in splendid form and had obviously pulled off something that pleased him.

"Hoppy," as he was affectionately called, was an amusing little man. Very short, with black wavy hair, he was very ambitious, and delighted at having been made up to a General.

He had, I felt, pulled a fast one on General Browning in avoiding him in North Africa, and I wondered, as I waited for him to send for me, just what he had been up to. I was more than certain that he had committed the Glider Force to something, and he most certainly had!

"Well, George," the General greeted me. "It's nice to see you. I have a very interesting operation for you to study."

I looked at him and wondered what on earth was coming next.

"I've been to see General Montgomery," he continued, "and he has agreed to use the 1st Airborne Division on a night assault on Sicily." I held my breath. I did not like the sound of the developments.

He motioned me to a map of the island that was hanging on the wall.

"I have agreed to land the Air Landing Brigade on the night of July 9th/10th on the beaches in the neighbourhood of Syracusa. Another force of parachutists will be dropped at Catania, and a further force, supported by a glider squadron, at Augusta."

I made a quick calculation. It was now April 1st. There was, roughly, about three months left; no time at all, when one considered that there were no airstrips, tugs or gliders.

"Now, let us have a look at these photographs." And he leaned over a table on which were a number of aerial photographs of the Sicilian beaches. I looked at them and, to my horror, saw that they were rock-strewn, with cliffs, and that the fields had stone walls.

"Well," said the General, looking hard at me, "what do you think?"

I hesitated a moment and then said, "You know, sir, that the pilots have had no flying practice for at least three months, and little or no experience of night flying at all."

"Oh," replied the General, "we will soon put that right. The U.S. Air Force are going to supply tugs and gliders."

"American gliders?" I asked incredulously.

"Yes, what difference will that make?"

"Difference, sir? Why, they hardly know our own gliders, let alone American!"

"Well, you'll have to put up with it, won't you," he said in some heat.

"Yes, sir, I will try to do so. But this looks a pretty stiff landing place, don't you think, sir?" I asked, and knew that I had made a mistake.

"Now look here, Colonel Chatterton," he said, sternly, "I'm going to leave you for half an hour, and in that time you can study the photographs. If at the end of that time you still think that this is too difficult, you can consider yourself relieved of your Command."

He walked to the door of the room and looked back at me.

"Half an hour. You see? I shall then return."

He left the room and closed the door, leaving me to my thoughts. And what thoughts! I was faced with an appalling situation. My glider pilots, whether in the temporary prison camp at Tizi or back in England, had had little or no flying experience, and there was no officer to take over from me with any more experience than the N.C.O.'s, if I resigned. Then, this frightening operation. Obviously I must keep my silly mouth shut and use all my experience to try to relieve the situation.

The minutes ticked by as I paced up and down, and finally I made up my mind that at all costs I must stand by the men, despite the fact that I considered the plan to be mad. The whole situation was astounding, and I felt sure that it had been "sold" to Monty, with the best saleman's manner, that airborne troops had to be used at all costs, otherwise they might never be used at all!

The General returned and I said nothing; neither did he. We continued to discuss the pros and cons. He was like a little boy, he was so pleased.

Immediately afterwards I returned to Mascara, for I had heard that there were some gliders on the Oran airfield. Sure enough there were; they were scattered all over the airfield in huge crates. I immediately sent about fifty glider pilots to uncrate them and build them on the airfield, being relieved beyond measure to give them work to perform which had something to do with aircraft again.

There was no accommodation for them on the airfield, but they began working hard, and as they uncrated the gliders they literally went into the crates and turned them into billets for themselves. In no time, with only the handbook to guide them and one U.S. corporal to show them, they erected about thirty gliders, and when an American tug appeared the gliders were flown out to the series of air strips which the U.S. Air Force had built for themselves.

I now had to think up some form of training programme. I divulged that if the flight was to be a night one the landing would have to be done without ground aids, but the only one who seemed at all perturbed was myself.

I decided to try a moonlight landing, so I took up a Waco, at it was called, and tried it out. It was entirely different from a Hotspur or Horsa, the British gliders, for whereas these were made of wood, the Waco was made of steel and fabric. Its glide was flat and the whole scheme of flight was different. It was dual-controlled, with a large cockpit capable of carrying thirteen men or one jeep. The nose lifted up so that the load could be run out of the glider, and it could land on a fixed undercarriage or on skids. It was a pleasant aircraft to fly and handled very easily.

On take off, perhaps the most disconcerting thing was the huge dust cloud that was blown up from the airstrips by the tug, for the strips were just lengths of dust cut into the corn. However, it was something that one got used to after a practice or two.

I took the glider up and released at about 2,000 feet. It was a thrilling feeling, and I found that I could see the ground quite clearly. We gradually descended and the moon was so bright it was very similar to landing by day. Gently turning into the airfield I brought her down as easily as if it had been lit up by the sun.

This gave me greater confidence for the aircrews, and I set about listing an intensive refresher course. It was imperative that the pilots should be given all the practice they could get, but apart from this I felt that after the treatment they had suffered in the last weeks, a flying environment was vital to the success of the whole operation, otherwise there was going to be a disaster.

During this period it was decided that the R.A.F. would bring out a number of Horsas from England, a hazardous operation called "Turkey Buzzard." It entailed towing the great Horsa gliders from the south-west coast of England to Sali in North Africa, and then across North Africa to the Mascara Plain. Each glider had three pilots for relief, and many and varied were the adventures of these pilots. It was during one of these flights that Alistair Cooper excelled himself.

He was piloting one of the gliders when his team was intercepted by German Condors. When it was seen that the Halifax bomber towing the glider had no chance with the glider on tow, Cooper pulled off and descended into the sea. The bomber flew on into the cloud and fought the Condors off. In the meantime Alistair Cooper and his two co-pilots launched dinghies and floated off. The Condors came back and machine-gunned them but they failed to register any hits and flew off.

Twenty-four hours later a corvette picked them up from the sea and in no time Alistair Cooper was back at the controls again, piloting another Horsa glider which arrived in time to be briefed for the attack on Sicily.

The true spirit of these remarkable men was now beginning to emerge. Later they were to be tested by many different aspects of war, but these early experiences gave an assurance that they would never be lacking in courage and endurance when put to the test.

The following two narratives are by glider pilots who took part in Operation Turkey Buzzard. The first is told by Staff-Sergeant Gordon Jenks, one-time jazz trumpeter in the Highland Light Infantry Dance Band.

We had settled down into a normal flying and military routine at Holmsley South when we were teamed up three glider pilots to a crew. At about the same time we began dinghy drill and "prepared for ditching" until we could do it with our eyes shut. I crewed up with my two special pals, Percy Attwood and Harry Flynn.

Percy was a charming, soft-spoken fellow. A little over medium height and solidly built, he tackled every job with the same calm, unshakeable thoroughness. An inveterate pipe-smoker, it was just impossible for him to panic—a comforting bloke for anybody to have around.

Harry Flynn was a small, slightly bandy-legged Cockney with an irrepressible sense of humour. He had a fascinating way of using the expression "Cowson" almost every other sentence, which never failed to amuse me.

One Friday lunchtime the three of us were contemplating whether or not to go up to town for the weekend when we were sent for by Major Cooper. He informed us that on the following day we were to do a ten-hour tow, the longest ever attempted by a tug-glider combination. A Halifax tug had been fitted up with overload fuel tanks enabling it to carry 2,400 gallons of petrol. Pilot of the Halifax and skipper of the tug-glider combination was Flight-Lieutenant "Buster" Briggs. Our instructions were to jettison the undercarriage immediately after take-off, and at the end of the tow, cast off and do a skid landing at R.A.F. Station, Hurn, a few miles away. In the pilot's cabin of a Horsa there are two seats side by side, and the aircraft can be flown from either seat. We arranged to each do one hour's actual flying in every three hours, and twenty minutes each on the final stages of the trip. But, in fact, it didn't work out quite that way. Soon after take-off poor Harry became airsick and was ill for practically the whole ten hours. Even Percy succumbed to air sickness after a few hours, with the result that I had to spend about seven hours continuously at the controls. It had its compensations, however, as I ate the whole of the sandwiches provided for the three of us. Nevertheless, I wasn't altogether sorry to see Hurn Aerodrome come into view after a triangular flight of something like 1,400 miles, about 1,000 miles of which I had spent at the controls. I landed on the grass beside the main runway and was glad to get out and stretch my legs. A utility van was waiting to take the three of us back to Holmsley South, where I proceeded without delay to the mess and downed a few pints of beer. Unfortunately this first long tow had a tragic sequel.

The next morning, we discussed the trip with Major Cooper and suggested one or two improvements to make things easier on future long tows. He was very pleased with the whole affair and told us to get off to London on a 36-hour pass. I mentioned the Horsa still at Hurn, and he told me not to worry about it as Sergeants Sunter and Davies had asked to go over and fly it back. I spoke to "Geordie" Sunter, a short, stocky little man from Durham, before he and Sergeant Davies climbed into the Halifax which was to take them to Hurn, pick up the Horsa and tow them back. Harry, Percy and I watched the Halifax as it headed for Hurn which lay just beyond some distant trees. It appeared to be in trouble, with smoke coming from the port outer engine. A minute or so later there was a terrific explosion and thick black smoke shot hundreds of feet in the air. There were no survivors. Needless to say, it was a very subdued trio that set off for London.

On arriving back at Holmsley the following night, I was approached by the R.A.F. sergeant who ran the station dance band, with a rather unusual request. He asked me if I would be willing to play the Last Post and Long Reveille on my trumpet at the funeral of the air crew and glider pilots who died in the Halifax crash. Naturally, I agreed to take part in what for me turned out to be a most moving and unforgettable experience.

A large contingent of R.A.F. aircrew and Glider Pilots turned out impeccably dressed for the funeral parade. They marched slowly into the cemetery with a precision that would have done credit to the Brigade of Guards, and stood in three ranks a few yards away from the freshly dug graves. The pall-bearers lowered the coffins gently into the earth as the R.A.F. padre spoke a few words. Relations of the dead aircrew looked at the coffins for a few moments alone with their thoughts and then stepped back as a firing party of aircrew and glider pilots lined up either side of the graves. They fired three volleys and I started to play. Never have I played with so much feeling as at that moment. The notes of my trumpet rang out over the quiet cemetery on that fine May morning. I noticed the relatives weeping softly. Birds were singing, and an aircraft droned overhead. As the mourners filed softly from the cemetery, I realized that a great and lasting bond between the R.A.F. and the Glider Pilot Regiment had finally been cemented.

Late one afternoon, a few days later, three glider crews, including our own, proceeded by road transport to Netheravon where we were given a lecture by the Intelligence Officer and issued with escape kits. After a somewhat hasty tea in the mess, each crew was given a brand new Horsa glider and flew down to Portreath in Cornwall, landing at dusk. We were allocated sleeping quarters and told to get as much sleep as possible as we were to be called at 0530 hours the following morning. Once in bed, we lay smoking and talking quietly, wondering where we would be the following night. It wouldn't be England, that was a dead cert.

Next morning, after an excellent breakfast, we assembled in the briefing room and were told that we were to fly to an American-held aerodrome called Salle, in French Morocco on the North African coast. We looked at each other, all thinking the same thing. The whole trip would be over sea and the tug's navigators would have to be spot on or else we would end up in the drink. With Salle approximately 1,200 miles away there wouldn't be any margin for error, even though the Halifaxes were carrying overload fuel tanks.

It was fitting that Major Cooper, as Squadron Commander, would be the first to take off at 0800 hours. He had two very good glider pilots with him—Sergeant Dennis Hall, a quiet sort of bloke, and Sergeant Antonopoulos, a very tough-looking Greek. Both these sergeant-pilots were later awarded the Air Force Medal.

Percy, Harry and myself were to take off at 0805 hours, and I was very pleased to know that once again we were to be towed by

"Buster" Briggs and crew. Somehow, I always felt supremely confident flying behind "Buster" and so far as I was concerned there wasn't a better Halifax pilot in the squadron.

The crew of the third Horsa, which was to take off at 0810 hours, consisted of a lieutenant, Sergeant Nigel Brown, a tall, sandy-haired fellow who sported a magnificent bushy moustache, and Staff-Sergeant Galpin ("Galp" as he was affectionately called by all who knew him), who typified the spirit of the Glider Pilot Regiment. An immensely powerful man of tremendous character, his aggressiveness, determination and courage couldn't fail to influence anyone with whom he came in contact.

Before leaving the briefing room we were warned to keep a sharp look-out for enemy aircraft, especially over the Bay of Biscay. Several aircraft had been shot down over the Bay recently by JU 88s hunting in packs of nine or twelve. Not that we in the gliders could do much about it if we were attacked. It would simply be a case of pulling the tow release lever, landing in the drink and hoping for the best. I didn't allow my thoughts to dwell on that unpleasant prospect.

Since we had crewed up in threes we had been taking it in turns to do the take-offs and landings and it was Percy's turn to do the take-off and first hour's flying, with me taking over for the second hour. Sitting in the Horsa, awaiting the signal to take off, I must confess I didn't envy him. Portreath aerodrome was situated literally on the top of the cliffs and was surrounded on three sides by sea, and on the other side by hills. About 300 yards from the end of the runway we were using for take off, there was a steep drop of some 400 feet into the Atlantic. The weather was not particularly inspiring. It was a very dull, menacing day with a strong squally wind, and thick black cumulus cloud, with a base of under a thousand feet.

After what seemed an interminable wait, Major Cooper's combination moved down the runway and became airborne. Operation Turkey Buzzard was under way. I looked at Percy, who was sitting there looking supremely confident and he gave me the "thumbs up" sign. "O.K., Lofty, here we go," he called to me, and we started to move. We must have been no more than halfway down the runway, when Percy eased the Horsa off the deck, and from then on we were in trouble. No sooner had we become airborne, than the Horsa flopped back on the runway with a solid thump. This procedure was repeated several times until Percy, with a last despairing heave on the controls, managed to get it to stay airborne only a few yards from the end of the runway. I had one hand on the undercarriage release lever and looked at Percy for the signal to pull it. He nodded to me just as we were about to pass over the cliff tops, and I pulled the lever. At once we were in a most fantastic flying position behind the Halifax. The starboard wing dropped viciously, and it was only by holding the control wheel hard over to port that Percy was able to get the wing up to anything like its correct position. Even so, it was taking all his strength to hold it there, and at the slightest sign of relaxing on his part, down would go the wing once again. Obviously something was seriously amiss, and we soon found out what it was. A very anxious-looking Harry poked his head in the control cabin and yelled at the top of his voice: "Stone the bleedin' crows. The ——ing Cowson undercart's stuck in the Cowson bleedin' starboard wing!" I suggested he went back to have another look while I tried the release lever again. After pulling the lever several times, I realized that the offending undercarriage was firmly embedded in the wing and there it intended to stay until we landed. Percy was sweating freely with his exertions, and it was obvious that something would have to be done. To add to his discomfiture, the Horsa started to swing with a violent pendulum motion from side to side of the tug. I decided to call "Buster" Briggs on the intercom. as he must have been wondering what the hell was going on. "Matchbox to Zero—Matchbox to Zero. Are you receiving me—are you receiving me—Over." "Zero to Matchbox—Zero to Matchbox—Receiving you loud and clear—Go ahead—Over." I explained briefly what had happened and Buster replied: "Bad luck, Glider. Do you think you can hold on; it seems a pity to turn back now we're airborne." I looked at Percy and he nodded. "O.K. Zero—will hang on and hope for the best—Out." I suggested to Percy that we fly half an hour spells instead of one hour, and he readily agreed. Just then there was a terrific burst of machine-gun fire, and I nearly died of fright. "The bastards are attacking us already," I yelled to Harry, who'd popped an anxious head into the control cabin once again. I must have left my intercom. on, because the Halifax rear-gunner came through with a laughing voice—"It's all right, Lofty boy, I was only testing my guns." "Well, next time tell us beforehand, you lousy bastard," I replied. "You scared the ——ing daylights out of me!"

We had been airborne for about fifteen to twenty minutes now, and were still only about 500 feet above an angry-looking sea. The cloud base was getting lower and lower. Ahead of us it looked as though it was down to almost sea level. "Buster" Briggs came through on the intercom.—"Zero to Matchbox—am going to have a shot at getting above the clouds, do you think you can hang on? Over." Percy nodded resignedly, and I answered—"O.K., Zero—will do our best and start praying—Out." This was terrible! Things had been bad enough already with the starboard wing as it was. What followed now was a sheer bloody nightmare. Had things been normal, before we entered cloud, Percy would have taken the Horsa down through the tug slipstream into a low-tow position. To have attempted it with the starboard wing placed as it was would have been madness, so he had no alternative but to stay in the high-tow position. The tug disappeared into the clouds and we followed. An eerie silence seemed to descend on us as we were surrounded by white, misty vapour, and the glider started to get tossed around violently like a cork in a whirlpool. After a few minutes I had lost all sense of direction. God alone knows whether we were flying upside down, sideways or what. I looked at the altimeter, 2,200 feet, so we were still climbing all right. Percy had been doing a magnificent job hanging on to the control column. He was sweating like mad, but his face looked as imperturbable as ever. I was glad to have him around. Just over 3,000 feet I looked at my watch. Time to give Percy a spell. I put my hands on my own control column in its unnatural position. "O.K., Percy, ready when you are." "Thanks, Lofty, she's all yours, and the best of luck!" With these comforting words he took his hands off his control column, and mine spun round in my hands back to its normal position. I felt like a tenderfoot cowboy being put on a bucking bronco for the first time, only this Horsa was more vicious than any bronco. It had to be broken in. No gentle handling of the controls for this glider! It could only be mastered by sheer bloody brute strength! By dint of considerable exertion, I somehow managed to get the control column back to where it had been when I had taken over from Percy.

Things looked pretty grim. Of the tug there was so sign. Where it was I hadn't a clue! We could be flying over the top of it for all I knew. It wouldn't be the first time that had happened in cloud. A few feet in front of the glider I could just make out the vee of the tow rope where it parted to join on to each wing of the Horsa. Every now and again the cloud would thin out slightly and I would catch a glimpse of the shadowy vague outline of the tug. Sometimes I could swear we were almost flying alongside it and I swore at the Horsa—"Where do you think you're going now, you bastard?" I couldn't get rid of the thought that was going through my mind with nagging persistence, that all the time we were in this cloud there was a chance of the tow rope snapping as easily as a piece of cotton thread. If that happened, there was only one direction we could travel. Downwards! Down and down until we would eventually have to come to terms with the unfriendly Atlantic. I didn't fancy our chances if we had to ditch in this weather. At 4,000 feet we were still in cloud and I was still struggling with the control column. Harry was now sitting in the seat next to me, as Percy had gone back for a well-earned rest. Not that I could imagine him getting much rest while we were being tossed around as we were. I was beginning to tire with the terrific concentration and effort needed to fly this Horsa, when at 5,200 feet we broke through the cloud ceiling to a scene of dazzling brilliance. Never before had the sky seemed such a beautiful blue. Seen from above, the clouds which had been so menacing to our safety a few seconds ago, now looked like pure white snow stretching in every direction as far as the naked eye could see. We were not yet out of trouble, however, as I still couldn't see the tug. When it finally emerged from the clouds, after what seemed like several minutes but was in fact only a few seconds, it was slightly ahead of us and a good fifty feet below. Now came the tricky job of manoeuvring the Horsa back into its correct flying position without breaking the tow rope, a job made considerably easier by the expert skill of "Buster" Briggs in the Halifax. Once we were back in our rightful position, I noticed that what had seemed such a hard job, keeping the starboard wing up, was now child's play after our nightmare antics climbing up through the clouds. I knew now that nothing short of a direct attack by JU 88s could stop us reaching Africa. At about the same time, although I didn't of course know it then, Major Cooper and his crew were going down in the "drink", having broken their tow rope attempting to climb through the same clouds we were now looking down upon.

I was very grateful to hand over to Harry when my half hour was up, as I was soaking wet with sweat. Percy took over my seat and I went back into the fuselage to change. It had been very cold at Portreath and I was wearing a vest, shirt, pullover and battledress. After my exertions of the previous half hour, I was glad to strip down to the waist and have a brisk rub down. Considerably refreshed, I donned a tropical shirt and went to have a look at the starboard wing through one of the port-holes in the fuselage. It was worse than I had expected. Not only was the wheel embedded in the main part of the wing, part of it was sticking in the flaps, so we wouldn't be able to use them while landing. I could see the undercarriage parachute half in and half out of the wing and shuddered to think what would happen if it worked loose and opened while we were still on tow. The steel leg of the undercarriage was pointing straight downward and causing a considerable amount of drag on the starboard wing. The end of the leg was below the level of the fuselage and would obviously touch the ground first when we landed. However, we would have to worry about that when the time came. It was easy to guess what had happened. The undercarriage, fixed for jettisoning after take-off, had only been attached by a thin wire. During our series of bumps on the runway, the wire had come adrift and the wheel had bounced, turned turtle and stuck in its present position. Having assessed the damage to the wing and deciding there was nothing we could do about it, I dismissed it from my mind, got out my trumpet and spent the remainder of my rest period blowing long notes in the high register. I thought this was great fun. Playing my trumpet in the fuselage of a Horsa glider at 5,000 feet over the Bay of Biscay must surely be something that no one else had ever done, or has done, since. This was terrific! I could play to my heart's content and as loudly as I liked without such comments as "Lofty, can't you practise in the wash house" or "For Pete's sake stick a mute in it, I'm trying to get some kip!"

After four or five hours flying a gap appeared in the clouds, and just off the port wing, and over 5,000 feet below, I saw a city. It looked absolutely magnificent, and I can only assume it was Lisbon. Indeed we were over the gap so quickly that I thought I had imagined it, but Percy had seen it too. Shortly after that the cloud started to thin out and eventually disappeared altogether. From then on it was just like a pleasure trip. The farther south we flew, the calmer the sea seemed to look and the bluer the sky. The sun got stronger and stronger, and the perspex windows of the control cabin were too hot to touch. Soon we were flying stripped to the waist and wearing anti-glare glasses. Flying with the control column in its unnatural position had now become almost second nature.

It was about this time that the Halifax rear-gunner suggested I played him a tune on the trumpet, and, using my intercom. as a microphone, I readily obliged. From then on it developed into a sort of aerial request programme with the Halifax crew supplying the requests. So passed a pleasant half hour, which ended only when "Buster" Briggs politely pointed out that he couldn't hear himself speak to his crew. We had been airborne for ten hours when I handed over to Harry and went back for a rest. Percy had just taken my seat when he called out, "Coastline ahead." It was indeed, and I could see the long low brown line of the African coast getting nearer every second. My heart beat faster and faster, and I didn't envy Harry Flynn who was going to have the job of landing on a strange airstrip with the handicap of the starboard wing and undercarriage. We crossed the coast and I could see the long straight coastal road stretching for miles. Less than four hundred yards to our right, and alongside the coastal road, was Salle airfield. Two or three miles beyond it was the gleaming white city of Rabat, capital of French

Morocco. It had been a first-class job of navigation, but then we wouldn't have expected anything less from "Buster" Brigg's navigator. We did a couple of circuits to size up the airfield, decreasing height as we did so, until finally Harry released at 600 feet on the downwind leg.

I stood in the doorway of the control cabin overlooking Harry's shoulder as he made his approach. He did a long gentle sweeping turn and lined himself up beautifully with the runway. Coming in for the touchdown, I thought that if anything we were a shade too fast at 80-85 m.p.h., but then, Harry was at the controls and better able to judge. He did, however, seem to be having a spot of trouble with the control colufn and Percy asked, "Want any help, Harry?" "Not me, mate," said Harry, "I can handle this Cowson—it's a piece of cake." We touched down at eighty, and things happened quickly after that. There was a tremendous tearing, screeching din as we belted down the iron mesh runway. Suddenly the undercarriage parachute worked loose and with a sharp crack it opened and pulled the Horsa round in a right-angled turn. The force of the 'chute opening jerked the wheel out of the wing and it bounced back and hit the tailplane with the parachute wrapping itself round the tailfin. At this stage I was hurled bodily on to the fuselage floor. We came to an abrupt halt in some sandy scrub at the runway intersection and the glider tipped slowly sideways with the starboard wing coming to rest on the sand. I picked myself up. Percy looked at Harry. I looked at Harry. We all looked at each other and I spoke —"It's a piece of ——ing cake!" We all burst out laughing as the tension was relieved. We had landed the first Horsa to fly all the way from England to Africa. Within minutes we were surrounded by a crowd of admiring American airmen whose attitude seemed to be— "Gee! You Limeys sure must be tough to land those gliders like that and walk away unhurt." We just couldn't convince them that this had not been a normal landing until a few minutes later another Horsa came in, made a beautiful landing and out stepped Galpin and Co! We spent a few pleasant days at Salle patching up our Horsa and being very hospitably entertained by our American allies and then flew back to England to be immediately sent off on a short leave.

Turkey Buzzard was now in full swing, and several Horsas had been successfully ferried to Salle. Not without mishaps, however, as quite a few had come to grief in the Bay of Biscay. Sergeants Antonopoulos and Hall, along with an Irishman, Sergeant Paddy Conway, had made a second attempt a week earlier, but had again come down in the Bay. They were still missing.

Captain Denholm was keeping things moving in England, leaving Major Cooper free to organize the ferrying from Salle across North Africa to the forward Air Strip. There now appeared to be a shortage of tugs, as quite a few crews were now at Portreath with the Horsas, waiting for Halifaxes to tow them out to Salle. Percy, Harry and I had only been back from leave three or four days, when Captain Denholm informed us that we were now a priority crew, having already done the trip, and that we would take off for Portreath that evening carrying some spare parts that were urgently needed in North Africa.

As we took off for the comparatively short trip to Portreath, we carried, apart from ourselves and the spare parts, ten passengers and a cardboard box containing a dozen eggs. The ten passengers consisted of three glider crews who were going to wait at Portreath, and one tiny black kitten, complete with a basket and a blue ribbon tied in a bow round its neck. I was flying the Horsa.

By the time we neared Portreath, I was getting a bit fed up with a few of the passengers who were standing in a bunch round the control cabin doorway and were literally breathing down my neck. Being glider pilots themselves, they were critically watching every move I made and from time to time passed good-natured sarcastic comments among themselves.

Arriving at Portreath, I could see that the runway in use would mean us coming in to land from the seaward side and over the cliffs. For the benefit of my colleagues, I decided to execute a landing which, although spectacular looking, was perfectly safe under normal conditions. I cast off over the sea at about six hundred feet on the crosswind leg with the runway on my left, and immediately put the Horsa into a steep climbing turn to port. Coming out at the top of the turn facing the runway, I levelled out, slammed on full flap and went straight into a vertical dive. All this had been carried out in more or less one single manoeuvre and there were grunts of approval from the glider pilots standing in the doorway! So far, so good! We appeared to be losing height rapidly in the dive. Far too rapidly! I glanced at the air speed indicator, saw that we were doing about 130 m.p.h. and realized to my dismay that the flaps hadn't worked. I pulled the flap lever up and down desperately, but to no avail.

The runway was by no means a long one and I could see that unless I could get the speed down to anything like landing speed we would overshoot. To make matters worse, there was virtually no wind and one of the blokes was laughing his head off as he pointed this out. We were nearly half way up the runway and still doing around 100 m.p.h. when I yanked the control column back and tried a touch down. We bounced and became airborne again. I tried once more.

Again we bounced and again we were airborne. So it went on in a series of bucking bronco leaps right across the airfield, until with a rending, tearing crash, we finally came to rest with the nose of the Horsa in an air-raid trench and the tail sticking in the air. The glider pilot passengers were all in a heap in the control cabin doorway, and there were many unprintable remarks as they picked themselves up and rubbed their bruises. The kitten was still fast asleep, and the eggs were intact. An R.A.F. corporal stuck his head in the fuselage doorway, surveyed the wreckage, and said—"Blimey, Sarge, you made a right bleedin' mess of that one!"

As we walked away from the wrecked Horsa, we were told that the spare parts would be transferred to another glider and that we could still take off for Africa the following morning as planned, so at 0800 hours next day we duly took off, with Percy at the controls and me in the co-pilot's seat.

This time the take-off was inland towards some hills. I was just about to pull the undercarriage release lever when there was a helluva lot of shouting on the intercom. from the tug. Both the rear gunner and the wireless operator were yelling at the tops of their voices and the words I could pick out most were "Release" and "Pull off". I glanced ahead, and the Halifax with its overload fuel tanks looked as though it would be unable to clear the hill tops, which were looming nearer every second and were now almost on top of us. In the face of this I cast off immediately and we were adrift with less than a couple of hundred feet of height to spare for Percy to find a landing place. The hillside seemed to be covered with tiny fields, each bounded by stone fences. Unfortunately, we hit one of these stone fences with a terrific crash and finished up with the Horsa standing on its nose. Percy and Harry were O.K., but my safety harness broke and I shot forward, my head going through the perspex roof of the control cabin. The Horsa itself was a complete write-off. Later, it transpired that the two aircrew had been shouting at me to release the undercarriage. Had they kept quiet and minded their own business it would have been jettisoned anyway and we would no doubt have carried on to North Africa. As it was, Harry and Percy went back to Holsmley South and I was kept in the station hospital for a few days, under observation for possible head injuries. Just to rub it in, on coming out of hospital, I decided to get back to Holmsley as quickly as possible, and a young sergeant-pilot offered to give me a lift in his Whitley bomber as far as Hurn, where he had to land for some reason or other. We took off just before dark, and an hour later everything seemed to be going wrong. First the wireless packed up, then all sorts of things happened, with the result that, with the aircrew hopelessly lost, we finally landed at a satellite fighter aerodrome in the early hours of the following morning. When I finally arrived at Holmsley, thoroughly fed up, Captain Denholm sent me off on a few days' leave.

Back at Holmsley, it was obvious that we were dead unlucky as a crew, so we reluctantly decided to part company and crew up with someone else. Harry Flynn's luck was still out and on his trip to Africa, his tug-glider combination was attacked and shot down over the Bay of Biscay by a pack of nine JU 88s. Fortunately for Harry and his crewmates, they were picked up by a destroyer a few hours later.

For my next trip to Salle, I crewed up with Sergeants Coombs and Hatton. Charlie Coombs, an ex-member of the Military Police, was a magnificent specimen. Over six-feet tall with wavy auburn hair and a splendid moustache, he looked every inch a soldier, and with his impressive physique he even managed to look smart in battledress. Dougie Hatton was a likeable character who hailed from Lancashire. Ruddy-complexioned, stockily built, of medium height, he had slightly protruding teeth and an infectious grin. We spent an idyllic week at Portreath awaiting a tug to tow us to Salle. The weather was glorious and we whiled away the days sunbathing and swimming on the lovely Cornish beaches, along with a few other glider pilots and some comely-looking Waafs. The evenings we spent in the local pub, where I even managed to get in a spot of trumpet-playing. A pleasant interlude indeed!

One evening, a couple of Halifaxes flew in and we were duly allocated one of them and briefed to take off the following morning. I was none too happy about the aircrew of the tug we were assigned to. There was something about them which just didn't inspire any confidence. The skipper was a young, jittery, flying officer I hadn't seen before, and he seemed to be constantly arguing and bickering with his crew. Still, I thought that perhaps I had come to expect too much having been towed so often by "Buster" Briggs.

We took off towards the sea from Portreath and climbed steadily to about 2,000 feet into a brilliant blue sky. How different the weather was compared to my first trip. Not a cloud as far as the eye could see, and the Atlantic below us looked like a millpond. As far as Dougie and Charlie were concerned this was their first trip and it looked as though they were in for a nice pleasant one. The Horsa was handling a treat and we had one-hourly spells each at the controls. We had been flying for something like four hours at 2,000 feet and I was at the controls when without warning the Halifax went into a dive. The dive got steeper and I snapped into the intercom.—"What the bloody hell's going on!" There was no reply, but I could hear the tug crew shouting at each other. I decided to hang on until the last possible moment before releasing, as with the sea as calm as it was I didn't anticipate any trouble if I had to ditch. The speed built up to a terrific rate but at the last second when it seemed certain that the Halifax must crash into the sea, it levelled out and both tug and glider were skimming across the top of the water. The names I called the tug pilot over the intercom, during the next few minutes were unprintable. It appeared that he had set the controls of the Halifax on "George", the automatic pilot, and had left his seat to go and talk to one of the crew. "George", of course, had chosen that inopportune moment to pack up and become unserviceable. We shakily climbed back to a couple of thousand feet and continued on our way. A few miles farther on we spotted a lone aircraft flying towards us. It turned out to be a German Focke-Wulf Condor. Apparently it was not looking for trouble, however, because after turning and flying parallel with us for a few miles (just out of range of the tug's machine-guns), it waggled its wings, turned again and flew on its way. The rest of the trip was without incident and we landed at Salle just nine hours, fifty-five minutes after take off. The first thing I did on landing was to seek out the tug skipper to tell him just what I thought of him, but he was so nervous and apologetic that I let it slide. However, I wasn't exactly looking forward to the next day, when we had to fly behind him for another ten hours over the Atlas Mountains right across North Africa.

Next morning the heat was terrific, and as I stood watching the Halifax being refuelled with its 2,400 gallons of high-octane fuel, I didn't envy the tug pilot his job of coaxing it up over the Atlas Mountains with a Horsa on the end of the tow-rope. The skipper told us that he proposed to do a sweeping circuit to the left on take-off which would take us over the coastline, climbing steadily all the time so that by the time we completed the circuit and arrived back over the aerodrome, we would have about 2,000 feet in hand before setting a course for the Atlas Mountains. We took off, with Charlie at the controls, and had climbed to about 500 feet when thick black smoke started pouring out of the tug's starboard inner engine. It didn't need much imagination to see that something was seriously wrong. I called the tug skipper to ask if he would like us to cast off, and as I did so the starboard outer engine started to smoke. The tug skipper managed to make himself heard above the frightened voices of the rest of the crew and told me to cast off as soon as I liked, to give him a chance to maintain what height he had to complete the circuit back to the runway. Charlie nodded and I released just as we crossed the flat coastline. Without hesitation he went into a steep climbing turn over the sea until the Horsa's nose was headed back towards the land and then went into a steep dive. I thought at first he intended landing on the beach, but Charlie had other ideas. As soon as he had built up a good speed he levelled out, crossed the coast, and executed a perfect landing in a flat field adjacent to the long coastal road which ran alongside Salle airstrip less than four miles distant.

From release to the actual landing had taken less than a couple of minutes, and we quickly jumped out to watch the Halifax which was going its slow, heavy, ponderous way round the circuit, with smoke still coming furiously from two of its engines and slowly but surely losing height. We stood silently watching it, each of us hoping desperately that it would make the runway, but it was not to be. From where we were standing, the Halifax appeared to touch down in the sandy scrub just short of the runway and bounce high in the air, something falling off it as it did so. At the height of the bounce the Halifax blew up with a tremendous explosion which we could feel from where we were standing nearly four miles away. In less than fifteen minutes (during which time we were surrounded by masses of excited Arabs and their offsprings, who seemed to appear from nowhere) a convoy of American jeeps, trailers and tractors arrived to convey us and the undamaged Horsa back to Salle airstrip, where the Halifax was still burning. The rear turret had fallen off when the Halifax bounced, and the rear gunner escaped with a few scratches. Of the rest of the crew, there was no trace. They just didn't stand a chance!

We were now stranded at Salle without a tug, so settled down to live in our Horsa, be entertained by the ever-hospitable Americans and wait patiently for a spare Halifax to arrive to tow us to our destination. I soon found a couple of Yank musicians, a guitarist and accordionist, and will always remember those few pleasant evenings playing in the middle of a circle of squatting Americans on that sandy, scrubby airstrip, eager for every note of music they could get. Harry James's version of "You made me Love You" was very popular at the time and requests for it were numerous.

However, I was only too pleased when a lone Halifax arrived about a week after the accident to tow us for the rest of the trip. The pilot, Flight-Sergeant "Duggie" Dougal, his co-pilot, Sergeant Arthur Berry, and the rest of the crew had been great friends of mine since long before the start of Turkey Buzzard and I was delighted to know that they were to tow us on to our destination. "Duggie" I knew to be an absolutely first-rate pilot and had been towed by him on many occasions. We wasted no time and took off for the advanced airstrip near Sousse the following morning.

Just as on the previous trip I'd had a feeling that something would go wrong, I had a feeling on this trip that everything would be O.K. Sure enough we landed at Sousse about ten hours after take off, following a magnificent flight over the Atlas Mountains entirely without incident. Having safely delivered the Horsa, we spent two or three pleasant days on the advanced airstrip at Sousse renewing old friendships, and then one morning climbed aboard "Duggie's" Halifax, homeward bound via Gibraltar.

We touched down at Gibraltar in the afternoon, where "Duggie" intended to refuel and take off for England that night. As it turned out there was a very heavy mist, and all aircraft were grounded. The weather conditions remained the same the following night and looked like being the same on the third night when the inevitable mist closed down early in the evening. In view of this we decided, after having wangled a fiver each advance of cash from a considerate Quartermaster, to look in at the station dance being held that evening. "Duggie" had been having tummy trouble all day, but elected to come along. On arrival at the recreation hall where the dance was in full swing, we went straight to the bar and proceeded to down a few pints, as there seemed little likelihood of us flying that night. Around ten o'clock, Arthur Berry, who by then had quite a "load on", wandered over to the band and had a few words with the leader, who, in turn, asked me to sit in with his group for a swing session. I was right in the mood by this time and didn't need to be asked twice. We went into an impromptu swing session, which was greatly appreciated by the dancers as they yelled for more after each number. I was in the middle of a chorus, and the time was around 11.30, when I noticed an airman rounding up "Duggie" and the rest of the boys. "Duggie" signed to me and I thanked the bandleader and went over to join him. The mist had cleared suddenly, and we were to take off for England at midnight.

A few last-minute instructions and we climbed aboard the Halifax, which had been loaded up with sacks of mail destined for England. We parked ourselves where we could and nervously awaited take-off. I don't think any of us were feeling very happy at that moment. The runway being used for take off ended literally in the sea, and none of us relished the prospect of ending up in the drink at this stage. We needn't have worried! Poor "Duggie" may not have been feeling too well with the effects of his tummy upset, but his capabilities as a Halifax pilot were by no means diminished. We cleared the end of the flarepath with about fifty yards to spare, and headed out to sea, climbing steadily. After about ten minutes, Arthur Berry took over to enable "Duggie" to have a few hours' rest in the fuselage. Charlie Coombs and Dougie Hatton were also fast asleep, and I was just about to settle down myself, when the Flight Engineer shook me on the shoulder and shouted in my ear—"Hey— Lofty! Arthur wants to know if you'd like to have a bash on the controls!" Ready to try anything once, I went up front to the pilot's cabin and got into the pilot's seat. I felt just great sitting there in control of the giant four-engined Halifax, and it just didn't seem possible that less than an hour previously I had been playing my trumpet in a swing session in Gibraltar. We were flying at about 9,000 feet, and the only light in the cabin came from the luminous dials on the control panel. It was just like sitting in a Link Trainer back in the old days of flying training. Every now and again the navigator's voice would come over the intercom, with a slight adjust- ment of course. After an hour or so I glanced back in the fuselage and noticed that Arthur Berry, too, was fast asleep next to "Duggie". I must confess I had one or two uneasy moments when I allowed myself to think what would happen if we were attacked by a prowling JU 88, 9,000 feet over the Bay of Biscay, with myself at the controls. However, all went well.

The second story concerns a Halifax-Horsa combination that was intercepted, again by Condors, and the glider forced to cast-off and "ditch" about 140 miles west of Cape Finisterre. The three-man crew, Sergeants Antonopoulus, Hall and Conway, were adrift in a small rubber dinghy for eleven nights and days, but their spirit never failed, despite extraordinary privations. Antonopoulas nar- rates their experiences quite simply. Here is his story in his own words:

The first few hours after the attack we were too occupied to give much thought to the series of incidents which had led to our being in a dinghy, buffeted by a rough swell, 140 miles west of Cape Finisterre. For two of us, Denis Hall and myself, this was a quasi- humorous repetition of a similar happening only a week previously, when the tow-rope snapped and forced us to ditch in the same spot of the ocean, in the company of Major Cooper, our Squadron Commander.

This second time, two enemy planes (which we took to be Condors) had finally compelled the tug pilot to request us to cast off, after a gallant but hopeless struggle. During the fight I did my utmost to assist the tug by following the evasive twists and turns with all possible accuracy, while Hall in the co-pilot's seat was alert to every move and ready to take control in case of any failure on my part. As for the third man, Paddy Conway, he had apparently been roused from a quiet rest, while eating a Mars Bar in the back of the glider. Good old Paddy! He dashed up and down the length of the glider, giving us a running commentary on the fight and hits (with appropriate epithets), and even going so far as to poke his rifle through one of the portholes.

The ditching went well and everyone acted as per drill. So much happening: the grabbing of odds and ends, the box with the Thermos flask, the ground sheet, the small haversack, all the time wrestling for footholds as we launched the dinghy, and fighting to keep away from the heaving wreck under which we drifted so persistently. The rope became entangled and we had to scamble back on to the fuselage to cut it free and hitch it to the small tail-plane, eventually cutting it loose altogether as the whole glider broke up, and salvaging a few odd sticks of wreckage as they floated by. Then came the endless drifting, our hopes still high, all eyes searching the horizon, still quite confident, at least outwardly, that we could not fail "to be picked up this evening".

The wind rose that night, and large waves swamped us repeatedly; the dinghy was full of water, we were soaked to the skin, and so we were to remain from then on. I lost my temper and told the elements what I thought of them. Denis grinned and Paddy laughed, and we huddled together, shivering, till morning.

All day we searched the horizon around us; once we heard a plane overhead but could see nothing. The sky was clouded over, the sea choppy, and towards evening it was unanimously decided that we should hoist sail, so I erected a Heath Robinson arrangement with two of the salvaged sticks stuck T-wise in the flask box and the ground sheet stretched over it, Paddy being very dubious of my Granny knots. Denis Hall took charge of the rationing and opened up one of the flasks of tea. The tea was horrible as the milk had curdled, and we had to throw the whole lot away, our stomachs being already upset by continual retching as we bobbed up and down hour after hour.

We felt a little happier that evening as the wind pushed us along, with the drogue leaving a tiny wake behind us; at least we were getting somewhere! The nearest land was east, and we were travelling south-east. We ended the day in full song, with Paddy as leader.

The third day dawned after a quiet, but very cold, night and we were glad to see the sun rising into a clearer sky; we sorely needed warmth for we were chilled and hungry. Denis distributed some food: a few raisins remaining from one of our aircrew rations, two Horlicks tablets each, and a little water from one of the packs. To while away the time Paddy began telling us the story of his life; we listened distractedly, with eyes on the horizon, until we heard a faint drone in the distance. All talking stopped and the sound grew louder. Yes! A plane was approaching! Two planes were approaching, and we were right on their track. I grabbed the Very light pistol and waited for the best moment to fire. We all three realized at the same instant that the two planes were really one of our own Halifaxes with a Horsa in tow. I fired ahead of the tug and again as best I could between the tug and the glider; surely the rear gunner or the glider pilots must see it! But there was not a sign from either, though they were lower than a thousand feet.

Another cold and rough night, longing for the dawn, to be able to see and hope and to be warm; these nights were frightening and we hated them.

In the morning Paddy informed us that he had a feeling we would be picked up that day; we believed him, for of course we wanted so much to believe that. We did see the ship, too, very close, less than 400 yards away, we thought. Paddy fired the pistol several times, and he fired *at* it. We waited. But no; he just sat back and called the crew a few names, and we were sure that they must be German anyway.

In the afternoon the wind grew stronger and the swell increased. We were hungry. Denis and I were childishly attempting to fish with bent pins and chewing-gum, when a huge wave came at us like a wall. The next thing I knew I was fighting my way from under the dinghy, amidst a shroud of ground sheets and strings; I got out at last and found Paddy beside me. Together we tried to right the dinghy, and with both our weights we pulled and heaved on the hand-grips and got the dinghy vertically on its side, but it flopped back the wrong way up. We succeeded at the second attempt, and then heard the voice of Denis, who had been missing all this time. He appeared, floating towards us with one of the ration packs in his arms; he had grabbed it as it sank, and we felt very grateful. After a great effort I managed to clamber back into the dinghy and help my two companions in turn, not forgetting the ration box.

What a sorry plight we were in, with the dinghy full to the brim, the sail hanging over the side, only one half-empty ration pack, and Paddy without a dry cigarette. It took us ages to bale all the water out of the dinghy, and how weak and exhausted it left us, but how thankful we were at having survived that dreadful ordeal; that evening we all joined in prayer as the sun was going down.

That night Paddy was very ill; the constant strain of sitting so long in the same position was affecting his back. He moaned quietly in a half-sleep. Denis and I put him between us and tried to make a rest for him by joining hands behind his back. I repaired the sail, when I thought the wind had dropped sufficiently.

From then on conditions grew worse. With little water left, we were rationing ourselves to an eggcupful a day, instinctively looking away while waiting for the tiny container; each one made his small mouthful last a long time and none of us could bear to watch another one drink. The Horlicks tablets were unchewable with so little saliva to dissolve them. We looked thin and haggard, and salt water rashes began to appear on the most tender parts of our bodies. Our tongues were thick; Paddy was often delirious. Denis kept very quiet, though he and I said much to each other with our eyes. The dinghy was losing air by this time, and topping her up three or four times a day with the bellows was an exhausting routine.

We saw a boat or a plane every day; but we had no Very pistol now, only fluorescent powder which we trailed hopefully behind us from time to time.

One day we saw a fine sailing boat, just the type of craft that would be sent in answer to our prayers, we thought, but no luck! The bright sun was now affecting my eyes, and at night I could see as many as six moons in a row. Paddy grew worse; very weak, at times unconscious, at times delirious, and always feeling that "today we would get picked up".

On the ninth night we saw a large ship with all lights ablaze and we regained hope. At the same time, all my limbs became completely and inexplicably paralysed, but I managed to drink the water with which we had all agreed to celebrate the occasion. Well, was it not obvious that we must be very near land! But in the morning there was nothing to be seen but the interminable ocean.

We had less water than ever now, and the dinghy was deflating fast. Every two hours I kept topping her up with the bellows. My heart would pound and my ears felt as if they would burst. Another plane appeared that day and once more we were not seen.

The eleventh morning dawned, very quietly, not a breath of wind. Soon fog enveloped us completely. I suggested paddling a little, but Denis was too weak and we gave it up after a short while. Besides it seemed useless. Then, about noon, Denis and I looked at each other; we had heard a sound, the sound of a motor, a slow beat. "It must be a ship!" We dare not whistle in case they should take it for a fog warning and turn away. Then suddenly we saw it, a small trawler, making straight for us. A man was leaning on the rail. We blew our whistles now all right, but with faint blows! Even Paddy stirred. At last we had been seen. The man at the rail shouted in some foreign language. I shouted back, "Non comprehendo, Englisis." I still do not know what language I was supposed to be speaking, but soon we were alongside and I was on board. Denis followed, and the sailors lifted Paddy out with ease. "Aqua," I said, remembering some long-forgotten Latin. "Agua" corrected one of the men. What did it matter! They did give us water.

We learned later that our rescuers were Spanish and that we had been picked up twenty miles off Oporto, Portugal.

The three of us have often wondered since if we should have made land by ourselves in two or three days, had we not been picked up, but at the time we certainly had no such ambition.

While the pilots were delivering the Horsa gliders to North Africa, the operational training was continuing in the Mascara Plain. The American wing of Dakotas and the Waco gliders were now in full supply, and the glider pilots were going through a makeshift training programme that I had drawn up. My main problem was to get the men into the air, for I alone knew the limitations of the glider pilots and the immensity of the task they had been set. I am the last person to suggest that risks should not be taken in war, but they must be undertaken only after full consideration of all the circumstances and with a complete knowledge of the facts. In this instance, as I judged it, the task my men had been set had been conceived in complete ignorance of the facts, and solely to gratify certain ambitions.

The plan that had been evolved was this. The glider force was to be towed 300 to 400 miles across the Mediterranean to Sicily. The complete force was to arrive at its target at about 10 p.m., and to do this the aircraft must fly three miles distant and parallel to the coast of Sicily before releasing the gliders, which would be required to land an air landing brigade, with arms and guns, on the rock-strewn shores of Sicily, close to Syracusa, by moonlight. Once on the ground this force was to disembark from the gliders, capture a bridge crossing the canal, and then move on and take the town of Syracusa. All this was to precede by some seven hours the main landings by the 8th Army on the beaches of Sicily.

Brigadier Pip Hicks and the 1st Air Landing Brigade were enthusiastic at the prospect, and they were confident they would be able to fulfil their task. But they never really understood the immensity of the task since they knew little or nothing of the technical requirements of an air landing by glider, let alone the added difficulties of landing by night in completely unknown territory.

The popular Major-General, "Hoppy" Hopkinson, had "sold" an airborne landing to General Montgomery, who knew even less than Hopkinson of the required conditions for success. All he knew was that there was an airborne force—therefore by all means let us use it. The sea was between him and Sicily, and I have no doubt that he saw in this unit a method of making a quick landing and a lead-in for the 8th Army. So far as the glider effort was concerned, he could not have known of its muddled background, the inadequacy of the training facilities, or whether the pilots were efficient or otherwise. He was given the possibility and he took it, solely on the advice of an amateur pilot who was bent on getting his force into action, come what may.

The conditions that the pilots lived under were similar to those of the ordinary Tommy—pup tents, into which they crawled at night. I feel sure they were as conscious as I was that we were regarded as a sort of privileged nuisance, and this being so we were given the minimum in transport and other help which would be the normal requirements of aviators. That a pilot needs certain conditions to make his life tolerable and to enable him to be in top flying form was beyond the comprehension of those who had set him this almost impossible task. Nevertheless, under these unhappy conditions the force made every effort to train itself. Their patience and enthusiasm was nothing short of miraculous. Only I knew how frighteningly inadequate it was, and the strain was appalling. All the training was concentrated on attempting to land a full load of guns, jeeps and men in complete darkness, and I know only too well that the necessary standard was never reached. How could it have been in the space of three weeks?

I was given permission to fly to Malta to pick up a lift in a night Beaufighter, so that I could fly along the coast and make observations of the target. This was a month before the intended attack, and it was an experience not easily forgotten.

I was flown by an Australian crew of an R.A.F. night fighter squadron, and stood between the pilot and the navigator, with intercom. earphones on my head. We roared into the night at about

4 a.m., and flew at fifty feet above the sea, which was lit by moonlight, and sped along the coast which lay in a dark mass below. We roared up and down, and I tried from my awkward position to make out where and how we were going to land, but I could see nothing.

Eventually, at dawn, we turned away and flew for home. At one point the Australian pilot spotted some shipping in the moonlit path of the sea and we had a few breathtaking moments as he started ship-strafing, but we began to lose our oil pressure in the port engine so decided to make for Malta as quickly as we could. I enjoyed all this excitement, but, alas, I knew that my journey had achieved nothing. I returned to my little force none the wiser and waited philosophically for the moon to change, for the next quarter would see us on our way. I need hardly say that I was deeply apprehensive.

The training continued and each night, standing on the flarepath, I was deeply moved by the enthusiasm and energy of the pilots, as one by one their gliders were slowly tugged off into the darkness and, later, landed safely.

At one airfield, Relizane, which was condemned as a danger spot for cholera infection, the pilots slept on the concrete floor, with mosquitoes stinging them all night. The food was limited and almost inedible. The heat was intense; by ten in the morning it was unbearable in the cockpits, and flying was out of the question. All the men could do was to lie about and sweat. It is to their everlasting credit that their sense of humour and their courage kept the training programme to schedule.

There was much to be done on the landing zones, for each time a glider landed it had to be man-handled so that another could land after it; many were the nights that I swung a tail or hung on to a wing-tip.

The flarepath presented an extraordinary problem. Not only were the flares put out by the Arabs, but they would come and steal the containers also, so that sometimes, when we arrived for training at night, we could not provide flares for the pilots to land by. Any pilot or member of the R.A.F. will know that such conditions must have been very exacting for men in the pupil stage of flying training. In spite of it all they carried out their duties like veterans.

While the men flew I had regular consultations with the Generals and Brigadiers about the main plan of the battle, for it was imperative that I should have an up-to-date picture of the military plan. The overall plan was that the assault on Sicily would be conducted by two armies, American and British. The British 8th Army were to attack the south-eastern corner, but move north via the east coast, and the Americans would do the same on the west coast.

So far as was known the German defensive plan was to use the majority of the Italian Army for defending the coast, with two Hermann Goering Divisions in mobile reserve. Thus, it was assumed that once these two divisions were committed, all troops in Sicily would be fully engaged.

The task of the 1st Airborne Division was divided into three brigade attacks. The first, on the night of July 9th/10th, was to be carried out by the 1st Air Landing Brigade—a lone glider operation with no parachutists included—with the object, as I have already mentioned, of taking the bridges near Syracusa and capturing Syracusa itself. The second attack would take place on the following night, when one parachute brigade would be dropped in the area of Augusta with the task of capturing the port. The third attack would be carried out by the 1st Parachute Brigade, supported by Horsa and Waco gliders, with guns and jeeps on board. This was to be a drop into the Catania Plain, round the Primasole bridge, which was to be held until the advancing 8th Army moved up the east coast road to meet them, when they would debouch on to the Catania Plain. So far as I was concerned the first operation was the major one, in that the whole of my force of glider pilots was committed to it.

In view of the shortage of aircraft the U.S. wing demanded that they should not be required to fly closer to the shore than 3,000 yards, because of the extensive radar reception, and that the entire flight of 400 miles should be made at 100 feet above the sea, climbing to 1,500 feet shortly before arriving on the Sicilian coast.

My task was as follows:

1. To give my pilots confidence enough in themselves to carry out the flight to Sicily and to land.
2. To land by moonlight on a rock-strewn beach, after being released at between 1,500 and 2,000 feet.
3. The gliders to be landed in groups of battalions, in order that the air landing brigade should be able to fight as a brigade group.
4. The loads in the gliders were to be infantry, jeeps and artillery.

For the Catania landings, the Horsas were to land jeeps and six-pounder guns in support of the parachute brigade. The total glider-borne effort in this second operation was to be eight Waco gliders and seven Horsas, towed by Halifaxes and Albemarles of the Royal Air Force. It was hoped that the Independent Parachute Company could be dropped on both beach heads to lay out flarepaths, so that the pilots could have some way of recognizing where they were to land.

As soon as I found that the operation was based on moonlight landings, I had a signal sent back to England, saying it was imperative that aircrews be practised in this form of landing. This instruction was completely disregarded and the pilots arrived without any night training whatever.

The whole of it covered a little under three weeks and to attain the requisite standard in the time seemed to me almost impossible.

As preparations for the Sicilian assault progressed so demands for more gliders for the air landing brigade increased, in consequence the pilots available had to be stretched out over the gliders, and my hair was turning grey with trying to ensure that each glider had a pilot capable of flying under the difficult conditions imposed on him. Today I am pretty well sure that many entered the cockpits who had had little or no training at all in Africa.

Our next move was to be a tow from the Mascara Plain to the airstrips at Sousse and Sfax on the Tunisian coast, from which bases we were to fly to Sicily and the assault. The tow to Tunisia was 600 miles in length over the Atlas Mountains. It was a long, long flight, and to us pilots it seemed endless. There was one fatal crash when the tail came off one of the Waco gliders and the entire crew and load of thirteen soldiers were killed. However, on the whole, the armada reached the landing strips well and in good order, and soon the aircraft were lined up for the great day which we awaited with excited anticipation.

I believe that our position had been sited to give the impression that our target was Sardinia, which was opposite the strips where we were stationed, and I had been told that Sardinia was packed with German troops expecting invasion.

Soon the moon came up to its first quarter and gradually grew larger and larger. Two or three days before the date of the operation a wind got up and blew at gale force. I was perplexed to know what height I should give for the gliders to cast off for landing, for to date we had been landing in dead-still air. Night after night we had practised in dead calm, and now we were faced with conditions for which we were completely unprepared.

I slept little those nights and waited for the wind to abate, but it didn't. I felt desperately alone in trying to make my decision and I left it to the very last moment. The difficulty was that I had no telephonic communications with the six strips on which the gliders were stationed. Somehow or other the height would have to be put round by word of mouth. I have to admit that I could not decide whether to instruct the pilots to go much higher or to keep to a lower height than 2,000 feet. The critics today say that one should always have too much height, and I think they are right. But I was faced with the fact that we could not put the gliders too far inland because of olive groves and cliffs, and I didn't want them to overshoot. Eventually, I put the height up 500 feet, making a total of 1,900 feet above the sea.

On the eve of the attack on Sicily the wind was blowing at forty-five miles an hour across our course. I went down to the shore to be alone, and there found the pilots eagerly waiting for the moment when the order to take-off would be given. All that remained was to brief them with the plan. As I looked at the wind whipping up the sea I wondered how many gliders would break away from the ropes which attached them to the tugs.

Those were strange times. We, the Glider Pilot Regiment, were to be towed by Americans, and the tugs and gliders would be Anglo-American; in consequence all the ground staff were from the United States Air Force. One day one of my officers asked me to come and have a look at his glider, and when I arrived he said:

"Please look at the intercom., sir. The union seems to have been tampered with." He pointed to the fitting and I saw black insulating tape bound round the wire.

"Well," I said, "what does that mean?"

"I will unwind the tape for you to see, sir." He did, and then I realized that the wire had been cut.

"What on earth is this," I exclaimed.

"Well, sir, I think you had better look at some of the others."

"Let's get hold of an American officer first," I said, and we did.

We then found that several aircraft had had the intercoms tampered with, and after some investigations it was discovered that

East of the Rhine with the 6th Airborne Division.   A German prisoner being marched away.

D-day + 1.   Hamilcar gliders landing near Raneville, Normandy.

Glider which crash-landed on the banks of the Caen Canal, June, 1944. Note how close to " Pegasus " Bridge the glider landed at night.

The tail of a Horsa glider comes away neatly if all goes to plan. If not, it is blown apart from the fuselage.

one of the fitters was an Italian-American who had taken action to prevent us attacking his country of origin. We rebound the intercom. connections and called it a day.

Another thing happened which at that time I shall always remember. One day I was passing the tent of one of the Wing-Commanders, Peter May, who had been an instructor in the Royal Air Force for some years and whom I knew well. As I passed, the ground flaps were up and he could see my feet, on which I was wearing a very nice pair of Chukka suede boots.

The Wing-Commander asked me into the tent.

"I say, George, I like those boots. May I have them if you don't come back?"

I was somewhat stunned for a moment, but said "Oh, yes, of course," as casually as possible. "Just ask my batman, Private Gaul, and he'll give them to you."

I mention this because it gives an idea of what another airman thought of the possibilities of our operation. The odd thing was, that when I did return from Sicily I found that my boots were missing, and my batman told me that Peter May had asked for them after I had gone. Perhaps the greater irony was that he put them on when he took off in his Albemarle, and was shot down and never seen again. Presumably, he went to the bottom of the sea wearing my boots.

My operations room was an old Nissen hut, and here were many photographs of the landing zones and beaches in Sicily. It was in this hut that I briefed the pilots for the flight plan.

One day in walked Alistair Cooper, having had many adventures since he left England. I asked him what his night-flying practice had been since he left, and he answered, "None." And neither had any of the pilots who had flown with him. It was incredible to think that not one Horsa pilot had had the chance to get in a full practice at night, despite the fact that it was known that he was going to be asked to land on a target 400 miles away from Africa with guns and jeeps, and in pitch darkness.

I hesitated before I gave Alistair his briefing. I told him he would have to carry a jeep and six-pounder gun and the Commander Royal Artillery through to the Catania Plain, and that he would have to land probably without lights.

He looked at me and said: "All right, sir. Don't worry, we won't let you down, sir."

F

He took off on the second night of the assault with a six-pounder anti-tank gun and its crew, and was never to return. In him I lost a wonderful officer and a friend. I was told that his tug, a Halifax, was hit by flak and exploded. The rope broke, and in attempting to land he crashed into the river bed, where he and all the occupants were killed.

One of the main points in the operation on the Ponte Grande was the attempt to land six Horsa gliders, three on one side of the canal and three on the other, in order that a *coup de main* might capture the bridge. The remaining 130-odd Wacos were to land, as had been originally planned, with the 1st Air Landing Brigade in battalion groups. And so the stage was set. Next day we were to try to carry out this most difficult of operations.

As I sat on the beach watching the wind and the blue of the sea and the whiteness of the wave tips, I thought back on all the air training at Tilshead, the military training, the speeches, the discipline, and so on, and I realized that all that remained was for the glider pilots to prove themselves in action—as "total" soldiers.

As I see it now, all those years ago, perhaps it was best that their patience had been tested to the limit during training, because if they had not had to joke about the tiresome limitations of the training, lack of equipment and inadequate airfields, they might not have proved so worthy as they were destined to be during the next few days.

At least I felt we had done our best, and all we could do now was to try to carry out our orders.

4

SICILY, 1943

I DROVE down to the strip in my jeep with my batman, Alec Gaul, accompanied by the brigade commander, Pip Hicks, the Senior Medical Officer and various staff officers. Silver wings glinting in the sun, thirty Dakotas and Waco gliders were waiting the signal to take off. Mine was the leading glider, and as I climbed into the cockpit with Peter Harding, my adjutant and second pilot, I looked down at the face of Alec Gaul for what I thought might be the last time. It was a tense moment. There was a strong wind blowing, the light was hard and brittle, and great waves seemed to leap into the air at the far end of the runway.

As the signal to take off was given, the propellors of the Dakotas started up with a whirl, dust flew off the runway and whipped into the air, and the tug slowly moved into position. Gripping the controls, I gave the thumbs-up signal, the rope taughtened, and I heard over the intercom. the faint sound of the Dakota pilot's voice, but the crackling and interference was so bad that from the beginning to end of the trip we were never able to hear each other clearly. We moved slowly forward, then faster and faster across the dusty strip until suddenly the Dakota disappeared in the dust and I was forced to hold the glider in position by the tow-rope's angle. Then, still gathering speed, we were out of the dust and in the clear, and there, below, was the silver Dakota tug, and below her again the sea, smothered in foam. It was extremely rough, the glider jumping up and down and from side to side, and I held on like grim death, concentrating on holding position above the Dakota. But soon I was able to relax as I became accustomed to the movements of the aircraft and its behaviour.

After a while I handed over to Peter Harding, but he was very sick and in no state to fly, so I took back the stick and without relief piloted the glider for the next 400 miles, a tow of four hours, for the time was 6 p.m. and we were scheduled to reach the target or landing zone at about ten o'clock.

71

Settling down to it I allowed myself a glance astern. It was an exhilarating sight, for there—stretching back in the evening light—was a great armada of well over two hundred aircraft. It was a great moment, one not to be missed, and all the hazards, risks and difficulties still to be faced seemed to dissolve into thin air. But it *was* rough! The spray seemed to be passing the very wing-tips, adding to the sensation of speed. I wondered if German fighters were likely to intercept, and I remember experiencing a sense of astonishment when they did not come, and, as the darkness descended, a feeling of elation that we had got away with it, for we would have been sitting ducks if a force of fighters had come across us. And what a target we would have made!

The storm did not abate, and as the sun went down, glowing red on the horizon, the foam still sweeping through the gloom, the sea changed from cold blue to dark green, and then to a menacing black.

By now my arms were aching intolerably from holding the glider in position and I felt my endurance ebbing. My eyes and my head throbbed from ceaselessly concentrating on formation flying and on the tug ahead. Then, as darkness came, the Dakota switched on a row of lights in the trailing edge of the wings, enabling me to see the tug clearly against the dark horizon.

It was a little later that I thought I was losing control, for the whole glider seemed to be sliding away to port. I tried the left rudder, then the right rudder, and then full aileron, but nothing happened. I seemed to be in a tremendous skid. I tried every flying trick I knew but could not alter the position, and as gradually we slid out and alongside the tug I felt sick with apprehension. How long could the rope last without snapping? Looking out I saw that the tug was level with us in the moonlight; we were flying side by side! What could I do? I think I must have been shouting at Peter Harding, for I could hear Brigadier Pip Hick's voice, deep and resonant, in the back: "I say, all is not well in front there!" Eventually (how I shall never know), the glider gradually came back into position. Had we gone down in that sea we most likely would never have been heard of again.

So we flew on until, looking down, I saw the cliffs of Malta below —dark, mystical and menacing—and as I passed over them I thought back to the night when I had flown from Sicily in the Beaufighter, and I wondered if the same aircraft was anywhere in the darkness, protecting us. This was our turning point. From here we flew north towards Sicily, gradually gaining height, and as we did so the air seemed to become calmer. The bright moonlight turned the water to silver and I began to experience a great peace and elation.

As we climbed I searched the darkness for Sicily and picked out the coast, recognizing its shape from the maps and charts we had studied. We changed course again and started to fly down the coast at some 1,900 feet, trying to discern exactly where we were, but it was very difficult to do this and fly the glider at the same time. Suddenly flak started to come up from Syracusa, which was being raided by the R.A.F. in order to divert the Italians' attention from us. Out of the corner of my eye I could see other aircraft behind me, for we were trying to fly in what might be termed "echelon right", so that we could land in formation on the coast.

"Can you see the release point, Peter?" I cried, trying to locate our position.

"Another five minutes or so, sir," he replied, looking at his watch.

Then, "There it is!" Peter shouted.

"I can't see a damned thing," I said, reaching for the release lever, and as I did so I saw the tug starting to turn and dive.

"My God, he's pushing off," I shouted, and heaved on the lever. The glider lifted up and after all that bucketing about seemed light and easy to handle. I turned towards the coast, and it was then I received a jolt. As we lost height it seemed as if a great wall of blackness was rising up to meet us, and at that moment the moonlight disappeared. I was devastated, for I realized that if this was happening to me, it was happening to the other pilots. What were we going to be able to do under these unforeseen conditions.

Afterwards, I discovered that the screen of blackness was a pall of dust created by the intensity and length of the gale; it completely obliterated our target. The only thing that could be said in its favour was that it made the night so bad that the Italians could never have expected we would be such fools as to come.

Descending into the darkness I had no idea where I was or what I was doing, but seeing a black object below, I turned my glider towards it, and at that moment out of the darkness came a burst of tracer bullets. There was a jolt, I saw the fabric tear open, and my port wing was hit as I began to turn. I straightened

her out and down we came, the sea rushing up to meet us. Somehow I levelled out as, with a great splash, we ditched. The water
came over my head, and as I came up I was aware of shouting and
scrambling figures as I fumbled with my straps, spitting out brine.
Then two hands grasped my armpits and I was hauled out of the
cockpit on to the fuselage.

"Are you all right, George?" I heard Pip Hicks call.

"Yes, sir, I think so," I answered, still in a daze. Then as the
mists cleared, I saw the dark forms of my passengers in the sea,
on the wings and on the fuselage.

"Everybody keep down on the wings," Hicks ordered, and we
lay flat, looking at the coast, the glider floating like a boat and giving
us something substantial to hang on to.

A searchlight suddenly shone from the shore, swung across the
sea, rested on us for a moment, and then swung out again.

"Keep still, dead still," hissed Hicks. We did. The light swung
out again and this time lingered on us. A brief moment, and then
a hail of tracer bullets streamed from the shore, and I remember
sinking in the sea, sick and terrified with an awful helpless feeling,
for there was no cover. The hail of bullets continued in bursts
but by some mercy none hit us; they were just too high and hit the
sea behind us.

"It's no good staying here," I said to Pip Hicks. "Shall we swim
for it?"

"O.K., George," he replied, "I think under these conditions it
would be best. Quietly as possible—come on, everybody."

And so we set off. I can remember my feeling of nakedness
even now, for the phosphorescence seemed to light up the night
as we made our way to shore.

Pip Hicks looked huge, like a Spanish galleon, as he ploughed
through the water, and I told him to keep down, but he said he
couldn't because his Mae West was blown up too high. Soon we
reached the shore, soaking and shaking with cold, and without
weapons for they had gone to the bottom. We felt quite helpless.
One of us—I can't remember who it was—climbed up the cliff
while the rest of us took refuge a few yards from the sea.

Suddenly there was an ear-splitting explosion, bombs dropped
all round us, and an aircraft hit the sea with a tremendous crash,
just where we had been swimming. The whole sea caught fire, and
I lay there paralysed with fear and shock watching the flames lapping

the shore. Incongruously, all I could think of was the brandy on a Christmas pudding.

By now the enemy had taken alarm, and spasmodic firing was going on all round us. We felt helpless, and I for my part was utterly dejected and despondent. All the planning and training exercises in the world could not have foreseen this situation. I wondered what had happened to the other gliders and their crews, and as I lay there one of them, white and ghostly, was caught in the searchlights. Flak burst all round it—and then there was another, and another, and another.

As it proved, some of these gliders, like ourselves, met with misfortune, and the ways their pilots faced their ordeals are worth recording here in their own words. Here is the story of Staff-Sergeant T. Ellis:

I had been one of a flight of four gliders, part of a force of 134 that had set out on the invasion of Sicily, and now my glider was down in the sea. After a quick survey of our predicament and a short conference with the officer in charge of the airborne troops that I was carrying, it was decided that being a fair swimmer I should strip and swim ashore to reconnoitre the coast, then swim back and report.

That was the intention, but the plan misfired sadly. The first part I carried out all right, and after resting I began the return journey. I had not noticed in the dark that a strong current was running and that I had drifted, and I was therefore surprised to find that when I reached what I thought to be my aircraft, it was in fact another from the squadron. I was greeted with the familiar voice of Arthur Baker murmuring "Hello, old boy! Where did you spring from?" I am afraid I wasn't in the mood to be chatty and just swore. Very soon I was back once again on land in company with Arthur and two more airborne troops who were in a similar position to myself. If I remember rightly, between us our total assets comprised two pairs of denim slacks, two shirts and two pairs of boots. My total contribution being goose pimples.

After a while we could hear the sounds of a patrol searching the rocky coast, so making up our minds quickly we decided to give ourselves up and wait for a favourable opportunity to escape, if and when we had a chance to get better equipped.

As soon as the patrol came within hailing distance, we made ourselves known and they then started to shepherd us up the cliffs to a machine-gun post at the top. We hadn't moved more than a dozen yards over the rocks when I sat down and flatly refused to go any farther.

The patrol kept on shouting at me "Avante" and motioning with their carbines, but I just shook my head, pointed to my feet and then at the rocky ground.

To my surprise one of the patrol stooped forward, pointed at me and then to his back, so without further ado, I climbed aboard and away we went. I hadn't a stitch of clothing on, and I wondered if I had full possession of all my faculties. There I was, a prisoner-of-war, looking like a bare-back rider in a circus, being pick-a-backed up a cliff by my captor.

Arthur Baker, who had been a school-teacher in civvy street, managed with his knowledge of Latin to be a fairly successful interpreter, and as a result I acquired an old greatcoat to cover my goose pimples which by now seemed to have doubled in size.

At dawn the next morning, after smoking all the Italians' cigarettes, clad immaculately in the greatcoat which just reached my knees, I, in company with the rest of my compatriots, moved off, presumably to be put behind the enemy's lines.

Just as we started I was surprised, and not a little amused, to see coming towards us one of my squadron officers. He it seems, had fared a little better than I; at least he did have a shirt. Occasionally the tail of it flapped in the breeze and exposed his hind quarters to all and sundry. Later he was provided with a blanket to conceal his nether parts from the startled stares of the women whose farmhouses and villages we passed through.

Just after mid-day and by many detours, we arrived at a farmhouse, just south of Syracusa Bridge. It proved to be the end of the line, because soon we were released by advance elements of the 8th Army who had landed at dawn.

My first reaction was to find some clothes and equipment, which I did by looting the baggage of the now-captured captors. All I could find were civilian clothes; after I had dressed, the net result was unique. A pair of lightweight boots, light grey slacks with a thin red stripe, brown-striped shirt and a green pullover, topped by the usual cherry beret, which had been given to me earlier. Across my shoulders was an Italian leather bandolier complete with ammunition. I had also acquired one of their short carbines. I must have looked a cross between an Italian onion vendor and a bandit (of which there were many) from the hills.

About a week later we were back in North Africa settling down once more to a more or less placid life in our tented camp among the olive groves.

By way of contrast, here is Staff-Sergeant A. H. Mills's story:

The North African coastline drew nearer, and in a few moments the blue ocean, turning to grey, seemed to stretch endlessly before us. I glanced at my watch and saw it was 7.15 p.m. What an impressive sight it was, as the other formations converged on us, forming a gigantic armada. I felt proud to be taking part in this great invasion. A flight of Mustangs wheeled above in the sunshine to give us a feeling of security.

Below us we observed odd ships here and there, their bows cutting large white vees in the water. I noticed that the crests of the waves were getting more pronounced, pointing to a strengthening of the wind. The sun sank rather quickly towards the sea as I handed over control to my co-pilot, and I looked round at my passengers. They seemed cheerful enough, munching barley sugar, but rather quiet, I thought. I glanced at the waves again. Yes, the crests were much larger. The wind must be getting very strong, almost up to gale force. The aircraft began to toss, but Dennis showed her that he was the master. I hoped that our navigator would make allowances for drift. Just in case I had had better warn him. I raised my "mike" but to my dismay it was completely dead. The nylon rope had probably stretched, snapping the intercom. cable which was carried along its length. All we could do now was hope.

"I have control," I shouted, and Dennis settled back for a well-earned rest. Darkness had fallen swiftly, so that I had to line up on small pinpoints of blue light arranged along the wings of the Dakota. I could still pick out the dim outline of the tug, and at intervals could see short flashes from the glowing exhausts. Then, just ahead, half a dozen powerful searchlights stabbed the night sky. Malta! We were dead on course. We approached the island low, and in the strange artificial half light I could see the preceding combinations banking into the turn to bring them on course for Sicily.

I began my turn, and the light became steadily weaker as we left Malta behind. It was dark again, and the glider began to buck in the turbulent air. I hoped that no one would be sick, as we wanted to be in a fit condition to do battle on landing. Over three hours had passed since we had left the dusty air-strip at El Djem, and I quickly calculated that we should be there in less than half an hour. Damn that intercom.!

Then, without warning, the sky became alive with searchlight beams, and streams of white-hot tracer began to form strangely fascinating criss-cross patterns on the dark backcloth of the Sicilian

sky. I quickly ordered Dennis and the troops to get on their equipment in readiness for the landing, so that we could be out as soon
as we touched down. I was in my gear already, having seen to
that earlier while Dennis had been at the controls.

Then—tragedy! My towing rope had run into trouble and to
my horror, it came tearing back towards us with its connecting
tackle striking the top of the cabin with a tremendous report, but
luckily not breaking the perspex. For a moment I was stunned, and
then as I pulled the cable release I quickly sized up the situation.
I judged that we were roughly two miles from the dark smudge that
I knew was Sicily, so now I had to carry out an action I dreaded—
ditching! And I was unable to swim!

As I gave the order to remove all equipment, remove the side
exits, and secure safety harness, I perceived a lone searchlight. It
was particularly noticeable as it was immensely powerful and had
an unusual blue beam. I turned away from it and saw that in the
strong off-shore wind we were losing altitude rapidly. I remembered
a training lecture we had had back home, when we were told that if
we ever had to ditch in a rough sea, the safest way was to land along
the troughs and not into wind which is the normal method. This
instructor, whose name I can't recollect, probably saved the lives of
us all. I sincerely thank him.

The angry sea reached up towards us, the white crests acting as
a flare path. We approached closer. I held off as long as possible
and, as we touched, it seemed as if a giant hand held us and tried
to drag us under. I pitched forward, nearly breaking my safety
harness. The sea surged in and in seconds was up to my waist. I
released myself and picking up a loose object—a rifle, I think—
I battered the cabin roof out. By now only my head was showing,
as I somehow dragged myself clear. Next minute I was sitting on
the wing, watching the cabin disappear below the waves. Only the
mainplanes now showed above the water. I wondered how long they
would remain like that; if they sank below the surface all we had to
support us were our small, now inflated, lifebelts. A quick count
told me that, so far, all had survived the ditching—Dennis having
escaped with me and the other six through the side doors. One
chap had banged his head on the way out, but fortunately this was
the only casualty.

We were all alone, I judged at least a mile from shore. The sea
was rough, tossing us up and down like a cork. When I look back
I wonder how we managed to stay on that wing, which is not an
ideal shape for sailing. We linked arms lest one of us slipped over
the side. Our legs were in the water, surprisingly quite warm, while

the rest of our bodies almost froze in the strong wind. I was fascinated by small points of light floating by on the surface of the water, later being told that this was caused by phosphorus.

I cursed my luck. To think that out of more than a hundred and thirty gliders, I would be the only one to come a cropper in the sea. Then the powerful blue searchlight I had seen earlier changed the direction of its beam to the horizontal, and began methodically to sweep the sea, to the accompaniment of glowing streams of tracer from shore-based machine-guns. There must be something else to shoot at besides us, I thought. Just then, to my dismay, a red glow from the glider's cabin began to show. Somehow, although under water, the instrument panel lights had come on, probably due to the action of the sea. I prayed that it would not give our position away. We tried to reach it but found that impossible. However, my prayers were being answered, as each time the beam stretched towards us, we sank with the swell, the powerful light either not reaching us or passing harmlessly overhead.

My luminous watch told me it was 11.30 p.m. An hour had passed since we had ditched, and almost five hours since we had left the sun-baked North African coast. I prayed again that there would be sufficient buoyancy in the wings to keep us afloat till dawn. I dreaded to think of our chances otherwise. The sound of aircraft engines, as the tugs wended their way back to their bases, had now ceased. Lucky devils those Dak crews, I thought. They would soon be having a good meal and a rest. Oh, for a nice soft bed now!

The activity on the island now increased in tempo. All the searchlights were out of action, but the sky was lit up by gunfire, tracer and explosions here and there. Then, against the light of a momentary explosion, I saw outlined something which appeared to be a ship. My heart leapt as, in unison, eight lusty voices cried, "Help! Help!" The shape grew larger and I wondered if the ship would be friendly or whether we would jump from the frying pan into the fire. Nearer it came but, to our disappointment, passed us by, disappearing into the gloom.

I knew that seaborne landings were also taking place, so I instructed my party to keep up a synchronized yell at regular intervals. If anything, we were now drifting farther away from the shore, the sounds of battle becoming quieter. By this time our throats were becoming dry and sore, our cries not carrying so far. We were cold and tired. I hoped we would have the strength to hold on. One of the men began to tremble violently and I had to keep as tight a hold on him as I was able under the circumstances.

We had been in the sea for almost five hours, the five longest hours

I had ever spent in my life. I kept imagining I could see ships in the murk, but my eyes were playing tricks on me. I saw another black smudge in front of me. Ah! This was different! "Shout as loud as you can, lads," I cried, and, straining our throats almost to breaking point, we let out a tremendous shout, and, to my delight, the ship came closer. A voice hailed us. "What nationality are you?" it queried, and as we replied, "British!" we knew with relief that they were on our side.

In minutes we saw a small boat being lowered over the side, soon being rowed towards us by rugged sailors, who helped us aboard. A short row back to the ship, and willing hands pulled us to safety. Cups of steaming tea, the best I had ever tasted, were brought to us, and after a hot shower we retired to lovely, soft, warm beds, with more tea and bars of chocolate.

I slept soundly and long, so much so that I never heard a sound of battle during the night, although in the immediate vicinity another ship had received a direct hit, sinking almost immediately.

Next morning, or rather the same morning, I arose to find that we had sailed in close to the island. As our own clothing had been ruined, we were issued with tropical kit of the Royal Navy. I went on deck and to my surprise there were several gliders still floating in the bay. I hadn't been the only one after all! I discovered that the ship was the *Ulster Monarch,* and that we had been picked up at 3.30 a.m. about three miles from Cap Murro di Porco. We must have drifted quite a way.

We spent some time sailing round to the wrecked gliders, and managed to salvage a fair amount of equipment. By this time the sea was calm, but on the mainland there was much activity, both on the ground and in the air. We had a grandstand, but rather dangerous, view of this, especially when the ships in the bay opened up with their Bofors and heavier ack-ack guns on low-flying F.W.190s and M.E.109s, which would appear from the island with very little or no warning.

We were waiting to go ashore to join up with the airborne forces, when a message came through telling us, to our chagrin, that we would not be required. Apparently all was going well.

Returning to my own troubles, even as the flak burst round the gliders caught in the searchlights I was confident that some of them at least would get through, that the Glider Pilot Regiment was making history, despite disaster, in more ways than one, and proving themselves to be the men I had envisaged. This indeed they did, for while I and my companions were lying helpless on the coast, men of the regiment were carrying out the tasks they had been set, as the accounts which follow amply testify. But by way of introduction I must explain what they had been briefed to do.

One of the major objectives of the operation was the bridge. Ponte Grande, which was of the utmost importance to both the British Army and the Italians who were defending Syracusa.

It had been planned that six Horsas should be released at 4,000 feet to land in the fields on either side of the bridge, and thus to capture the bridge from either end.

It seems incredible that such a demand should have been made, for it required the pilots to fly four or five miles from 4,000 feet, in pitch darkness, and to find two fields a couple of acres in extent. Only a pilot can appreciate the immensity of such an order. It is not surprising that only two out of the six reached the target. One of these, piloted by Captain Denholm, forced to land down wind, hit the bank of the canal at speed, and part of his load—a bangalore torpedo—exploded and killed him, his crew and his passengers.

Three more were forced to land two miles away (their stories follow later) and it took some time for their passengers to make their way to the bridge.

Glider 133, however, piloted by Staff-Sergeant Galpin, D.F.M., actually managed to land exactly on the target, by the bridge—a remarkable effort of piloting, requiring immense tenacity and courage. This is his story as he related it:

In order to effect the greatest possible surprise on the enemy defending Syracusa, eight Horsas, each carrying a platoon of the South Staffordshire Regiment, were instructed to land in a field right on top of the objectives.

At the briefing taken by the wing-commander of the R.A.F. wing who were doing the towing for all the Horsa operations on Sicily, we were told that we would be released at 5,000 feet, one mile out at sea from Cap Murro di Porco, whence we would glide to the objective five to six miles away, and arrive there with plenty of height to spare. Being in free flight we would be less vulnerable to opposition from the ground defences around the harbour and from ack-ack fire of any naval vessels that happened to be in port. We had been told to expect little or no opposition from the ground but, as it turned out, I am afraid our intelligence was not quite accurate on this point. To my mind the most valuable information given at the briefing was the course that we were to fly once we had been released from the tug; in my case, without that information, I do not think I could have reached the objective.

For all the pilots flying Horsas this was to be their first operation and it was only the fourth time I had flown solo at night, the last occasion, as first pilot, having been many months before. I cannot say whether all the other pilots were in the same category, but I do know that none of us had many night hours to our credit or had done any night flying for many months.

The spirit among the pilots and the air landing troops we were carrying was wonderful; everybody's main anxiety seemed to be that they might be left behind. I do not think that any of us realized what we were about to undertake, and we treated this operation as just another exercise with a good scrap at the end.

As was always the case on the North African air-strips the take-off was done in a cloud of red dust. My tug seemed to be in trouble right from the start, but the pilot got her off just at the end of the runway and we set course for Malta. After we had been flying for a few minutes, having gained very little height, I heard over the intercom. that the tug pilot was taking us back to the air-strip as his aircraft had developed engine trouble. Immediately, the tug went into a very steep turn as it headed back to the drome and we were taken down wind doing a left-hand circuit. Just as I was about to pull off I heard with joy that the engine had picked up and that we were setting out on course again.

This delay, however, put my glider well behind the others, but we did not mind, realizing how near we had been to being out of the show completely. As we left the coast of Africa it was beginning to get dark. We couldn't see any Horsas in front of us but there were a few Wacos in sight. By the time we reached Malta it was quite dark. So far the flight had been uneventful and conditions were quite perfect. Leaving Malta, we began to climb, and by the time we had reached Cape Passero we were at 6,000 feet. Through the intercom. I heard the navigator giving the courses and landmarks to the pilot, and this was a great help, as I knew exactly where we were and how long it would take to reach the objective. Flying up the coast of Sicily, heading for Syracusa, I could see that someone was getting a reception, but so far we had not been detected.

Just short of our casting-off point the skipper said he would take us a litle nearer to the objective because of the increased wind strength, thus making sure we had enough height. The outline of Cap Murro di Porco was just in front, and below us, when the tug turned to the right and I was given the signal to cast off.

Once I had cast off it was impossible for either my co-pilot or myself to see anything except the dim outline of Cap Murro di Porco below us, so my co-pilot set the pre-determined course on the compass and we set off hoping for the best. We had been flying for what seemed quite a few minutes when I at last recognized where I was. I had flown too far north and was over Syracusa itself, so I turned towards where I imagined the objective lay. Very soon I recognized our landing zone, just as depicted on the night map. We were then flying at about 2,000 feet. I was just congratulating myself on having aimed right when a searchlight caught us in its beam and quite a few guns gave us their undivided attention. I took violent evasive action, but failed to shake off the searchlight, and by so doing I was out at sea again, so I decided to come down low and approach the bridge with a little speed in hand, flying parallel with the canal and river, knowing I would come to the field sooner or later.

The searchlight followed my glider right down to the deck level and as I was crossing the coast it very kindly showed me exactly where the field lay, lighting up the bridge at the same time. As soon as I saw this I pulled the nose of the glider up to reduce speed, put on full flap and flew the aircraft right down to the ground. The glider touched down fairly smoothly, but after it had run a few yards the nose wheel went into a ditch and broke, and the under part of the nose was damaged. The pilot's kit and arms were pinned under the nose, but luckily nothing was badly damaged, and the only casualty was the platoon commander, who sprained his ankle.

The platoon soon assembled at the rendezvous and lost no time in setting about the capture of the bridge. Splitting up into two parties, one crossing the river and the canal to attack from the flank, and the other making a frontal attack, in a very short time we were in complete control of our objective. But where were the other seven gliders? We knew that our glider should have been the last to arrive and we made every effort to contact any of our own troops in the vicinity, but we found none, and I began to imagine that I had landed by the wrong bridge.

Nothing much happened during the night except that a few Italians were found hiding in the cellar below one of the pill-boxes, and the R.A.F. gave Syracusa a good pasting, dropping a chandelier flare right over us. It would have been just too bad if they had demolished the bridge after all our trouble.

Round about dawn the first few of the air landing brigade began to trickle through to us; a few sappers and, I am pleased to say, quite a few glider pilots had used their initiative and got through to the bridge as ordered. At 8 a.m. the brigade was due to march through to us on their way to capture Syracusa itself, but there was no sign of them as yet; at the time we were unaware that the majority of the brigade had been cast off too early and had landed in the sea, and that those who had managed to get on land were held back at several strong points about a mile away.

So far, the defenders of Sicily had put in no real attack, but were worrying us with intermittent sniping and machine-gun fire. We used some of our precious mortar bombs in an attempt to neutralize the nearest and more troublesome ones, and our efforts were not entirely wasted as firing from those points stopped for some time.

By mid-morning I should say that the force on the bridge amounted to some eighty men of all branches of the brigade, and again the regiment was very well represented. Before long the Italians put in a big attack on our position; they completely surrounded us and the bridge took very heavy mortar fire. Luckily quite a number of their bombs were falling in the river and canal. Now, of course, it was impossible for any small force to get through to help our hard-pressed band and unfortunately there were too few of us to defend the bridge adequately for long. We were attacked from all sides; we were unable to increase our defensive positions in depth and it was necessary to sit on the bridge, which was the one thing we had to keep intact. Later in the afternoon our outlying defences were over-run and the enemy gained a foothold on the bridge itself. It was not long before we ourselves were completely over-run and lost the bridge we had tried so hard to hold. However, a small force gallantly held out in a position near the river mouth until relieved by the 8th Army.

So successful were the airborne landings in their disruption of the enemy communications that our captors marched us straight into the advance elements of the 8th Army, and we were able to escape, taking some of our guards prisoner in the process. Much to my delight the enemy had not had time to lay fresh explosive charges on the bridge, and so our success was complete after all.

Thus, a remarkable feat of arms was accomplished, one of the first of its kind in history. I must add a tribute to the Royal Air Force. The courage of Flight-Lieutenant Tommy Grant, Royal Air Force, Sergeant Galpin's pilot, must be mentioned, for after the long and extremely hazardous flight, on arriving over the coast his wing, which had been hit by flak, caught fire, but still he flew on and delivered the glider to the right spot and at the right height before turning to fly back to his base, 400 miles away. Luckily

H.R.H. Princess Elizabeth watching parachutists dropping, 1944, with Brigadier Hill, Commander, 3rd Parachute Brigade.

H.M. the King inspects glider-borne lorry, May, 1944.

A Horsa glider in flight. This unusual picture was taken from the gunner's position in an R.A.F. Albemarle which tows the glider.

the fire in his engine was put out and he arrived back safely. His courage in delivering the glider to Sicily and other feats of endurance earned him the Distinguished Service Order, and Galpin was awarded the Distinguished Flying Medal.

Many were the actions described by glider pilots that night, and among them is this extraordinary account by Captain A. F. Boucher-Giles, D.F.C.

One of my most vivid memories of the Sicily operation was the air crossing. My glider was one of the first to take off from landing strip "F" near Sousse, in Tunisia, towed by an Albemarle bomber flown by Squadron-Leader Bartram. The day had been scorchingly hot and when we took off at 19.00 hours it was necessary to cruise around 2,000 feet for nearly half an hour while the rest of the air-lift got into formation. The bumps and air turbulence were so bad that both my second pilot (Sergeant Miller) and myself were soaked with perspiration with the effort of keeping the glider on an even keel, and our telephone intercommunication system broke down within the first ten minutes.

After that came the long crossing of the Mediterranean at a height of 200 feet above the sea to avoid any danger of the enemy's radio-location picking us up. As darkness fell things became worse, due to a heavy storm springing up. The Border Regiment boys in the back of the glider were very calm and extremely happy, and someone produced a bottle of whisky which cheered us up all round. At 22.30 hours we sighted Cape Passero, which was the signal for the turning-in run. Gaining height to cast off, we flew in. As I was sitting on the left of the cockpit as first pilot, I got Staff-Sergeant Miller to fly the glider for this run-up while I looked out for the cast-off point which was some two and a half miles short of Cap Murro di Porco. We were subject to spasmodic firing from heavy ack-ack guns during the run-up, and as we approached the cast-off point at 22.45 hours there seemed to be a good deal going on in the way of flak and searchlights. Indeed, it was like Blackpool on Illuminations Night, the fireworks party being at our expense. We got caught in a searchlight shortly after casting off at 1,800 feet and had the utmost difficulty in getting the glider out. Subsequently I found out that my tug pilot had flown down and shot the searchlight out for me. However, both Miller (who was a tower of strength throughout the whole operation) and I were far too busy to worry about anything but getting the glider down safely. On the landing zone itself below I could see several aircraft in flames and the criss-cross of tracer bullets. It seemed no safe place to land as obviously quite a battle

G

was raging down there, so I simply kept my lift-spoilers up and landed a few hundred yards farther on in a field west of the landing zone.

It was rather a heavy landing due to the dazzling effects of the searchlight and the fact that there was only a quarter moon, and a wind of some considerable strength. We were all a little bruised and shaken, but the only serious injury was to Sergeant Hodge of the Border Regiment. The gun had worked loose in its mooring during the bumpy crossing and when we landed had slipped forward and dealt him a frightful blow in the back.

We came under pretty heavy fire from small arms, as we lay still under the wings of the glider for about a quarter of an hour, hoping that a jeep would connect up with us so that we could get the six-pounder away. As nobody, either friend or foe, came to us, we made Staff-Sergeant Hodge as comfortable as possible, left one man to guard him, and setting my compass for a night march, in the best O.T.U. tradition, Miller and I and the other two Border Regiment boys marched in the direction of the bridge which was some five miles across country. I will not go into details about our adventures that night, though they were many and varied. A high spot during the night was when we crossed a field of what, on inspection, proved to be small water melons. We waited in the shadow of a wall while the R.A.F. did a good job of work bombing Syracusa once more. Then we heard shouts of a large party coming down the road. To our relief, they proved to be English, and to my delight were a platoon of the 2nd Battalion South Staffordshire Regiment, whom I knew very well, having trained with them in the past. Their officer had been killed and I was only too pleased to lead them. We had a few spasmodic fights with Italians, who did not stay to argue, and a few of our people were wounded.

As dawn approached we joined up, in an orchard a mile or so south of the bridge, with another party of troops who had made their way from the landing zone. Lieutenant-Colonel Walch, O.B.E., took command as the senior officer present, and we found after a little recce that the bridge itself had already been taken and was in the hands of the South Staffordshires. There was a gauntlet of sniping and fairly heavy machine-gun fire to run before we could get through, but we made the bridge in two waves, with only one or two casualties. It was now about five o'clock in the morning, and we were a party of some seven officers and eighty other ranks on the bridge. Colonel Walch proceeded to place his men in defensive positions. This bridge, the Ponte Grande, spans two canals on the south side of Syracusa, and it was of the utmost importance that we should hold it until

Montgomery's sea landing force came in from the beaches in order that the tanks and heavy transport could proceed over it into Syracusa. In the briefing, 500 men had been allowed for this task. We were only eighty-seven, so we could see things were going to be a bit tricky, especially as we had only two Bren guns, one 3-in. mortar and one 2-in. mortar, both with very little ammunition, and the usual Sten guns and rifles—much of the ammunition for these had been used up in the night fighting.

The proceedings started comically enough as a large Italian staff car stopped at the barricade of the bridge and the officer in charge, resplendent in gold braid and fancy uniform, proceeded haughtily to command the barrier to be lifted. He obviously had no idea that the British had captured the bridge. But a second afterwards pandemonium was let loose as every single weapon was fired into the wretched car. The prisoners were put in the blockhouse on the bridge and all settled down as before. As the sun rose in the sky, it quickly became apparent that we were to be attacked in some strength. The Italians, keeping, as was their custom, at a very healthy distance, were bringing up lorry-borne troops from Syracusa. We were heavily mortared and shelled by a small field gun which made a direct hit on the blockhouse on the bridge, killing all the prisoners therein.

I was myself given command of the glider pilots and some four or five others, amounting to some twenty men, to hold the south bank of the southernmost canal. This canal led straight into the sea, and the only cover was actually on the bank. This was fortunate in a way because the Italians so outnumbered us that if they had had the courage to come in as good German infantry would undoubtedly have done they would have overrun us by sheer weight of numbers alone. The greatest difficulty was to keep the men from expending all their ammunition, as we did not know how many hours we should have to hold the bridge until Monty's forces came up. However, early direct hits wiped out both Bren guns and annihilated the crews. The second-in-command, Major Beasley, Royal Engineers, came over to my side of the canal, and was unfortunately killed by a burst of machine-gun fire, which also killed one of my staff-sergeants, and incidentally put a bullet through my pack and knocked my rifle out of my hand. Things were getting pretty grim and we were by now suffering quite a lot of casualties. We had no machine-guns and very small supplies of ammunition, so we could not easily put in a counter-attack. Had we been able to do so I feel sure the Italians would have melted away with shrieks of terror. As it was, all we could do was occasionally to knock off one or two of the bolder ones when they showed themselves within reasonable range; but as they were in excellent cover and extremely cautious, this was not easy.

The morning had its comic moments. Some of the wags among our party scoured the road leading up from the beaches for signs of dust that would mark the progress of the sea landing troops, calling out, "Sister Ann, Sister Ann, do you see anyone coming?" I remember Lieutenant Dale of the Glider Pilot Regiment climbing a tree for the same purpose but having quickly to scramble down again as the bark of the tree was ripped away just above his hands with a burst of machine-gun fire. Unfortunately this sort of thing could not go on indefinitely, and by a quarter to three things were looking pretty bad as the enemy had been able to enfilade the north bank of the canal, and some of the South Staffordshires had been killed in the water trying to cross to my side. The rest were over-run and taken prisoner as they were without any ammunition at all. My own little party had now been reduced to some thirteen men, several of whom were wounded, and to avoid the enfilade and grenades which the now emboldened Italians were throwing in considerable quantities, we took cover in a small, dry ditch to the south of the canal bank, and here we held on for another half hour or so, several attempts to rush us being stopped.

It was a bitter blow to have to surrender eventually, especially to the Italians; but I could see no other course as we were now entirely without ammunition and our ditch provided no cover. We had no machine-guns to cover us for a bayonet charge and had we made such a charge we should have been wiped out within a few seconds, for by now the Italians had at least half a dozen machine-guns firing at point-blank range, the nearest some forty yards away. However, our captors treated us, rather to our surprise, quite kindly, disarming us only and not taking the men's personal possessions, giving us water for our wounded and allowing us to dress their wounds before marching the rest of us off to the woods, under heavy guard led by a pompous little man with a coil of hangman's rope round his shoulders. I did not like him. We all knew that, with any luck, all our party of thirty-odd men could escape quite easily, and this proved to be so when, after half an hour's march, we met a fighting patrol of the Northamptonshire Regiment. They immediately opened fire on our Italian guards, who were speedily put out of action and disarmed. After a brief spell for mutual congratulations we returned to the bridge to find that this had, in our absence, been recaptured by troops of the Royal Scots Fusiliers, who had come up from the beaches.

The Italians, to judge by the numbers of their dead who now

littered the bridge itself and its surrounds, had paid a very high price for their half hour or so of triumph.

And just one more narrative describing the Sicilian adventure. The reader will remember Major T. D. B. McMillen's exploit with an overloaded Horsa at Netheravon. Here is the sequel to it:

We took off in a more or less orderly manner, though by the time it came to my turn to start the whole area was so shrouded in a pall of thick yellow dust that it was impossible to see the tug and it was a pure coincidence that we both happened to be heading in the same direction when we emerged. The first part of the flight went without a hitch, though it soon became obvious that the loose formation called for in the briefing was more loose than formation. I had time to take stock of my load, consisting of a sergeant, ten men of the South Staffords, a medical orderly, a trailer of ammunition and a folding bicycle. My second pilot, a great friend of mine called Bernard Halsall, had not had a lot of experience on Wacos, so we used the hours of daylight left to run through his duties on coming in to land. These consisted mainly of calling out the height and air-speed at ten-second intervals.

I checked the intercom. and found it still to be working, and then settled down to await the dark. When it did come we were due for a shock. I called up Captain Smith and asked him to switch on his station-keeping lights to which he replied plaintively that they had been on for a quarter of an hour: obviously there was an electrical failure somewhere. By this time it was inky black and we were over the sea, so it behoved us not to get out of position to such an extent that the tow rope might snap. I remembered that sometimes it was easier to see in the darkness if there was no intervening glass window so, with the South Stafford's axe, I cut away the front panel of my perspex canopy. The wind was appalling but I was enabled to see slightly more clearly the dim blur which was the American white star on the starboard wing of the Dakota.

After what seemed a lifetime we saw flak, flares and a red glow over on our port bow and Captain Smith said laconically "I guess that's Sicily."

We turned in towards the land but the darkness was so great that it was impossible to make out any of the landmarks which hours of studying air photos of the area had led us to believe should be prominent. Captain Smith was equally bewildered, so he turned north along the coast, heading for what was quite conspicuously a strongly defended area. As we flew steadily along we became the focus of attention of the enemy A.A. gunners and I remember wondering whether, if an A.A. shell hit us, it would go straight through without exploding, and then realizing that it would be asking rather too much of Providence. Our attention was suddenly distracted by the Dakota's electrical system choosing that moment to spring to life and it seemed to us that the enemy gunners could not fail to take advantage of the aerial Christmas tree we had become. I rang up Captain Smith and the lights went out, but it left us feeling strangely weak. Just then another frenzy of enemy A.A. surrounded us, but apart from frightening us out of our wits, had no effect. Captain Smith called up to say that he had no idea where we were, and suggested taking us back to Malta. I protested strongly, so he said that he had guessed that the first lot of flak was from Syracusa and the second lot was from Catania but to make sure we'd better go and have another look. Without further ado, he turned round and we repeated the performance, but in reverse. Again we flew through the first and second barrage without being hit, but fearing that Captain Smith's inquisitiveness might prompt him to try a third run I decided to part company.

I had seen a large fire burning down below so I decided to go and join the other gliders which must be down there, even if I didn't know where it was.

I thanked Captain Smith for the ride and released the rope. The rush of the wind died away and we circled to lose height, with Bernard chanting monotonously our height and air-speed. I kept the large fire on my right and headed downwards into the unknown dark.

Suddenly some tree-tops loomed up and I just managed to pull up and avoid them. I pushed the stick forward to gain flying speed and then levelled off for a landing. I remember Bernard saying "Nought feet, eighty-five miles an hour" when we hit something very solid and I passed out. When I came to, the glider was at rest, the cockpit was full of dust and the whole of the tubular steel struts in the nose of the glider were snugly wrapped round my waist instead of being in their proper place. Bernard was leaning forward with his head on the splintered wreckage of the instrument panel. (I learnt later that he had foolishly undone his harness, the better to read the instruments.)

I shook him and asked if he was all right. He came to quickly and shook his head to clear it. "Yes, I'm O.K. but I bet I've got the thickest bloody lip in Sicily." He was silhouetted against the glow of the fire and from what I could see, I was sure that he was right.

I realized that this was no place to linger and, as my passengers showed no sign of coming to life I heaved myself out of the wreckage. It was then that I discovered that all was not well with my left leg, which had no feeling in it at all. However, the other one was all right so I hopped to the door of the glider and fell out into the arms of Captain Alec Dale. He told me afterwards that his glider had been set alight by incendiaries and had caused the tomato field in which he landed to blaze merrily.

He and his crew were unhurt, so he led them across an open field adjacent. While he was crossing it he heard the unmistakable whistle of a glider coming in fast and took cover behind a stout tree. As luck would have it, it was the same tree which my glider struck at 85 m.p.h. A considerably shaken Alec waited hopefully for a few minutes for signs of life and then forced himself to go and have a look to see if there was anyone still alive. Imagine his relief when the door burst open and I hopped into his arms. My passengers, who had all been concussed, came to and we set off cross-country towards our objective, the bridge at Syracusa. I could not walk so they put me on the bicycle which we had carried and gave me the nineteen-year-old medical orderly to act as my means of pro-pulsion. We travelled at the tail of my little party, with Alec Dale leading. Unfortunately, every time there was a louder bang than usual my escort dived for the ditch, leaving me and my bicycle to carry on as best we could. Inevitably we ran over at least one prostrate soldier each time and collapsed in a heap on another, through sheer lack of momentum. The bangs became more and more frequent and the night sky was split by brilliant explosions every few seconds. I eventually got so fed up with my involuntary nose-dives that I begged to be left behind in a ditch with a rifle. By this time my damaged foot was beginning to cause me considerable pain and I couldn't really have cared less what happened to me. They refused my very reasonable request, so we pushed on.

Dawn was just beginning to break when one of our patrols came back with the news that they had located a parachute brigade regi-mental aid post in an orchard, and in this I was finally deposited while the others made their way to the bridge.

As the day warmed up, more and more wounded were brought in until we had a pretty fair cross-section of the Airborne Division. We lay there all day, waiting for the relieving sea-borne forces of the 8th Army to catch up with us. The only bit of excitement was when a force of Italians, taking it for granted that it was fairly safe for them to attack a place where the Red Cross flag was hanging con-spicuously, put in an assault but were beaten off without further casualties to ourselves.

Towards evening the battle around us died down, and the R.A.P. became more organized. It was then that I had my second meeting with Colonel Jones. A shadow fell across my stretcher and I looked up to see him standing over me. With a twisted grin he said "Oh, so it's you, is it? Now it's your turn to go through the hoop!"

Then, and only then, did it occur to me how appropriate was his nickname of "Jonah".

While the contest for the bridge was taking place, my party was also having its adventures. We had been lying underneath the cliff wondering what to do next when we heard a boat approaching, and a naval pinnace appeared. Out of it leapt a number of armed men of the Special Air Service, who were following up our attack by a sea landing. By some miraculous chance they had missed the point where they should have landed and hit just where we were, under the rocks. Thankfully we joined in with them and advanced up the cliff. During the night we had various adventures while engaging strong-points and pillboxes, I acting as an ordinary trooper, and by dawn we had captured some 100 to 150 prisoners.

The Italians in Sicily had all manner of queer ways of fighting, some of which had to be dealt with quite ruthlessly, as the following incident illustrates.

I was acting as an escort for some prisoners and was dressed in my sea-soaked battle-dress, with an Italian topee on my head, and armed with a British rifle. Winding down a narrow lane, the guards out in front of the column and a dozen or so of us on either side of it, we were brought to an abrupt halt by the crack of a rifle, one of the guards in front falling mortally wounded. Momentarily we were stunned, then, seemingly without reason, one of the S.A.S. guards in front of me, whose head had been half turned towards the prisoners, turned right round and pushed his way into the column. Without a word, he stopped in front of one of the men, lifted his rifle by the barrel, and, without warning, swung it up and brought it down with a crack on the man's head. The Italian sank to the ground without uttering a sound, his skull crushed in.

"Why on earth did you do that?" I asked incredulously.

"Didn't you see the bastard?" he replied.

"No," I answered. "Why?"

"Well," he continued, wiping the butt of his rifle, "He was up that tree. He shot my chum in the back and then dropped into the column. I happened to turn round just as he dropped."

The column proceeded until, finally, we came to a small farm, where we put all the prisoners in a pig sty, in which they crouched in terror, while we climbed on the sty's flat roof to observe the firing which was coming towards us. The dawn had broken and it was a beautiful morning—already blazing hot. I shall never forget the sight that met our eyes as we turned towards the sea. The farm was not far from the sea, and there, between Cap Passero and Cap Murro di Porco, was the greatest fleet yet to be assembled in the world. It was a fantastic sight. Ship upon ship of every kind— a thousand of them—and I was spellbound, despite the shelling. I remembered having talked to a naval captain in Algiers some weeks before, and his telling me of the enormous fleet that had had to sail unnoticed from London and Alexandria to rendezvous in the middle of the Mediterranean, and then, on a common course, to converge on Sicily. And here I was looking at it—the result of years of work and planning.

It was then that shells began to fall all round us, both from an Italian battery inland and from Allied ships at sea. We noticed a British destroyer, tearing up and down the anchored convoy, ranging on the farm house where we were, and frantically we signalled to it with an Aldis lamp. After a nerve-racking ten minutes we succeeded in getting the firing diverted on to the Italian batteries, and thus had the satisfaction of being relieved of both pests at once!

The Special Air Service Force in which I was temporarily enlisted was led by an incredible and romantic character named Paddy Mayne. I only saw him once, and that was when we were moving into the island and came upon a group of very senior-looking officers—Italian, judging by the magnificence of their uniforms. Mayne was going forward to accept their surrender when there was a shot which seemed to come from the back of the group of officers. Without hesitation Mayne drew his revolver, pushed an officer violently aside, and fired at someone in the rear rank. An officer fell. There was no more trouble, but it left no one in doubt as to the character of Paddy Mayne—why he was what he was, and why he had done what he had done.

As the day drew on I found gliders everywhere, many in the fantastic positions where they had crashed in the night. I remember one which had obviously hit the top of a tree and tipped up, the load—a jeep—remaining in the glider, the cockpit having pitched forward on to the ground. The amazing thing was that the dead driver of the jeep was still in his seat at the wheel. He had been killed outright.

Later I found another glider, carrying a six-pounder anti-tank gun. This time the gun had burst through into the cockpit, crushing the pilot, who was dead underneath. Another I discovered fixed in the side of a cliff. Obviously the pilots must have been killed on impact, but the load of troops had survived. Everywhere there were remarkable examples of what the glider could put up with, if given a reasonable chance.

During my wanderings I went in search of food, for we had had nothing to eat for a day and a night. I gathered four tough chaps round me and we sortied down the road. Suddenly an Italian jumped out of the hedge and we all crouched, Tommy guns at the ready. To our surprise, he threw down his rifle and with his hands in the air shouted: "All right, all right, don't be fright."

I don't know which of us was the more surprised, but it was little incidents like this that kept up one's morale.

Later the next day we came to the bridge, Ponte Grande, where we found the aftermath of the battle. Galpin's glider was still in the field, a memorial to an epic piece of glider piloting, and the pattern of so much that was to come.

On the other side of the canal I could see the tail of Captain Denholm's glider. I crossed over and the sight which met my eyes was indeed terrible. The glider had hit the bank, and the effects of the explosion inside the glider could clearly be seen. The crew and passengers had been blown forward as if down a funnel, but of the pilot there was no sign. As I stood looking at this macabre and tragic pile of bodies I thought back to the gay Denholm. I remembered that as I was briefing the pilots, he had appeared at the door. His beret was at a jaunty angle and his long fair hair showed beneath. He had just arrived, after having been towed 1,500 miles across the sea and desert in one of the Horsa gliders. As he leaned on the door, he said, in his typical drawl: "I say, I've come to see a man about an operation."

He had shown that nonchalance which is of such immense value in the British officer, which sometimes startles, but brings with it calm confidence. Although he had been asked to carry out an almost impossible task, his death was not in vain, but I walked back to the bridge deeply affected, and somewhat overwhelmed.

I arrived at the bridge almost at the same time as a jeep, in which was the divisional commander, as dapper as ever, despite the fact that his glider had been landed in the sea.

"Ah, George," he shouted, "there you are. I've been looking for you everywhere. Come on, get in. I want to have a talk with you." I climbed in feeling very weary, and wondering what was going to happen next. There was much to talk about, and as we drove into Syracusa we found the British Army everywhere. After leaving the General, I found Colonel Jonah Jones, second-in-command of the air landing brigade. He had landed successfully and carried out a meritorious action. His glider had been filled with the staff and clerks of the brigade headquarters. They had landed close by a strongly defended shore battery of five field guns surrounded by barbed wire and ditches. Realizing that to attempt to attack the battery by night would be an impossibility, Colonel Jones and his party lay up in a near-by farm. The following morning, however, the little party of glider pilots, staff officers and clerks attacked the position so vigorously that by 11.15 a.m. it was captured. Jones subsequently was to receive the D.S.O. for his courageous action. But he was also, apart from being brave, a very amusing man, always with an eye for the girls.

"I say, George," he said, on meeting me, "I've got an invitation to lunch."

"Don't be silly," I answered. "What do you mean?"

"Well," he replied, smiling, "after I had captured the guns, I saw a villa, so I decided to capture that too. Lo and behold, there emerged from the door a lovely American girl. Her husband was in the cellar, but he was an Italian and didn't like the sound of the battle raging round the villa. She was tickled that we were British, and I got on with her so well that she asked me to lunch today. I said I would come as soon as I had finished fighting, and I also asked if I could bring a friend. I thought you would like to come, too. Will you?"

"O.K., I'd love to," I answered, "but what about transport?"

"Well," said Jonah, "all I could find was the Syracusa fire-engine."

I looked at him incredulously. Leading me to a shed he showed me a real, live fire-engine of about 1900 vintage, brass fittings and all, and attached to the rear was a six-pounder anti-tank gun. Collecting several men we all climbed on the fire-engine, armed to the teeth, and sped down the lanes to lunch with an American lady. It was an amazing sight, and when we roared into the courtyard the owner and his entourage set up a cheer. With sentries at strategic points we then proceeded to a wonderful lunch, while all around us were the sounds of the diminishing battle, the rattle of machine-guns and explosions. I don't know how many bottles of Chianti we drank that afternoon, or how much spaghetti we ate, but it was a large and very, very good lunch.

Forty-eight hours after the main landings on the beaches, a second airborne landing was made in the area of Catania. Catania is a town or port situated on a coastal plain, backed by a range of mountains—the greatest of these being Mount Etna. To reach it from Syracusa it is necessary to cross some hills and then to come down on to the plain via a road. A river, the Surento, flows through this plain, and at one point is the Primasole bridge, which carries the road from Syracusa across the river and then continues northwards.

In order that the 8th Army should be able to race unimpeded to the north of the island, it had been deemed essential that the Primasole bridge should be captured, and with that in view the 1st Parachute Brigade, under the command of Brigadier Gerald Lathbury, was instructed to drop on three zones in the vicinity of the Primasole bridge and to carry out the following plan. Three parachute battalions were to drop west of the bridge near the river, and one near the Gornalunga Canal. Two platoons of parachutists were to capture the bridge by *coup de main* while others were engaged on other tasks, such as eliminating anti-aircraft batteries.

Having taken the bridge it was to be held in depth, the 1st Parachute Battalion organizing the defence of the bridge itself while the 2nd Battalion held the high ground south of the bridge. In support of this attack were units of the airborne anti-tank Royal Artillery.

The whole force was to be carried in 105 Dakotas, the glider force consisting of eight Waco gliders and eleven Horsas, towed by Halifaxes and Albemarles of the Royal Air Force.

The raid took off from the strips in North Africa and headed for Sicily and the dropping zones, 500 odd miles distant, but as the armada of over one hundred aircraft came upon Cap Murro di Porco, misfortune overtook them and nearly wrecked the expedition. Anti-aircraft fire opened up on the air fleet, considerable damage was done and a number of aircraft shot down. I heard a rumour that the Germans had obtained the call-sign of the day from aircraft to ships and had, shortly before the approach of the armada, given the sign and had bombed the British Fleet. Shortly after, the British airborne forces arrived and gave the same signal, only to be greeted by murderous fire. Whatever the cause, disorder and confusion reigned everywhere and the main strength of the force was dispersed. However, a number of aircraft found the targets and parachutists and gliders were landed in the area soon after 10 p.m. on the 13th July, the battle continuing until the 14th.

During this time, in the dark, officers and men searched for each other, and having gathered sufficient members they had to find their way to the bridge. By 2.15 a.m. a defensive position had been established around the bridge. One extraordinary and confusing factor was that both German and British parachutists were dropped in the same zones, and became mixed up in the darkness.

To say there was no confusion in the British force would be an exaggeration. The unfortunate incident of the fleet had thrown everything into turmoil in the air, and still greater confusion prevailed on the ground, so that Brigadier Lathbury, the brigade commander, had great difficulty in centralizing his force.

Staff-Sergeant White, one of the glider pilots, reported that the enemy's ack-ack fire, with flaming tracer shells and bullets, was so bright that it lit up the landing zones. It is astonishing to think that many of the pilots who landed under these conditions, being shot at by all and everything and trying to land into the darkness, had had no training at all in England, and that, for some of them, this was their first experience of night landing since they had been flying gliders. The ironical point is that the R.A.F. considered it too dangerous to land without flare paths, when training at home.

It was here that Major Alistair Cooper, A.F.C., met his death when he was carrying the regimental commander and his headquarters. Apparently the tug aircraft was hit by ack-ack and exploded, and in the pitch darkness Alistair Cooper tried to land his heavily loaded aircraft in a river bed. They were only at 500 feet when the tug blew up, so he had little or no time to make up his mind when and how to land, and he and all his passengers were killed.

His loss was my own, for I have never had an officer who showed such complete loyalty and self-sacrifice. He gave up rank and flying training so that the regiment might be shaped efficiently. He saw others pass on to coveted courses at the R.A.F. training schools and come back and receive promotion over his head. Many of these were Territorials, whereas he was a Regular officer. He never complained, and he continued to show the same spirit throughout, even to sacrificing his life, for Alistair Cooper was fully aware of the limitations of his flying experience and that he had had no training whatsoever for landing under the conditions forced upon him, but he never faltered.

In the action of the defence of the Primasole bridge, the first glimpses of the total soldier were to appear. Anti-tank guns were served and operated by Sergeants Anderson, Atkinson and Doig, glider pilots, and they fought with these guns after being shown how to operate them when they were actually on the bridge. In another instance glider pilots insisted on making use of a captured 88 m.m. German gun.

The following is the story of one of the glider pilots who took part in this assault:

> Just before approaching Malta we passed over elements of our fleet and I must confess to a few anxious moments. I knew that should the Albemarle, our tug, fail to give the correct signal we would soon be doing our best to carry out forced landing procedure on Malta. But, thanks once again to the tug crew, all we received from the Royal Navy was "Bon Voyage".
>
> At last we were ready for the run in to the landing zone. We climbed to 1,000 feet and began the run in, losing height again until we were at 500 feet. We had been told at the briefing that a path-finder force of the 21st Independent Parachute Company would have dropped flares to lay out a skeleton flarepath for us, but the lights on the landing zone were much too brilliant for flares; they included several searchlights and the odd machine-gun, with light ack-ack for good measure. By this time we were over the area and could see numerous fires which seemed to have been placed at uniform intervals. Having seen photographs of our particular landing zone, which showed the field to be corn or hay, and as our intelligence had assured us that the only opposition we were likely to encounter would be from the local Home Guard, we were perhaps just a little doubtful whether we were in the right area, or even in the right country! The air around us was getting quite warm; one burst of small arms fire had passed between the cockpit and the passengers and, as we later discovered, made rather a mess of the undercarriage and fuselage and the left front wheel of the jeep.

We were now circling the area and did so twice before the tug crew, who had played their part wonderfully, said that we must depart down to the ground. We realized now that we really were over the target. We released, and dived to avoid the small arms fire. The enemy must have thought that we were finished because the fire suddenly ceased, so we attempted to carry out a landing between the fires still blazing in a building and the fields. All went well for a time. We could see that the fires had been started by haystacks set alight by ack-ack fire. Unfortunately one stack had not been set on fire, so we didn't see it until we hit it with the port mainplane. In the end this turned out to be an advantage, as it afforded perfect cover from the fire of the enemy and gave time to unload the glider and move for cover. The only casualty was some of the equipment of the cameraman, a sergeant of the Film and Photographic Unit; he lost a camera lens and went about, crawling on hands and knees, trying to locate it, but without any luck.

At last everyone was safely in the jeep and we decided to put as many miles as we could between us and the haysack before dawn. After several miles the only contact we had made was a paratrooper, who appeared to be the only survivor of his "stick".

At dawn we arrived at what seemed to be a deserted farmhouse, still in complete ignorance of what had happened to the artillery units we were supposed to join. We decided to put the jeep into a barn and wait for full daylight. About an hour later we were favoured with machine-gun fire from the river, but not wishing to give ourselves away, we made no reply. This appeared to satisfy the opposition, who withdrew.

Knowing that our troops were to the south, we decided to try to get through to them. The only way across the river was by a narrow bridge, about a mile along the bank, guarded by a single sentry. We were prevented from reaching the bridge, however, by concentrated small-arms fire from the south bank of the river and had to take cover in the river bed, returning their fire. Very soon we suffered our first casualty, the Royal Artillery gunner, who was fatally wounded, and within a short time we were surrounded and made prisoners. Our captors turned out to be not Italian Home Guard units but German paratroopers who had been dropped the previous day to await our arrival.

Later that day we were forced to march with the retreating German forces, and at one stage I began to doubt whether the Germans intended to continue to be burdened with us. We were herded together into a small hole, the sentries fingering grenades with obvious intentions, but something or someone must have made them change their minds.

The next day we were constantly shelled by our own artillery and strafed by the American Air Force which was responsible for several casualties, one of them being my co-pilot, Staff-Sergeant Montagu, who was fatally wounded.

The following morning saw us on our way across the Straits of Messina to Italy, this time to be bombed by Flying Fortresses.

About nine days later we reached Stalag VIIA, a prisoner-of-war camp near Munich. It was in this and similar camps that I spent the remainder of the war until liberated by the Russians in May, 1945.

The operation against the Primasole bridge was successful, but the margin between success and failure was small. Fewer than one-fifth of the brigade were dropped at the right place and at the right time. The remainder were scattered over a wide area, for reasons already given. To these must be added the loss of eleven aircraft shot down and the return to base, for one cause or another, of twenty-seven without dropping their parachutists. Thus, the numbers of those available to capture the objective and then to repel counter-attacks was very small.

And so the first airborne operation in which gliders were used came to a successful, if costly end, and it taught us many lessons. One of the most important features, so far as I am concerned, was that the men of the Glider Pilot Regiment had proved themselves to be the men I had wanted them to be. Despite the fact that they were pilots first, they had also shown remarkable adaptability, courage and self-discipline in the battle. Here is the epic story of Staff-Sergeant T. N. Moore, M.M., to prove my point.

About 6 p.m. on July 9th, 1943, Ivan Garrett and I took off in our Waco glider, No. 47, from Tunisia, bound for Sicily. We carried a load of twelve infantrymen, four handcarts of ammunition and a Bangalore torpedo. It was Ivan's twenty-ninth birthday.

Shortly after take-off a perspex panel in the front of the cockpit blew out. The intake of cold air caused great discomfort to the troops and the noise made it extremely difficult to maintain telephonic communication with the towing Dakotas. After passing over Malta, gliders numbered 47 and 48, the latter flown by Lieutenant Whittington-Steiner, became detached from the main stream and it was some forty minutes after our estimated time of arrival that we reached the Sicilian coast. We were near Augusta and well to the north of the intended landing area, and we could see the glow from Mount Etna to the north-west. We turned south and flew down the coast towards the landing zone near Syracusa and were caught in a searchlight beam. Our tug pilot dived and we followed him down almost to sea level. As we levelled out I caught a glimpse of Whittington-Steiner still in the beam at about 2,000 feet: it was the last we saw or heard of him.

We cast off at about 2,300 feet, a mile and a half from the coast, but in the teeth of a 40 m.p.h. off-shore gale, made little headway. The beam caught us again but we had no choice, in view of our limited height and poor ground speed, but to fly down it. We crossed the coast at an indicated height of about 300 feet, but in the absence of the moonlight which the meteorological experts had promised, the actual crossing was scarcely discernible. The ground came up at an alarming angle and I made a heavy landing. By daylight next day we saw we had landed on a boulder-strewn slope, about thirty yards from an Italian pillbox. The wheels were smashed on landing and the glider came to an abrupt stop as the nose hit a large rock. This penetrated the nose of the machine, broke my ankle and pinned my legs under the cockpit seat. Garrett was unhurt and he kicked his way through the side of the cockpit.

Within a few seconds of landing the fabric top of the fuselage was in flames. Later we discovered that the fire was caused by grenades thrown by the Italians in the pillbox. Flaming patches of fabric fell into the handcarts of ammunition in the centre of the glider and before all the troops could escape there was a series of explosions, caused by the ignition of phosphorous grenades and mortar bombs. Six of the airborne infantry managed to get out but the remainder perished. Those who did escape took cover among the rocks and shrubs, but the explosions were so violent that one man was killed well over a hundred yards away. I saw Garrett help one injured man from the burning machine and then stumble. A piece of flying grenade or bomb struck his left arm and tore away practically the whole of the elbow joint. Meanwhile I was unable to move and the cushion on my seat was beginning to burn. Garrett struggled to the nose of the glider and with his right arm lifted it a little. I knew this was my only chance. As he lifted I threw myself forward and wrenched my leg free. As I did so I felt the bone in my leg break. Once free, Garrett and I, tried, but without success, to pull another man from the wreckage. He was unconscious and already burnt. We scrambled about thirty yards away and took cover in the rocks as protection from the explosions. They continued for about two hours until one particularly violent one scattered the blazing skeleton of the glider far and wide. We thought this final explosion was due to the ignition of the Bangalore torpedo. Later we learned that the fire had acted as a landmark for many of our unfortunate comrades who were down in the sea.

During the night Garrett lost a lot of blood (he was given a transfusion of seven pints when he reached hospital in Tripoli) and he suffered from the intense cold. I used a puttee as a tourniquet to control the bleeding, but by morning his forearm was completely black and it was evident that even if we were rescued quickly he would lose his arm. As the sun got up our hopes rose, for as the sea mist cleared we could see the invasion fleet mast to mast along the horizon about three miles away. Presently infantry landing barges began nosing into Avola about five miles away to the south and we hoped our position would soon be over-run by the invading forces.

The immediate area around us and the coastal strip to Avola were held by Italian troops and dominated by fire from a large tower, which appeared to be in the direction of the landing zone. Soon after dawn German fighter aircraft began strafing the beaches and landing craft around Avola.

About 7 a.m. we were pleased to see a fellow glider pilot and an American who had managed to swim ashore from their glider which had been forced down in the sea. They approached us from the beach and enquired as to the direction of the landing zone, but in view of our information about the enemy positions they decided to proceed along the coast to Avola where they hoped to obtain help for us.

Shortly after their visit we heard a cry from some fifty yards away and saw someone propelling himself towards us on his back by the use of his elbows. After what seemed an age he reached us and we recognized him to be the corporal from our glider. He had been struck between the knees by an exploding grenade. I ripped the legs off his trousers and tried to dress his wounds but it was almost hopeless, for the hole in each knee was larger than a field dressing. Meanwhile Garrett grew weaker and by noon I had given up hope of aid from Avola reaching us.

I decided that, to avoid his having to spend another night in the open, I must reach either the landing base at Avola or the shipping. I dragged myself towards the wreck of our Waco and came across a dead Italian. He was undoubtedly one of the party who had previously occupied the pill-box and who had thrown grenades at the glider. He still had a grenade cap in his hand and had been wounded in the head, no doubt by the explosions. I took his carbine and bayonet and found that together they would serve as a crutch, and on this contraption I was able to make my way to the beach. I found great difficulty in crossing two wire apron fences but fortunately I was quite unaware, at the time, that they marked the limits of a minefield. On reaching the beach I lay there for some time half submerged in the sea. In this attitude I dozed for a time and when I awoke found a large fish nosing around my legs. It had no doubt been attracted by the blood oozing from my trousers into the water. I thought of tickling trout in the Cumbrian hills, but without the finesse such as I had been taught there I scooped it out of the sea on to the bank. I ate it raw with great gusto.

I swallowed two benzedrene tablets and set out to swim to the shipping. When about quarter of a mile out I saw the corporal had reached the first apron fence and procured himself a couple of wooden sticks (wooden staves used by the Italians in place of our iron ones for building barbed wire fences). He began to hobble along in a southerly direction towards Avola. Although he had agreed to remain with Garrett he had for some reason decided to seek help on his own. I could see a farmhouse about three quarters of a mile ahead of the corporal, and near the beach, and I decided to swim along the beach and contact him at the farmhouse. I scrambled ashore near the farm and hauled myself towards it along a wire fence. I noticed imprints of both English and Italian stud markings in the dust and hoped that our own troops might be occupying the farm. It proved to be completely deserted, however, and everything was in a state of disorder; it was evident that there had been fighting there earlier in the day. The corporal followed slowly and was obviously in great pain as he pushed himself along with his sticks. By the time he reached the farm it was quite dark. Whilst waiting for him I was surprised by an Italian patrol advancing through the tomato patch at the side of the farm. When they entered the courtyard of the farm I hid under a pile of beans in the kitchen but no one came inside and after a few minutes they left dragging a machine-gun on wheels after them. When the corporal hobbled in he was obviously at the end of his strength. He lay down in front of a smouldering charcoal fire built on a sheet of metal resting on a few bricks in the centre of the room and proceeded to fortify himself with the only food we could find—an enormous piece of cheese.

We discussed means of getting Garrett under cover. The corporal had found a path which led quite near the glider and we made plans to use a couple of donkeys from the stable. I had made myself a splint for my injured leg and found that with a stick I could get along. We decided to take some bedding from the farm to keep

Garrett warm in case it was not possible to move him. All these plans, however, were upset by an action of the corporal.

He wanted some water from the well in the courtyard and on his way out poked the smouldering charcoal fire. It immediately burst into flame and the glow must have been plainly visible for quite a distance, for the door was open and the shutters had not been placed over the windows. With the Italian patrol in mind I cursed him for his folly but he took little heed and continued on into the courtyard. In a few moments I heard voices. I realized we had visitors who were speaking in a foreign tongue which I did not recognize, so once again I hid under the friendly pile of beans. I heard the sound of approaching footsteps and someone stood in the doorway silhouetted against the evening sky. For a few anxious moments there was silence and then I realized that the visitor was wearing a British steel helmet. Help from Avola had arrived at last. A medical officer and a stretcher party from an Indian Division having spent all day searching for us had given up and were returning to Avola when they were attracted by the light at the farm.

They found Garrett and brought him in an hour later. He was conscious but suffering from gangrene, loss of blood and exposure. The Indians sent for additional stretcher bearers and we were carried to Avola. The cross-country journey was most arduous because of the rocky terrain, innumerable stone walls and Italian cross-fire. On the journey to the field dressing station in Avola we saw the farm where we had taken refuge completely destroyed by naval gun fire.

Later we were evacuated to Tripoli, and the three of us spent four months in hospital there. Garrett lost him arm and the corporal found he would never bend his knees again. Garrett, by his bravery and self-sacrifice, had undoubtedly saved my life. As time passes I realize more than ever what this sacrifice on his twenty-ninth birthday really cost him, but like to feel that in some way my actions on that day helped in his own rescue.

He was very deservedly awarded the D.C.M. and I was proud to receive the M.M. To-day I am proud to write that there were such men as Ivan Garrett and that I served with them.

Many similar stories were told by the men who returned, but the main theme of them all was courage and self-discipline. Nevertheless, I was deeply distressed and worried, for I, and I alone, had any real comprehension of just what they had done, and done with less than the minimum of necessary practice and training.

When we returned to the shores of North Africa I was met by a staff officer and told: "On no account will you allow any of your officers and men to get into any argument with the Americans about this operation."

I was given no reason, but I was under no illusions, for there were many reasons why the subject of our allies was very hot and controversial. There were many unpleasant rumours in the air that they let us cast-off too early, but I tried not to listen to them, for recriminations seemed useless. I even had trouble among my own officers, some of whom wished to make me the scapegoat for the fact that so many gliders had landed in the sea. In fact such an ugly situation arose that two officers had to be dealt with. Even today, one senior officer (who incidentally took no part in the training or the operation) is a severe critic of mine.

I was under no illusions concerning the main reason for the near-disaster. Whatever mistakes I may have made, and no doubt I did make many, what I could not help was the limited training and, therefore, the limitations of the glider pilots.

As I lay in my tent I meditated on all that had come to pass and I was determined that I would get to the highest authority and put my point of view. By good fortune, just at this time I was informed that the Glider Pilot Regiment was temporarily to come under the command of the United States Air Force, and I realized that my opportunity had come. But what must I do to get the right people to hear what I had to say about the state of the regiment. I wondered. Then I remembered that, buried in the sand, was a bottle of Johnny Walker whisky—my monthly ration. I dug it up and decided to go down to the tent of the local U.S. Air Force commander, Colonel Dunne. It was about seven in the evening, and he too was lying on his bed.

"Good evening, sir," I said politely.

"Oh, hullo, Colonel. Come on in," answered Colonel Dunne.

"Thank you, sir. Look, I've got a bottle of whisky here. I thought you might like a drink."

"You bet I would," he cried, and jumped off his bed. "Come on. Here are two mugs and some water."

I entered the tent and we both sat down at the table and I poured out the whisky. We talked of this and that and, inevitably, of the recent operations in Sicily. Gradually the bottle emptied and I said: "Colonel, may I tell you what I feel?"

"O.K.," he answered, "Go ahead."

"Well, sir," I continued, "I am sure that a great deal of the trouble on this operation was due to the fact that those in charge had no idea what we were being asked to do."

"Well, so what?" he said, rather unsteadily.

"I feel that before further mistakes are made through sheer ignorance and lack of training, the top people should be made aware of what happened."

"How do you think that can be done?" he asked.

"Well, sir, I think that if you would send me to England I could do it."

"O.K., boy, you can go. I'll fix it. I think it's a good idea."

"There's one thing, sir," I said.

"Yes?"

"If I go, could you get me the backing of a very high general? I have had too much experience of trying to do it without any real power behind me."

"Who do you want then?" he said.

I took a deep breath and said: "General Eisenhower, sir. Is it possible?"

"Boy, you shall have Ike himself."

We went on drinking and talking, and I cannot remember what happened next, but I know we parted very good friends.

5

REORGANIZATION

A few days later I received orders to proceed to England immediately, and before leaving I said goodbye to General Hopkinson. He wished me good luck on my venture and said: "Do all you can to make them see the real importance of airborne operations; how much can be done if one has aircraft and training."

"I will, sir. That is my main purpose," I said.

I was never to see him again, for the Airborne Division moved to Italy while I was away and he was killed in one of the forward positions. General Hopkinson was followed by Major-General Downes, another very determined character.

I arrived in England and went to ground. By now the 2nd Battalion the Glider Pilot Regiment was beginning to take shape. Lieutenant-Colonel Ian Murray had his headquarters in the new Nissen hut at Camp Fargo. This was complete folly. It was in the middle of Salisbury Plain, and although it had several huts laid out to suit the squadrons of the Glider Pilot Regiment, it created an entirely wrong atmosphere.

A very high standard of discipline and *esprit de corps* had been established in this camp, but there is discipline and discipline, and now the difficulty was to show those at home that a new approach to the subject was necessary. Having seen the remarkable flexibility of the glider pilots in the field, I knew that although strict discipline and *esprit de corps* were very important, a greater respect for the intelligence, integrity and purpose of these exceptional men must also be shown.

Soon I was informed that I must report to the Director of Training at the Air Ministry. The Director was Air Chief Marshal Sir Peter Drummond, who had been one of my station commanders in the Royal Air Force, and when I arrived at the Air Ministry I was treated with a great deal more respect than usual. An Air Commodore came up to me and said: "Will you come this way, please, Colonel," which was a rather different approach from the usual, "This way, please."

Entering the lift I was taken to a top floor and there ushered into the office of Sir Peter Drummond, who sat writing at his desk. Looking up, in a startled voice he said: "Good God, George, what on earth are you dressed up like that for?"

I explained. Then he said rather loudly: "And what the hell is the meaning of this cable? I'll read it to you: 'Give every assistance to Colonel George Chatterton, United States Air Force. Make available a number of lectures and follow the advice of this officer on glider operations. Signed, Whigglesworth, Air Commodore, for General Dwight Eisenhower.' What does all this mean? You a colonel in the U.S.A.A.F. However, I shall have to give you every assistance, as directed!"

I then explained the whole set up, and my difficulty in making generals understand that the air was not like green pastures. I said, "What amazes me is that when this regiment was started a colonel who had never flown was selected to command the outfit, which is much the same as deciding that the Horse Guards, or the 12th Lancers, should have a commander who has never ridden a horse!"

The Air Marshal said, "I see no difference."

Gradually I brought out my story, and he sat there listening. Finally he said, "Good God, I cannot believe it! Well, you must have *carte blanche* immediately." And he gave it to me. From that moment things began to happen. I lectured at many headquarters and began to create a new attitude towards glider operations.

It was interesting to see how little anybody knew of this form of warfare, and I could see all was not going to be plain sailing, for we are, as a nation, suspicious of new ideas and demand long experience before we are convinced. Airborne forces were no exception to the rule.

I gradually forced the authorities to see that it was wrong for each battalion of the Glider Pilot Regiment to be separated because the 1st and 6th Airborne Divisions wanted them to be. I argued that centralization was the only hope of making the force adequate and that the 1st Battalion must join the 2nd Battalion. This meant there would have to be a Commander Glider Pilots, whose status would be similar to that of a Commander Royal Artillery. In this way the whole regiment would have, in the Commander Glider Pilots, one officer who would look after all their interests.

During this time I visited Salisbury Plain to see an exercise carried out by the 2nd Battalion, The Glider Pilot Regiment. Eleven Whitley bombers tugged eleven Horsa gliders to an airfield at Shrewton, and the gliders landed on the airfield. As I watched, it was clear that little or no advance had been made in over a year. I thought back to the demonstration before Winston Churchill when six Hotspur gliders had landed. Now, a little over a year later, only eleven Horsas could be landed in front of him if he asked for it. Indeed, all those present were delighted with the result, but it was more than apprehensive. If the airborne lift was to be effective many hundreds of gliders must be landed *en masse* and here we were still at the same stage of only a few at a time.

One other point became clear to me and that was that the dispositions of the two battalions of the Glider Pilot Regiment were wrong. The 1st Battalion, of which I was in command, had been despatched to Italy, under command of the 1st Airborne Division, and was being used as ground troops—an appalling conception. The 2nd Battalion was nearly ready, so far as flying training by the R.A.F. was concerned, and it was now at Camp Fargo wrapping iteslf up in red tape. If glider pilots wanted flying practice they were instructed to mount waiting lorries to take them to the station at Netheravon. Here they had to sign-in at the guard-room gate before being driven to the Glider Training Unit Establishment, which was equipped with a number of Hotspur 8-seater gliders. A certain amount of flying practice would then be allowed, after which they were driven back to the military camp. No fraternization with the R.A.F. was allowed. The whole picture was wrong, wrong in every respect, and I felt that I must do something to change it.

By now I had been in England a few weeks and "conventional" elements were beginning to criticize me. Why had I not gone back to my battalion? Why was I interfering with that which did not concern me? But I was trying to find the answer to one question: How was I going to establish the regiment in the right environment and give it the right status, providing the maximum training for the pilots and fiinding maximum opportunity for planning whatever operation was required—as required it must be in the near future?

At this time the regiment was still established as an R.A.F. wing. Group-Captain Sir Nigel Norman, who was one of the original commanders, was killed while a passenger in a Hudson aircraft belonging to the Communication Flight of 38 Wing. To date the casualty list of officers killed during the development of airborne forces was indeed a long one. Lieut.-Colonel John Rock, Major Lander, a pioneer parachutist, Major Alistair Cooper, Squadron-Leader Wilkinson, an expert in glider towing, Major-General Hopkinson, and now Sir Nigel Norman. These men would be difficult to replace.

I succeeded in convincing the Air Force that it was imperative that the Headquarters of the R.A.F. should have an officer who knew what he was talking about, and the weight of my R.A.F. background impressed them enough to encourage them to ask for my services. Without any justification on establishment, I invented the name "Commander Glider Pilots", similar to Commander Royal Artillery, the two rôles being very similar. Whereas the Commander Royal Artillery controlled all things pertaining to artillery, I would advise on and control all things pertaining to glider pilots.

I managed to obtain an office in the headquarters of 38 Wing. It was a compromise, for one end of it was a coal cellar and at the other end I had a small table and a blotter and ink. My thoughts and work were often interrupted by the entry of a Waaf who came to collect coal for the fires in other offices, and quite naturally I became covered in coal dust, as did all my papers!

In January 1944, Air Vice Marshal Leonard Hollinghurst, C.B., C.B.E., D.F.C., was appointed to command 38 Group, which was originally 38 Wing. It had been decided to increase the establishment, and as a result some Halifax and Stirling bombers were transferred, with crews, to 38 Group. This was a major step forward, and it became clear that things were really about to move. The Air Vice Marshal was a determined type, and I do not think that he relished being handed this command, particularly as he knew that he would have to be mixed up with the Army.

Through my half-open door I would watch him pass along the passage to his office and hear the door slam, and I thought, "God, this is not going to be easy!"

One day I decided to take the bull by the horns, and by careful timing I managed to be in the passage when he was on his way to his office. It was fairly narrow, which meant that we would meet head on.

"After you, sir," I said politely.

"Thanks," replied the Air Vice Marshal, with hardly a look, but owing to the limited space he had to glance up at me and in doing so he saw the R.A.F. wings on my tunic.

"Hullo, what are these?" he asked, rather truculently.

"I was in Fighter Command, 1930-35, sir," I answered quickly and purposefully.

"Oh, ex-R.A.F. What the hell are you dressed like that for?" he asked, his keen eyes searching my face.

"Well, sir, I am in command of the glider pilots—or I am supposed to be!"

"Supposed to be! What do you mean?" he demanded.

"Well, sir, it is a long story," I replied hesitantly, for I was playing a tricky hand.

"Come in. I've only a moment," he said, opening the door of his office.

"My God," I thought, "I'm in! And where I want to be, too!"

"Well," he said, looking up from his desk, "what is all this? What are you doing wandering about my headquarters? I don't see any establishment for your presence here."

"No, sir," I answered. "I invented the rank, and the position on your staff."

"You what!" he cried.

"I invented the whole scheme. It was the only way to make any headway."

"Well I'm bitched!" he cried. "Well, I've no time now. Got a date this evening? Come and have a drink with me in my quarters."

"Thank you, sir. About 6.30, sir?"

"Yes, that's right. Come in then," he said.

I saluted smartly and left his room. But I knew now that I had a chance to play my cards, and if I played them right, all would be well.

That evening we sat long and talked for many hours. I explained to him all my experiences in Fighter Command and how I had come to be in the Glider Pilot Regiment.

I told him of the whole amazing plan to build a regiment of soldier pilots, and what had happened. How, against my advice, the glider pilots had been sent out without training and, even worse, without night-flying experience.

"In my opinion," I continued, "there is a misconception as to the true status and value of glider pilots so far as the Army is concerned, and if it is not changed it could be disastrous.

"It is extremely difficult for the average soldier, whether officer or other rank, to understand that these men are expensive luxuries.

In the first years I could only obtain one in twenty-five who seemed really satisfactory. We lost quite a few in the Sicilian operations. There is no question that the selection and basic training were right, and I was impressed with the flying training that the Royal Air Force had given. However, I have had good grounds for alarm since.

"Why?" the Air Vice Marshal asked.

"Well, sir, you will understand what I mean when I say that it is imperative that a pilot should live in the environment of the air. After all, a horseman must live with and around the atmosphere of horses. Is it not the same with pilots? Whatever their employment or the type of aircraft they fly, they must live with and around aircraft."

"I couldn't agree with you more. What are you driving at?" said the Air Vice Marshal, looking me straight in the eye.

"At the moment several hundred glider pilots are messing about in Italy under the command of the 1st Airborne Division; many have not been near an airfield for months and months. The rest are in the R.A.F. training pipeline, which is all right, but I feel that the glider pilots in the Salisbury Plain area are completely in the wrong environment."

"It is all right to have a base depot, as the R.A.F. has, but the active pilots who are flying should live on the airfields."

"Yes, that is very true. Go on," he observed.

"Another point is this. You know better than I that your best air crews are a team: pilots, navigators, forward and rear-gunners and engineers, understanding each other perfectly. Well, sir, now you have two extra—the glider pilots—on the end of the rope. The two must be part of the team, and in my opinion there can be only one way to do this . . . " I paused.

"What is that?" he queried, with a twinkle in his eye.

"Well, sir . . ." I hesitated, and then said, "Within reason the glider pilots must live on the airfields, with your own air crews—live, drink, laugh and womanize with them. It is only in this way that they will really come to understand each other, and the air, as well. Anyway, that it how I feel about it, and feel strongly, too, sir!"

The Air Vice Marshal leaned back in his chair and said nothing. I can still feel the silence that crept into the room. The clock ticked and the fire moved in the grate. I wondered what he thought and what he was going to say. Some time elapsed before he spoke, and then he got up and moved over to the fireplace.

He looked at the fire for a moment and then turned: "Well, all that is very interesting," he said. "I will give it considerable thought."

I realized that nothing more was to be said, and I got up. "Well, sir, I am very grateful to you for all your interest. I am very grateful to you indeed."

He showed me out and that was that, for the moment.

It was in those moments that I felt the responsibility of my position very keenly, for I had a difficult path to tread. Had I been *too* disloyal to the Army? But what else was I to do? How could I put the situation over otherwise? I could not. It was imperative that the status of the regiment should be examined realistically.

Well, it was done, and that was that. I could not change my view and I was determined not to!

I was now left with the generals to deal with. Would they see the situation in the same way? Was it possible that they could agree with the air marshal?

In this particular case they were considering an aspect of war which was new. They had to adapt their own attitude to a new military arm, a new vehicle. They understood the normal application of the conventional war machine, the inspiration which was needed, the normal practice of all that goes to make war and all that it demands. But, however good they were at their job, as they understood it, they were completely ignorant of the potential of the new airborne army.

I have already referred, in Chapter 2, to differences in outlook between the Army and the R.A.F., but it is necessary here to examine these differences more closely so that the problems I and the Glider Pilot Regiment had to solve shall be fully understood.

During the "in-between" years the Air Force had expanded beyond recognition, and many of the officers I had served with had gained high rank and great recognition for their services. In fact, the Air Force had gained a dominating position. They were popular with both Government and nation, and had adopted a "never again" attitude to life. By that I mean that between the wars they had experienced frustration at the hands of both Army and Navy. This had produced in them a "superiority plus inferiority complex", leading to a belief that they knew all the answers, and a tendency to ridicule the rival Services, particularly the Army. Most of the senior officers of both Army and R.A.F. were trying to overcome this, but were handicapped by their natural in-bred rivalry.

Millions of pounds had been spent on the R.A.F. airfields, and on some there was something approaching luxury in all rank messes. This tended to spoil discipline, but it was easy to understand the Air Force attitude. Officers and men who had to spend hours cramped in various types of aircraft were bound to develop a completely new comradeship and discipline, but not only that, they evolved a new language of their own and a new outlook.

The Army, on the other hand, had to continue with what they knew to be the only way for them, especially in the field. This demanded a high standard of discipline for which there is no substitute on the battlefield, where, once committed, there is no going back.

It was clear to me that we, the Glider Pilot Regiment, must try to seek a compromise between Army and R.A.F. While we must try to emulate the freedom granted to R.A.F. air crews—the relaxed outlook—we must also inculcate the necessary discipline to which the pilots would be subjected on landing in enemy country. The glider pilots would have no hot water, fried eggs, and Waafs and a bar to come back to, such as the R.A.F. stations offered to returning air-crews, instead, once committed, they would have to stay on and fight in all weathers with the rest of the Airborne Division, and face all that was demanded of them on the battlefield.

I found myself handling the two groups of senior officers with their different outlooks well enough, yet to try to persuade both sides that there had to be an intelligent compromise was not easy. But not only had I to win over the senior officers of both Services; my own officers also had to be persuaded, and already I found that there were some on each side of the fence.

One of the biggest obstacles I had to surmount stemmed from the haphazard organization under which the Glider Pilot Regiment had grown up, since it meant, inevitably, that my ideas would clash with those of high-ranking officers under whose command oddments of the regiment, as then constituted, were distributed.

In my absence in North Africa and Sicily the 6th Airborne Division had been formed, and in its Commander, Major-General Richard Gale, it had an inspired man who intended to build up his new division to the highest possible standard. He set out from the beginning to make it the best and had no intention of making it a copy of the 1st Airborne Division. He had the advantage of having the unit as a whole, and he knew that if and when it went into action it would not have the disadvantages of the 1st Airborne Division, since it would operate as one formation, not in parcels of units or brigades, as the 1st Airborne Division had done.

By now the full invasion of Europe was an established goal, and all the arms and equipment available were being allocated to Gale, who it was clear was determined not to make any mistake. Added to his accomplishments he had all the experience and political "know how" of the War Office behind him, which his brigade commanders well knew. One of his brigade commanders, Brigadier Hugh Kindersley, O.B.E., M.C., was a brilliant officer, rich and confident, with the Brigade of Guards as a background, who was determined to make his brigade second to none. This was all to his credit, but so far as I was concerned he represented a danger for two reasons: one, he had been an amateur pilot; two, he believed that the 2nd Battalion Glider Pilot Regiment should be under his direct command, and he had obviously convinced the officers of that battalion that his was the right policy. I completely disagreed. At all costs the Glider Pilot Regiment had to be independent of any command, of this I was certain. It was a force on its own, with its own outlook, its own training, and its own planning. I was determined that it should remain so.

What might have been plain sailing for me was confused by the fact that Major-General "Boy" Browning had been made Major-General airborne Forces—which seemed to me to be more in the nature of a political appointment, since it acted as a curb on a potentially brilliant leader. Major-General Gale, after all, was neither junior to him nor under command. What little influence I had hoped for in furthering my plans for the regiment was to have come from General Browning. I now knew he was tremendously handicapped. So, therefore, was I.

There was nothing for it but to play a lone hand, so I put my arguments for the independent status of the Glider Pilot Regiment both to the War Office and to the Royal Air Force, and the latter backed me up because they knew I was right.

At last I was appointed Commander Glider Pilots, with two wings under command, and with the rank of full colonel, but I was given only one staff officer. I chose Peter Harding.

In order that my forces could be fully concentrated, I made the

strongest representations to the War Office for the return of the
1st Battalion from Italy, for, as explained earlier, they were trailing
along behind the 1st Airborne Division in an absolutely useless
rôle.

At this time 38 Wing of the R.A.F. had been promoted to that
of a Group, and a further Group—No. 46 Group Royal Air Force
—was to be utilized for operations. The latter group came under
Air Transport Command and it was equipped with Dakotas. It
was upon these two formations that I wanted to base the whole of
the Glider Pilot Regiment. The titles "battalions", "companies",
"troops", were, in my opinion, ill-conceived, since the Glider Pilot
Regiment was a flying force. I therefore proposed they should be
called "wings", "squadrons" and "flights". These ideas were accepted, and at last the regiment became unique in the British Army,
a dream come true.

The main feature of the reorganization was that the H.Q. Commander, Glider Pilots, should be independent in nature, and those
subordinate to that H.Q. should also be independent. I therefore
organized my own H.Q. as follows:

As I had been given only one staff officer I had to compromise
and I set up my H.Q. at the base of 38 Group, a new organization.
Here I placed an officer and two glider pilot sergeants whose rôle
was responsibility for all air training and operations. From their
office I controlled all things necessary to flying. All flying instructions came from this office and from my H.Q., and thus we were a
liaison between the Glider Pilot Regiment and the Royal Air Force.

I placed two officers in charge of all administration and equipment and they dealt with the Wing Quartermaster and became
liaison for all matters of administration and the link between the
War Office and the Glider Pilot Regiment.

I also designed Wing H.Q. to be such that it was independent
in every way, and, should it be sent overseas independently, it would
be adaptable and able to work on its own.

The Wing H.Q. had a number of flexible squadrons. These were
so planned as to be able to fall in line with the Royal Air Force
stations on which they were placed. Thus, the commander of the
squadron on one of the airfields of 38 Group or 46 Group was
completely at the disposal of the station commander.

Each squadron had a number of Flight H.Q.s which were also
"blue printed" on to the R.A.F. Squadron H.Q. In each flight

would be a glider crew. This crew would be teamed up with a bomber crew of the Royal Air Force. They consisted of a first pilot and a second co-pilot. Thus, to the bomber pilot, navigator, engineer and gunner was added an extra crew, namely the glider pilot in his glider on the end of the rope.

Because of the rapidity with which this scheme was developed it was impossible to train enough pilots. Thus, I devised the idea of a first pilot and a second-grade pilot. I considered that if a pilot could have a short term of flying instruction—some thirty to forty hours in all—he, the second pilot, would have sufficient training to take over from the first pilot under certain conditions when they were in flight, or in a case of emergency, and, if necessary, he could land the glider. The second pilot was given simple training and when he had achieved the required standard he received a pair of wings, but different from the first pilot's wings. He was given the rank of sergeant, as compared with the rank of staff-sergeant, held by the first pilot. From this reorganization the glider pilot emerged like a moth from a chrysalis, his position in the general scheme now settled.

I also believed that glider pilots should be able to maintain their own gliders, and proposed to the Air Ministry that they should be given maintenance courses. These proved an unqualified success, as was shown by the high standard the glider pilots achieved in examinations. In this way the glider pilot became completely independent if his glider needed servicing.

Having given a background to the flying life of the glider pilot, I then had to organize their military formation and armaments, for it could not be forgotten for an instant that the pilots were also soldiers who would have to fight on the ground in every capacity.

The Wing H.Q. was equivalent to a Battalion H.Q. on the ground, and was so organized, with the subsidiary squadrons corresponding to the requirements of the Royal Air Force. For example, a flight consisted of four officers and forty other ranks, all pilots of the gliders. Their armament was four pistols, two tommy guns, two light machine-guns and thirty-two rifles. This force would be under command of the Squadron H.Q., and each squadron could command up to five flights of four officers and forty other ranks.

The squadron was completely independent and so equipped that it had a staff and transport that could make it self-supporting under any conditions. Thus a wing, on entering battle, if it commanded

J

say three squadrons, represented in fire-power 38 pistols, 12 bren guns, 12 tommy guns and 192 rifles. As can be seen this force, as created, was armed and trained to fight on its own as a lightly-armed infantry battalion, or in co-operation with other forces on the ground.

In view of its military rôle, the highest standards of discipline were maintained at all times by the Glider Pilot Regiment, and it was an inspiration to visit the stations of the R.A.F. groups to see how well the Glider Pilot Regiment worked with the Royal Air Force.

During the period January—April 1944, all the glider pilot squadrons were trained intensively on the ground for the battles that lay ahead of them, and it was in January 1944 that, with many other officers, I entered a certain room in St. James's Square to be briefed for the coming invasion. There, in front of us, was a long map covered by a baize curtain, and as we sat there I wondered, as many others must have done, what my feelings would be when I left it.

A general came in, stood in front of us and addressed us as follows: "Gentlemen, there are two things I want you to remember before I draw the baize curtain. The first is that if we do not get ashore or land in some way to defeat the enemy, the war may continue for many years. The second point is this: I am aware that I am addressing British and Canadian officers and therefore I must ask you to be ready to understand that the contribution made by the British and Canadians is small beside that of the United States. Let us have no illusions about this".

He turned and motioned for the curtain to be drawn back. And there was the line of the coast of Normandy. And there was the beach-head which was to be the graveyard of so many courageous men.

"You will see, gentlemen, what I mean. On the left we have the 2nd British Army, to which is added the Canadian Forces, but to the right are five American Armies—not only ready for the beaches when the time comes, but also re-supplied from the sea, and, beyond the seas, from the United States."

As I looked, I remembered my conversation with Randolph Churchill and how he had said that Winston Churchill had another plan in his mind and that the American forces were essential to that plan.

I was now made aware of the contribution the 6th Airborne Division would have to make to the main landing. It was in fact to land by air, parachute and glider on the left flank of the 2nd British Army, to protect this flank from counter-attack, and to hold up, if possible, any reserve which might endanger the seaborne landing on the shores of Normandy.

It was clear that a parachute/glider force would be expected to land on certain chosen target areas. The first part would probably have to be done at night and then be reinforced by another force on D-Day of the invasion. The positions the 6th Airborne Division were to hold lay in the area of the Caen Canal and the River Orne.

Having been briefed, and conscious of the great responsibility that rested on me, I felt that it was now my duty to see that impossible tasks were not demanded of the Glider Pilot Regiment without adequate training and practice, and to that end I pledged myself.

As I have said, there was a strained atmosphere in the whole set up of H.Q. Airborne Forces, and even at this late date, when one might have expected encouragement from all taking part in the coming operations, I was sometimes rebuffed, as the following incident shows. Shortly after I had been promoted to the rank of full colonel I was asked to dine at a certain H.Q. At one moment during the evening I walked into a room, rather conscious of my new red tabs, and came face to face with a very senior officer accompanied by a number of his staff.

"Hullo! What is this?" cried the very senior officer. "Oh! It's this new-fangled rank 'Commander Glider Pilots', is it? Is that what you are?"

"Yes, sir," I answered, and there followed a tense silence of a kind that I had learned this particular officer was an expert at creating.

"Well, what does it *mean*? What the hell *do* you think you are? Why do you *need* such a rank?" he went on belligerently.

So I tried to explain.

"Well, all I can say is it all seems damned unnecessary to me, and I'll give you six months before you blow up and find that you're quite superfluous!"

I said goodnight and turned on my heel.

6

PREPARATIONS FOR D-DAY

The last exercise of any size had taken place in September 1943, since when the men had had little or no opportunities of flying. The situation at the time of reorganization was, therefore, to say the least, dismaying. What I had was two wings, neither of which had had much flying experience. No. 1 Wing, operating with 38 Group, had only the training the R.A.F. training schools had given the glider pilots. Other than this they had been hanging about with little or no flying at all.

No. 2 Wing, which had been following the 1st Airborne Division in Italy, was in an even worse state. One-third of this wing had been on the Sicilian operation but had had no flying for many months. Luckily a number of glider pilots had been engaged in towing gliders across the Bay of Biscay to North Africa and had gathered useful experience as a result. However, the majority had not been on an airfield for six to nine months.

It was an astonishing fact that the Glider Pilot Regiment in January 1944 had had little or no training, yet here we were facing one of the major operations of our time, and this only six months ahead. Six months may seem to some a long while, but when one considers that in that space of time 1,500 glider pilots had to be trained, exercised and fitted into a most complicated operation, it was far too short.

Apart from anything else, only Iain Murray, Who commanded No. 1 Wing, and myself had any experience of what flying really meant. The average glider pilot had a little over 150 flying hours to his credit, and most of that in a training school. We had operational training programmes, but I knew that the officers who had to conduct the programmes had little more experience than the men they were to command. Yet they would have to set the men an example, direct their training and gather confidence as they went along.

I was painfully aware, also, of the problems of the Royal Air Force, who not only had to be used for training the glider pilots, but also to give parachute training and this prompted me to devise a scheme whereby instead of thinking in terms of flying hours we thought in terms of "lifts" and landings, for I felt that the most important part of glider flying was the take-off and landing. Added to this, of course, was the most important of all—night flying. The take-off was easy, but far more important was the landing. I therefore insisted that my H.Q. at 38 Group should constantly determine the number of "lifts" which had been achieved on the R.A.F. station.

Another idea was the "funnel system", which was evolved to meet the problem of a large number of gliders arriving over the target at the same time. In such an event, to avoid collisions and haphazard landings, the gliders would need to follow each other down as through a "funnel" on to the airfield or air landing strips. If the gliders arrived in a particular area a given number of yards from the far end of the landing zone, and at a controlled height, they would have no difficulty in selecting a landing place within the zone since it could be calculated on the basis of distance of glide from the release height. At least the system gave the pilots something to hang their hats on. The result of it was that landings improved, and although some of the pilots despised the funnel system I am quite sure they carried it in their *heads*, with remarkable results.

It must be understood that the task set was to land several hundred gliders, at thirty-second intervals, on the battlefields. Our aim, therefore, was to put into the air as many gliders as possible, and for 38 and 46 Groups to train themselves to manoeuvre this unwieldy force into a long stream, and finally run on to the target in such a way that the gliders could release and land as accurately as possible.

While the glider pilots were receiving as much refresher training as possible, I had to think out a system that would satisfy the Army that what we were doing would suit them when their troops arrived on the ground. The forces to be carried by gliders consisted of infantry battalions, tank squadrons, Royal Artillery and other arms, and these forces could not be landed all over the place anyhow. We had to have some practicable system for when they arrived on the ground or on the target they were attacking.

To complicate matters, when trying to plan exercises to test our efficiency, we could not make glider landings away from our training airfields because of the money and time spent in retrieving the gliders. To overcome this difficulty I produced the idea of using an overlay on the aerial photographs of the airfields we used. This overlay, a sheet of transparent paper, was placed over the photograph of the airfield, and roads, fields, lanes and hedges drawn on it. This was then presented to the military commander of the exercise who would state how he wanted his forces disposed on the area or airfield. The height of release of the gliders would then be agreed with the Royal Air Force, the glider pilot squadrons told the area in which they were to land, and each glider pilot given a spot to land on. Thus, infantry, guns and jeeps could be placed on the airfield as though it were the landing zone in an actual battle.

Under this system of briefing, training really made progress, the three organizations—the Army, the R.A.F. and the Glider Pilot Regiment—gaining confidence, as they worked together, that they would be able to carry out the tasks allotted them when actual operations began.

The loading and unloading of gliders was most difficult, for when the Horsa glider was designed, such loads as jeeps and six-pounder guns had not been considered. This had been one of the great problems in Sicily. One of the most extraordinary stories of the Sicilian landing was that of the glider crew who, having landed in the far north of Sicily, found great difficulty in getting the jeep and gun out of their glider. They had in fact flown their glider across the Bay of Biscay, along the coast of North Africa, over the Mediterranean, and now, when they were on their target, were unable to unload. At this time in such a difficulty it was the custom to put a belt of explosive round the tail and blow it off. This they did, but not only did they blow off the tail, but they also blew up the glider, the jeep, the ammunition, and, in fact, everything. The remarks of the two glider pilots have not been recorded, but they can be imagined!

With this problem on my mind, I remember one day sitting in a Horsa glider in one of the hangars at Netheravon with the engineer officer of 38 Group. I had been telling him this story, and as we sat there I was staring at the stern bulkhead. It was then I noticed a number of bolts which anchored the tail of the glider to the main body.

"My God," I cried, "do you think those bolts unscrew?"

"I'll soon find out," answered the engineer officer, sending for an adjustable spanner. In a short time the bolts were undone and pulled out to release the whole tail unit. This meeting, which revolutionized the whole method of unloading the Horsa glider, led to the soldier's equipment, including, for the first and probably the last time, a spanner—rear glider unscrewing for the use of.

And so the training went on, and still more ideas were thought up and tried out. We decided that it would be good to have "target gliders". These were gliders with special markings or streamers, which on being landed at a particular target could be followed by others who would land as near as possible to them. Thereby we hoped Army formations could be landed nearer their rendezvous as one body.

All these experiments and discoveries took time to try out, but at last we felt we were ready to begin large-scale exercises, which by February 1944 were in full swing. On 2nd March the first large-scale mass landing was made at Welford airfield. Ninety-seven bomber glider units took part, in which there were British and American troops as loads. It was immensely satisfying, as only three gliders failed to reach the target.

The scale of these landings soon built up and we had the satisfaction of seeing 154 land by daylight, and 135 land on a standard flarepath at night. Then, on April 23rd, the greatest mass landing ever carried out in training was flown in by 38 and 46 Groups, 185 gliders landing at Southrop, Brize Norton and Harwell. This was the first time that No. 2 Wing and 46 Group tugs had taken part in a major exercise, and their performance was most creditable.

Finally, moonlight landings of between 90 to 100 gliders were made with complete success.

The climax of this type of flying was a mass night landing on an operational flarepath. It shall always remember this landing. I took off as second pilot to Ian Toler from Brize Norton. It was a magnificent night as the great armada rose into the darkness, and soon we had crossed the countryside to the landing zone at Netheravon, where a great stream of gliders were to land on a flarepath which had been laid out by parachutists. The method of laying a flarepath was for each parachutist to set out a number of small lamps, in the shape of a letter "T", and, as a rule, the path was laid into the wind. For some unknown reason, possibly because the wind was slight that night, the flarepath was laid into the opposite direction to that expected by the air-crews. As there were some 150 gliders trying to land at the same time, the situation was nothing short of bizarre, half the pilots deciding to land in one direction and the other half in the opposite direction. Never could I have imagined such a sight as gliders bore down on the flare path from every direction. The miracle was that there were no collisions.

I was now reasonably content that mass landings were more or less possible on the landing zones in Normany. The glider pilots had reached an astonishingly high standard of flying in a very short time, and to achieve this there had been a complete inter-Service understanding. This was one of the remarkable results of the whole scheme. Thanks to the co-operation and wisdom of Air Vice Marshal Hollinghurst in allowing the Glider Pilot Regiment to live and mess with the R.A.F., all that had been hoped for had been achieved. Both the Army and the R.A.F. can be proud of the fact that inter-Service rivalry—and all that goes with it—was completely buried, and an unsurpassed flying efficiency, the like of which had never been seen before, emerged.

Now I must turn to one of the more amazing experiments with aircraft and with towing crews: the advent of the Hamilcar glider, the R.A.F. crews who towed it, and the glider pilots who flew it. This goliath came from the drawing boards of the General Aircraft Company. It was a huge aircraft which weighed fourteen tons with its full load, and had a wing span greater than a Halifax or a Stirling. The height of the cockpit from the ground was well over twenty-five feet, and the pilots climbed up to it on a wooden ladder in the hull, where they sat one behind the other, "in tandem" as it was called. The whole monstrous structure was made of wood and metal, and the hull was not unlike a square cave. Huge nose doors opened outwards to take such loads as Tetrarch tanks (light tanks), Morris trucks, 17 and 25-pounder guns, Bren carriers and jeeps.

I remember deciding to try one of these monsters out and arranging with Peter Cranmer, one of our top glider test pilots, to fly with me from Netheravon to Tarrant Rushton, which was to be the headquarters of the Hamilcar flights.

I found the Halifax Mark V and the Hamilcar at one end of the airfield. The disparity in their size made them look unreal. I climbed up the ladder nervously, and sat myself down in the front cockpit. It was a strange sensation looking out at the huge wing span, at a great height from the ground, and even more strange was seeing the Halifax—looking like a toy—ticking over, far ahead, with the thick tow rope lying on the ground between the two aircraft.

Soon the tug pilot was calling through the head phones, the rope tautened, and we moved across the grass. As the airfield hurtled past it seemed unreal and ridiculous, then the Hamilcar jumped once, twice, and was airborne. She handled remarkably lightly in the air—surprisingly so—and then the Halifax became airborne, and the whole combination was away.

The flight was uneventful. We sailed down to the south coast calmly enough, then, arriving over the airfield at Tarrant Rushton we released from the tug—and she was alone. How smoothly she flew. How the wind swished past the cockpit. How light she seemed to handle. It was remarkable to think that this huge wooden monster had been built completely "on spec"—a masterly achievement by General Aircraft.

We circled the airfield and turned into the runway. It seemed a steep descent, and as we levelled out the great nose almost obliterated the view of the runway. She sailed, or rather, floated, and then settled smoothly on terra firma. We experienced a great thrill of satisfaction as we climbed out of the cockpit.

I chose Major Dickie Dale, D.F.C. to command the Hamilcar squadron, and with him went the majority of the pilots that had ferried the gliders across the Bay of Biscay, for they had at least 150 glider hours to their credit; more than the rest of the regiment. Training on the Hamilcars began in November 1943 but by January 1944, owing to bad weather, little had been done.

Through the genius and drive of Group-Captain Tom Cooper, D.F.C., and such flight commanders as Squadron-Leader "Buster" Briggs, D.F.C., flying thereafter increased at a great rate, for it was realized that if the Hamilcar, with its immensely important loads of tanks and Bren carriers, was to be landed in support of the parachute and glider landings, much had to be done. And much was done, for in the period February to March 1,200 lifts were made, as against 311 lifts to that date. The landing speeds were reduced from 105 to 75 miles an hour and soon spot landings were introduced. Nearly 400 of these flights were made by night, and the flying standards rose to remarkable heights.

In April the mass take-offs and landings were increased. I remember going down to Tarrant Rushton to witness the first ever air landings of tanks. The glider pilots had not before taken up these loads, consisting of a light tank and the tank crew, and as the gliders came in to land my heart was in my mouth. The last glider to come in, a Hamilcar, came in somewhat fast, at about 110 miles an hour. She bounced, half took off again, landed again and bounced, then careered across the airfield and crashed into a group of Nissen huts, which disintegrated. The two pilots in their cockpit remained to top of the rubble, but the tank, which must have hit the building at eighty miles an hour, went straight on before coming to a stop some fifty yards away. I rushed over and found the tank covered in wood and tin and the remains of the huts. The driver's visor was open and he was handing out bricks and bits of old tin.

Rather anxiously, I said to him: "Are you all right?"

He looked up, with a soot-covered face, and said: "Yes, but I'm coovered in bloody moock!"

He must have been one of the fastest tank drivers in history.

When the training of the Hamilcar squadron was finished, over 2,800 lifts had been made, which was an average of fifty lifts per glider crew—a superb effort. For this, credit must go to the Royal Air Force. Few knew how difficult it was to fly a Halifax with a huge Hamilcar on its tail, and I am told that sometimes the pilot had little more than ten miles an hour on his air-speed between stalling and flying on. It must be to the eternal credit of the Halifax crews that their calmness and courage never faltered.

Throughout this training there were only seven fatal accidents to the glider pilots, and three where carried troops were killed.

7

THE EVE OF D-DAY

DURING the period of flying training the commander of the 6th Airborne Division, Major-General R. N. Gale, D.S.O., O.B.E., M.C., was gradually preparing his military plan. In a small shed not far from the R.A.F., Netheravon, he had a large-scale model of the Normandy beachhead, and upon this excellent model the plan developed.

In the main, the task of the 6th Airborne Division was to land on the night preceding D-Day and capture certain positions on the left flank of the main invasion forces to protect the 1st British Corps from flank counter-attack. As part of this task the division would have to capture and hold the bridges crossing the River Orne and the Caen Canal, and to attack and delay any counter-attack made by the German Army. The whole operation was to be carried out by the 5th Parachute Brigade Group, the 3rd Parachute Brigade Group, and the Air Landing Brigade, which was to be glider borne.

It is not the purpose of this book to discuss the military plan, but it *is* my purpose to show how the Glider Pilot Regiment carried out the flying and military tasks allotted to it. General Gale sent for me and outlined these tasks. The first two were indeed formidable for they required, in the first instance, the landing of six gliders in two separate fields alongside the bridges crossing the River Orne and the Caen Canal respectively—in order that the bridges could be captured intact. To be successful, the gliders would have to be released at a great height and land, in the darkness, as near as possible to the bridges.

I immediately ordered concentrated training for this task, and asked the Air Vice Marshal if Flight-Lieutenant Tom Grant, D.S.O., could be placed in charge of this training. It was he who had been so courageous in North Africa and who had successfully released Sergeant Galpin on to the bridge at Ponte Grande.

Six glider crews were selected from C Squadron and began training at Tarrant Rushton, and, in order that the gliders might reach the height required, Halifax bombers were chosen as the tug aircraft. A trial was arranged to see if the landing could be done in so small an area, and a field similar to those in Normany was marked out on the Netheravon airfield. Into this, a landing was to be made by selected air crews in front of General Gale and General Browning. The gliders landed perfectly. This was in broad daylight, however, but flying some six miles in free flight and finding the fields in pitch darkness was likely to be a different proposition. However, I had full confidence that Tommy Grant would be able to train glider crews to do this.

It was agreed that the closest co-operation would be needed between air crews of the Royal Air Force and the Glider Pilot Regiment, and that perfect navigation and flying would be needed. In fact, the whole success of the operation depended on the teamwork between both crews. The most vital requirement was that the tug-aircraft should tow the glider to an exact spot and then be able to give a course over the intercom. on which the crews could fly to the target. This course and air-speed would have to be given accurately, and all the training was therefore concentrated to that end.

One night, nearing D-Day, a demonstration of the results of this training was given. It was arranged that six gliders should carry out a night landing over a group of trees at Netheravon. The load carried by each of the six was the steel spar of a Bailey Bridge, which was approximately the weight of the armed men to be carried on the night of the attack. We all stood in a group looking up into the hazy moonlight, when there was a rushing sound and, with a suddenness which was startling, one Horsa came in over the trees— then another—and then another. Suddenly the sixth glider came hurtling out of the darkness and, mistaking the angle of the trees, landed with an ear-splitting crash on top of the others. There was a frightening rending of wood and metal as they crushed and split, and we rushed over to the heap of wreckage. Astonishingly, except for a sprained ankle, no one was injured. This incident gives just a little idea of the risks the glider pilots took night after night while training for the invasion.

The second group of gliders had been allotted a very different but similarly difficult task. It had been ascertained that just by a village called Merville, in Normandy, there was a battery of 6-inch guns which could create havoc on the beach head, and it was imperative that the battery be eliminated before it could blast the seaborne landings and damage them irreparably. The battery was surrounded by a ditch and was full manned, and, what made it more formidable was that the ditch was mined. A scale model of the Merville battery was built with the double object of allowing the parachutists to practise on it and for the gliders to fly over and look at it.

The request was for three gliders to crash-land into the middle of this group of guns, and it was to be done at night—again a formidable task. I considered this was such a risk that it must be a volunteer job, and I went down to B Squadron at Brize Norton and called for volunteers. The entire squadron stepped forward and I had to ask the squadron commander, Ian Toler, to choose the crews.

Here again very special training had to be done, and the aim was to achieve perfection. It was decided that a radio aid called Rebecca-Eureka should be used. This was a simple unit in which Rebecca, carried by the glider, could contact Eureka in the possession of a caller on the ground. It was intended that the calling end, Eureka, should be carried by a parachutist, who would be dropped close to the wire surrounding the battery and call the gliders down on to the battery. Ambitious, but hopeful!

While the glider crews were doing intensive training, mass landings and so on, on the full-scale model of the battery, we received our first shock, for one day there appeared on the aerial photographs, which reconnaisance aircraft were taking every day, strange white marks, which proved to be holes for poles. These marks were making their appearance all along the Normandy coast, and inland, and it was clear that the Germans were constructing anti-airborne defences.

I spent hours gazing at these marks, and eventually we decided that the poles must be about twenty feet high and two to three feet in diameter. This, of course, caused considerable consternation. What were the poles meant to do? Were they mined? Would they fall over? Would they smash the gliders very badly?

To give us some idea, we built a replica of what we assumed the holes to be, and I remember Major John Royal landing a Horsa into a lane formed by the poles, and hoping that it represented something like the hazards the glider pilots would have to face.

The whole divisional plan, however, had to be changed, and it was decided to land the parachutists first, among them parchutist engineers who would have the job of blasting down the poles. Some such plan was inevitable, for even if the poles *were* blown down, and were *not* laid in rows, they would still be a hazard to the gliders, which would be badly damaged and might turn over if the poles were of large diameter.

We therefore arranged, for practice purposes, lanes made by putting poles end to end, and the gliders tried to land in the lanes. The parachutists had the job of placing the poles end to end after first taking them down, a sweat-making business as the poles were a tidy weight. The whole answer to the landings, so far as I was concerned, lay in the training and briefing; nothing was left to the imagination.

At 38 Group there was an officer, Squadron-Leader Lawrence Wright, who was an architect in civilian life, and a brilliant and amusing artist. He conceived the wonderful idea of making a film of the model of the Normandy beach head. By using a blue filter on his 16-mm. camera, and by holding the camera at a calculated height, he produced a remarkable film for the briefing. It gave a complete picture of a glider coming in from 1,000 feet, down to about 100 feet, and provided a most realistic impression of what the landing in Normandy might be like. There is no doubt that it assisted the pilots no end.

The Glider Pilot Regiment had now taken real shape. No. 1 Wing was commanded by Lieut.-Colonel Iain Murray—a remarkable man. He was older than most of us, an ex-Guardsman who had also served in the Auxiliary Air Force before the war. In him I had a man of much experience and worth, and he was able to bring to the wing a very high standard indeed. No. 2 Wing was under the command of Lieut.-Colonel John Place, who had originally been in the Commandos and had taken part in the Sicilian campaign.

The two wings were now distributed between 38 and 46 Groups. A great change had come over the regiment, and I felt it was really something worth while now—well-trained, well-equipped and highly organized. Nothing had been left to the imagination in the way of equipment and transport. Everything had been made available. It was, I felt, now ready for war.

We thus approached the eve of the invasion of Normandy. The practised massed landings had been done, and new headquarters of the glider pilots had been tested to the full and was "operational" in every sense. The regiment carried out three major ground exercises before D-Day, all of which were designed to assist the wing commanders in taking up positions after landing into battle. One of these exercises had an interesting aspect. I found that on the map there was an area near Hinton, Buckland and Bampton Aston which almost completely corresponded to the area of the River Orne and the Caen Canal near the village of Ranville, and thus the Glider Pilot Regiment was able to practise their withdrawal from the battle under realistic conditions.

During these months the regiment was given a signal honour. General Sir Alan Brooke, the C.I.G.S., was appointed Colonel Commandant of the Regiment, and to have such a man as this was a wonderful inspiration, especially for me. Another vivid memory of those days before the invasion was the visit of the Royal Family to the 6th Airborne Division. Those who served in the division will never forget the day.

I was privileged to spend some time with the Queen and Princess Elizabeth as she then was, and during tea I related to them an amusing story of the occasion when two of my sergeants met Queen Mary. This story was bound up with what we called initiative training. These two sergeants were taken in a closed truck to the New Forest in full battle-dress and were allowed only half-a-crown between them. They were given one written order: "Find the Master of the Beaufort Hounds and ask him to sign your pay book." Somehow the two men found their way through the forest right across the countryside to Badminton House and, walking up to the door, rang the bell. The butler answered and was about to refuse the glider pilots entry, when a lady's voice behind him said: "Don't send them away. Let me speak to them first."

To the amazement of the glider pilots they saw that it was Queen Mary.

On being informed of the instructions they had been given, she said: "As the Duke is out, will my signature do instead?"

The sergeants were speechless. However, she led them into the study and wrote both the men's names and numbers down, and added—

Certified that they came to Badminton House,
(Signed) *MARY R.*

The Queen and Princess Elizabeth seemed delighted with the story and made me send for the book which Queen Mary had signed. They laughed a great deal, and of course charmed me and everyone else into the bargain.

We had another visitor: General Montgomery. On this occasion the 6th Airborne Division was drawn up in a hollow square, beside the Royal Air Force station at Netheravon, the senior officers lining up in the middle of the square. The general arrived in a huge car with outriders on motor-cycles bearing enormous Union Jacks. He himself was dressed in a red beret—with the two badges—a gold windcheater jacket, mackintosh trousers over his battle dress, and huge woollen driving gloves.

After inspecting the senior officers he said to Major-General Gale: "Turn the men facing inwards. I will walk through the centre of two ranks."

There was some hesitation and a strange look came over Gale's face; then a series of rather odd orders rang out, and we followed Monty as he walked slowly and silently up the line of two ranks of red-bereted soldiers.

Calling for his jeep he had a microphone placed on the flat bonnet, then he stood up on the bonnet and beckoned the entire division to gather round his jeep. Again there was momentary hesitation, then a mad rush of officers and men who made a massive circle round his jeep. He motioned us all to sit down on the ground.

"Well," General Montgomery said, "you have seen me and I have seen you, and we should now have confidence in each other." He then gave us a stirring speech. He certainly had the right ideas, for he made a deep impression on us all.

His visit was not the least of the excitement which was ever present in those days, days not to be forgotten, for one of the greatest military feats in history was about to take place, and the whole nation felt it in its blood.

By now the Glider Pilot Regiment was dispersed on the airfields of 38 Group and 46 Group. No. 1 Wing had four squadrons on such stations as Harwell, Brize Norton, Tarrant Rushton and Fairford; and No. 2 Wing had three squadrons at Broadwell, Down Ampney and Keevil. It can be seen that the Glider Pilot Regiment was dispersed over a wide area, and it was complicated to operate and administer. It can be seen also how necessary it was for the wings and squadrons, and even flights, to be independent and self-accounting.

On these stations well over 1,000 Horsa gliders and some 80 Hamilcars were standing—a formidable force. I often feel that we were never really able to discover the glider's full potential as a weapon of war. The main reason for this was that there were insufficient gliders for the actual operations, and therefore, during training, they could not be allowed to land in places from which it would be difficult to retrieve them, or risk any likelihood of damage. As a result, we became very airfield-minded, and did not appreciate that the glider was capable of being put down in quite extraordinary places. This, I think, affected the planning later on.

During the training build-up much experimental flying was being done at Farnborough to test the various combinations that might provide more efficient towing. I spent many days trying out these experimental tows. Not the least of these was the Beaufighter and Horsa combination, and the Spitfire and Hotspur combination. The latter was exciting and had many possibilities. Perhaps the most extraordinary experience was being towed by two Miles Masters, I myself flying a Horsa glider.

Another interesting experiment was the "snatch", in which an aircraft flew over and snatched the glider from the ground. I tried this in an American Waco and in a British Horsa. The tug-aircraft was fitted up with an endless wire drum in its fuselage from which hung a hook, and the towing rope of the glider was attached to a looped nylon rope which hung between two poles about fifty feet in front of the glider. The tug aircraft, flying with a flat trajectory, picked up the loop with its snatch hook and snatched the glider into the air. It was strangely exhilarating experience. At one moment we were standing still, the next we were flying through the air at 120 miles an hour. There was no jerk or feeling of unpleasantness, and I believe one could have held a glass of water in one's hand without spilling it.

A few weeks before the assault I was given the order to parade the Glider Pilot Regiment in front of General Sir Alan Brooke at Brize Norton R.A.F. Station. It was a memorable day and the first time the regiment had been on a ceremonial parade in full strength. The general inspected the ranks and then the whole regiment marched past. It was a magnificent sight and the marching and bearing were remarkable. General Sir Alan Brooke made a special remark to me on their bearing, and I think that he more than realized the true significance of this amazing force of men.

As I watched them pass, rank upon rank, I thought back to the days when there was nothing but an old camp on a hill on Salisbury Plain at Tilshead. It was stimulating to think that this Regiment, which only a few months before had been ill-trained and lacking in practice, was now an efficient force. In little over six months it had not only re-established itself, but now possessed all the attributes required of it. Everything was there: flying ability, discipline and battle training. *And* it had also won the full confidence of both the Army and the Royal Air Force, and that perhaps was its most hard-won achievement.

I do not believe that the Army, as a whole, ever fully appreciated quite what had happened. Possibly this was because they had little or no idea of the magnitude of the flying tasks set, and the vital necessity for flying and more flying, and more flying practice. Nevertheless, every gun, every jeep, all the heavy ammunition, and every soldier of the Air Landing Brigade arrived safely on the field of battle because of the understanding between the Royal Air Force and the Glider Pilot Regiment.

Close on D-Day I found myself in a difficult position. The Army had decided that all serving in the 6th Airborne Division should be gated nine days before the invasion in order that they might be briefed in all the details concerning the attack. On the other hand, the Royal Air Force decided that they needed only three days. As the glider crews lived on the airfields and messed with the Royal Air Force it was impossible for these crews to be gated if the R.A.F. were not, for it was humanly impossible to stop men talking, and thus there would be a leak of information which was deadly secret. I decided, therefore, to follow the R.A.F. and brief the glider crews three days before. This irritated the higher command and I was informed that I should be held responsible if anything went wrong, for in their opinion the glider pilots were being briefed too late. I stood by my decision and was finally proved right by the result of the battle, that is, so far as the glider landings were concerned, which after all was my chief job. The R.A.F. gave me full support in this problem and insisted that the glider pilots should be given the same treatment as the R.A.F. air-crews. I have a feeling I paid for it in the end—one of the mistakes of being right at the wrong time!

The briefing proceeded, nothing was left to chance, and I consider my staff surpassed themselves. There will always be a criticism of any headquarters, but the proof of the pudding is in the eating!

On the operational side the work of Major Andy Andrews was unsurpassed. I had selected him to be my operations officer and to be stationed at 38 Group Headquarters. His job was to control flying and training. He was tireless in his energy and worked with the Royal Air Force excellently. It was through him that the lift system was watched and developed; also Andrews gave me constant assistance in developing new ideas on how to improve training and to step up flying practice. The final results, the standard of flying and the amazing landings in Normandy were very much due to his hard work, popularity and loyalty.

With regard to administration, the regiment was now very well equipped, and invaluable assistance and help was given to me in the complete reorganization by Major Peter Harding. He had been my co-pilot in Sicily, and had been in the sea with me and had swum ashore in the first battle. Now he had helped me realize completely the new conception of things. There will always be "moans" and criticism when men are under stress, and Peter Harding came in for his full share of it, but in all fairness I cannot believe that anyone who served in the regiment in the early days and during its transformation could really have grumbled at our state in 1944. The transformation had been made and Peter Harding had had a great deal to do with the result from which all benefited. Another excellent officer was Captain Ian MacArthur who worked endlessly to keep the office organization going efficiently. Finally, I come to Captain George Roztzorowski, a Polish officer of extraordinary capacity. He was my intelligence officer, and it was his duty to look after all operational orders and information. The excellence of the briefing and information glider pilots received was mainly due to his efforts.

As D-Day approached I flew round the airfields and shook hands with most of the air-crews, who were keen and confident and gave me a feeling of elation. My one misfortune was that I was unable to go with them. The reason for this was that it had been decided that part of No. 2 Wing should wait behind and follow up when required. Air Vice Marshal Hollinghurst insisted that I should be available and not in the battle. I was happy, however, in the knowledge that No. 1 Wing had an intrepid leader in Iain Murray, who was to more than prove himself in the coming events.

The scene was set. Thousands upon thousands of men waited in the camps quietly and confidently, cleaning rifles and Bren guns, writing home, reading, playing games, sleeping, waiting for the hour.

8

NORMANDY

ON 6TH JUNE, 1944, the great invasion armada began to move, and among the first formations to go were three bomber/glider combinations at Tarrant Rushton, which included the crews of Gliders 27, 28 and 28A, who were to crash-land on the Merville battery. Weather conditions were very poor and Glider No. 28A broke a tow-rope over the sea coast and had to land in England. The other two aircraft combinations weaved in and out of the clouds and the rain, the glider pilots having considerable trouble in keeping on tow. However, as they cleared the English coast the weather seemed to improve and they crossed the Channel.

The combination, which included Glider 27, piloted by Staff-Sergeant Kerr, had to make a 360 degree turn at Worthing in order to lose time before arriving over the French coast. When it arrived there in the pitch darkness flak pounded up from the defences and several parachutists were badly wounded. However, the tug and the glider pressed on. In Glider No. 28, piloted by Staff-Sergeant Bone, the parachute arrester gear came undone from the tail and streamed out behind. This stalled the entire combination and considerable height was lost, but they released at 1,800 feet and circled the area. Now a great snag arose. The radio aid Rebecca-Eureka failed. I have described before how the Eureka was to be carried by a parachutist in a sack, and he was to set up his position near the battery and call the gliders down. When the operator jumped he had Eureka in the kit-bag attached to his leg. As the Rebecca-Eureka was top secret, it had a small explosive charge in it to destroy it, should there be a risk of its falling into enemy hands. Unfortunately, the plunger on the charge was out when the parachutist's kit-bag hit the ground and Eureka exploded, leaving the air crews without the hoped for ground aid. As a result, the combination found it impossible to pick up the battery in the darkness and the smoke, and circled four times round the area before finally releasing the gliders.

Staff-Sergeant Bone mistook a heavily bombed village for the battery. As he descended through the darkness and murk he searched and searched, but could see nothing until he got down to 500 feet, when he realized he was in the wrong place. It was too late then to turn away and so he landed in a field, which, on the following day, he found was only a quarter of a mile from the battery.

Finding the battery proved easier for Staff-Sergeant Kerr, but he realized that, in the darkness, he could not land in the middle of it and, to avoid touching down in the mine-field in the pit surrounding the battery, he crash-landed into a near-by orchard. He and his passengers, however, were able to take part in the assault on the battery, which was taken.

It was an extremely hazardous affair and one of the greatest difficulties, of which both crews complained, was the immense cloud of dust and smoke and sleet which made inspection of the ground impossible. They were unanimous in praising the Royal Air Force tug crews, who flew round and round the area despite heavy flak, and it was amazing that both the gliders were able to land, with their loads, fit and capable of taking part in the battle, without prior casualties. Great credit must go to Staff-Sergeants Bone, D.F.M., and Kerr, D.F.M., and to their second pilots Sergeants L. G. Dean and J. M. Mickey, for their courage. When these four were making their way to the rendezvous later to pick up the rest of the Glider Pilot Regiment they encountered two German patrols, engaged them and took a number of prisoners. Later they took part in an action against some tanks which, with the aid of some Canadians, they defeated. Thus, through this exciting night, they fought on without casualty, and finally returned to England triumphant.

Six more gliders of C Squadron were now about to take off. Their targets were the bridges over the Orne and Caen Canal. The taking of these bridges was an essential feature of the invasion plan, for if captured intact, the Second Army would be able to swing out into the open country on the far side of their left flank. On the other hand, if they were not captured, they were a potential source of danger from counter-attacks launched across them by German armour. It was therefore imperative that the bridges should be captured intact, *and* held *and* defended.

It had been ascertained that there were two fields alongside each bridge into which the Germans had not driven their anti-invasion poles because they believed the fields too small for gliders to land in, but the information provided by our reconnaisance patrols led us to believe that it *was* possible to land in these fields, and we hoped, therefore, that our surprise would be complete.

These gliders were to carry a company of the Oxford and Buckinghamshire Light Infantry, commanded by Major R. J. Howard, but extra equipment had to be carried in the gliders because of the nature of the operation. This equipment in the end proved so cumbersome that it weighed 7,330 pounds, which well exceeded the safe maximum, and to help in landing it an arrester parachute, similar to that used for the Merville Bridge battery landings, was provided.

The six combinations took off into the night and, strangely enough, the conditions were completely different from those prevailing at the first operation. In the leading glider were Staff-Sergeants Wallwork and Ainsworth, M.M. As the aircraft climbed to the maximum height of 4,000 to 5,000 feet the moonlight reflected the Channel below and revealed the dark mass of the French coast, as the glider pilots, through their intercoms, maintained contact with the navigator and captain of the Halifax tug.

The pilots grew tense as the warning of the release point came nearer, and soon the instructions for the landing were being delivered by the navigator. It was imperative that the glider crews made no mistake, so they set their stop-watches to synchronise with that of the navigator of the Halifax, who gave them the wind speed, course and airspeed. Tense with excitement, they warned their passengers that they were about to release, and the ribald singing and joking gave way to a dead silence.

"Good luck!" shouted the Halifax captain, through the intercom, and the first glider was in free flight.

Wallwork lifted the nose to lose airspeed and then, as she slowed, turned on to course. Ainsworth kept his eyes on the small gyro-compass, which he had set, and also on his stop-watch, calling off the height and the airspeed as they flew down course, which was about six to seven miles long, representing about three and a half minutes' flying. It was difficult to see outside, or recognise any landmark, and the figures on the instruments illuminated the cockpit with an unholy blue. As they descended, however, the moonlight lit up the coast and the River Orne and the Caen Canal.

Silently they flew down the track, checking as they went, and soon came to the spot where, according to their briefing, they should make a great circular turn. The check-point was the Bois de Bavons, one of the largest woods in Normandy. It should have been straight ahead on the port bow, but it was not there, so Wallwork had to put his glider through a 90 degree turn on to the crosswind leg. As he did so the bridges appeared below, picked out by the moonlight. Passing over them at 3,000 feet, half-flap was operated until they had reached about 1,000 feet, at which height they released the arrester parachute gear. Braking action was immediate, and the glider steadied up to the right airspeed for landing. As he touched down, the pilot jettisoned the parachute gear, and veered across towards the bridge embankment, the glider careering through the first of the barbed wire fences.

As it came to rest Wallwork and Ainsworth were thrown through the cockpit into the perimeter wire of the bridge itself, and in rapid succession there were two bumps behind them as two other gliders landed. The first of these two gliders was piloted by Staff-Sergeants O. F. Boland and P. Hobbs, D.F.M., who had gone though the same nerve-racking experience of the flight down to the bridges, and the third glider was piloted by Staff-Sergeants Barkaway and Boyle. All of them took part in the assault on the bridge led by Major Howard, the commanding officer of the raiding troops. Resistance there was fierce, although the enemy had been completely surprised; indeed the Germans were unaware that such huge craft could be used in such silence and with such accuracy.

While the assault on this bridge was in progress, the next three gliders were landing for an assault on the other bridge. The leading glider was given the wrong target and landed in the darkness on a bridge crossing the River Dives. It must be said that Staff-Sergeants Lawrence and Shorter carried out a remarkable piece of airmanship in safely landing in the dark at all.

The crew of the next glider, Staff-Sergeants Pearson and Guthrie, achieved a remarkable piece of flying. Their target was a field near the bridge surrounded by thirty-foot trees, and they came over the top of these trees and landed smack in the middle of the field. Their party was able to get out and overwhelm the defenders of the bridge within a few minutes. Staff-Sergeants P. A. Howard, D.F.M. and Back also landed, but they were about 400 yards short. Nevertheless, they were able to take part in the successful assault on the bridge.

At about 0300 hours the first elements of the 7th Parachute Battalion reinforcements arrived in time to help overwhelm the last desperately-defended bridge, which wase kept intact for the rest of the battle and became known as Pegasus Bridge.

While these battles were being fought eleven more gliders were carrying close support weapons for the parachutists. Their job was to land, without aids, so that the paratroopers could use the weapons and jeeps they carried. Crews for this operation were provided by E Squadron. Despite the hazards of this flight, no special training had been given. The weather was not good and all eleven crews experienced serious difficulty in keeping going behind the tugs. Again, they had to put up with a low cloud base and turbulence in the air. When they arrived at the landing zone it was completely obscured by the dust and smoke thrown up from the vigorous bombing of a battery by the R.A.F.

A further equipment-carrying operation was in progress in which four Horsas of A Squadron and seven of E Squadron landed in the darkness. Only five out of the eleven were able to find the target and these, hindered by the smoke, crashed into the obstruction poles. Because of the appalling conditions under which these gliders landed, some of them jammed their tail bolts and were at first unable to unload. Somehow they contrived to get the equipment out piecemeal, the pilots then fighting as infantry on the ground with great courage.

Another six gliders of F Squadron attempted, again without aids, to land in fields. Leaving Blakehill Farm at 22.50 hours on the 5th June, they also encountered very bad weather, but crossed the French coast about thirty-five minutes past midnight. Here again heavy bombardments had caused a great deal of smoke, and low cloud drifted across their tracks. As a result map-reading was impossible, and only two reached the target, the others being dropped in wrong places. Even so, they managed to fight in the battle, as the others were doing.

There then followed a much bigger operation led by Colonel Iain Murray, D.S.O., Commander of No. 1 Glider Wing. This consisted of sixty-eight Horsas carrying elements of the 6th Airborne Division, accompanied by four Hamilcars carrying heavy equipment. The seventy-two gliders took off early in the morning of the 6th June. The weather over England was very rough, and all pilots had to concentrate on keeping on tow. They all experienced low cloud and heavy rain. As they crossed the Channel the conditions moderated and continued to improve until France was in sight.

Heavy flak went up from the French coast as they crossed, but only a few of the passengers were wounded, which was extraordinary. This small armada was able to land on strips cut through the poles by parachute engineers, who had been instructed to lay out flarepaths. The air strips themselves were some 1,000 yards by 60 yards, and one strip was to be 1,000 yards by 90 yards, for the Hamilcars.

Soon, forty-seven Horsas and two of the four Hamilcars arrived over the target and landed, crashing into the poles where they could not get on to the strips. It was indeed an appallingly difficult landing to make because there was a cross-wind, and as a result there were numbers of collisions. Taken as a whole, however, it was a successful operation.

Major-General Gale, as Commander of the 6th Airborne Division, was the chief passenger in this flight, his pilot being Major S. C. Griffith, D.F.C., the Test Cricketer, who acted as Col. Murray's Second-in-Command, and formed a defensive position round the headquarters of the 6th Airborne Division. They were soon engaged with enemy patrols and snipers while the 6th Airborne troops unloaded themselves and their jeeps and guns and prepared for the battle, during which the glider pilots fought in every capacity and showed immense initiative in getting to the rendezvous from widely-scattered areas. Not a single glider pilot failed to take part in some action or another, either as gunners, jeep drivers or infantry.

I have already referred to the calmness with which the glider pilots met near-disaster in their training days, and the same attitude was apparent even in the most horrifying circumstances when in action. It needed to be seen to be believed, but their own accounts, written after the events, give just an inkling of their imperturbability. The following are three such accounts, the first taken by a pilot who landed among the poles:

There was nothing unusual in the take-off. I flew long enough to assure myself that the plane had been correctly loaded, then handed over to Paddy while I had a look at our passengers. They looked rather stern and were very young. Just the two of them, with their two jeeps fully loaded with special wireless equipment and medical supplies, together with the personal kit of Brigadier Hill. I remember that the night before he had asked me to be particularly careful with the contents.

Dusk was giving place to darkness as we droned over Oxford and towards the coast. I estimated that we were approaching the channel and checked with the tug crew, more for company and to test my intercom. than with any real interest. The air seemed very still, and the horizon was so well defined that at one stage I had to take over from Paddy, not because it was my turn but to satisfy myself we were in the right position behind the tug. This was just about the time we crossed the coast. Then continuing with our normal drill of twenty minutes each at the controls, which seemed quite long enough with a fully-loaded Horsa, we droned on.

Later the tug pilot told us we were getting close, and almost at once, we spotted another Horsa a few hundred feet above us. It puzzled us for the moment, as it seemed to be flying across our own course and we concluded it must have been one of the four gliders from Harwell going to the same landing zone. Then we ran into what we thought was mist, and that put all further calculation out of our mind. We soon realized it was smoke from the bombing of a coastal gun-battery, after the Lancasters had finished with it, which was to be the target of yet another glider and parachutist attack under Brigadier Hill. The smoke got thicker and demanded extreme concentration on the part of the tug-pilot, Paddy and myself; we didn't fancy landing in the Channel at any time, especially this night. Paddy was talking over the intercom., and I tried to observe the lights on the wings of the tug. Just when everything was disappearing and I was preparing to go into the low-tow position the smoke gradually began to clear until, quite suddenly, we were in comparatively good night visibility. Almost at once the observer, speaking calmly as if ordering another beer, said "Oh, there are the two houses—bang on time too." This was very comforting and a great relief. The flak was coming up lazily but didn't seem to be interested in us until just before the tracer burnt itself out. Almost unconsciously Paddy, who was flying now, skidded away slightly out of position, but he soon corrected and I concentrated on finding those lights. Our normal practice was to let Paddy fly the glider until I was quite certain of my landmarks, then I would say goodbye to the tug and take over for the landing. Between us we had calculated that at the operational height and at the time of crossing the coast, between the two houses we should fly at approximately ninety seconds before pulling off, and then whether the lights were visible or not we could fly straight ahead and land within reach of our rendezvous. Well the best made plans do seem to go astray. There were no lights! In a voice which sounded rather unreal I could hear myself asking Major Joubert about it, and he in a very cheery manner replying, "Don't worry, hang on, we have bags of time, I'll go round again in a second or two.' Just then over to the right and, so far as I could calculate, at the same distance from the coast as our landing zone should have been, we saw the "T". I knew it wasn't ours but it was a chance. Joubert spoke just at that moment and pointed them out and I asked him to fly a little to the right to give me more height in case of emergency.

Within five seconds it was just the right spot, I said goodbye, and someone wished us good luck, and then there was the familiar jerk with the noise of the wind gradually receding to the background, the speed dropping back to a modest 80 m.p.h. Paddy had handed over the controls and was intently watching an ack-ack battery on our right, whose tracer seemed to be a bit too near. He drew my attention to it and almost at once, as I put on half flap, the flak turned and seemed to have found another target. Then we saw the target, and another Horsa, well below us, flying towards the flak. Just a second afterwards it switched its emergency lights on and illuminated a small row of trees between ourselves and the "T" along which it was flying. I had to forget it then, but Paddy said later it seemed to crash into some trees to the right of the "T". Then we were coming in just right. A little bump, and then another, something like a ditch, I thought. Then a wheel seemed to stick and start to swing the glider round. I applied opposite rudder and my brake quickly, and no sooner had we straightened out than we stopped. I heaved a sigh and then immediately shot out of my seat; we were on the first light and not in our correct position on the extreme left of the "T". Having been forewarned, by a training mishap, that this might happen, we had arranged that Paddy should jump out and wave his torch to show the rear of the glider. This he did while with feverish haste I collected our personal kit and rifles and jumped out. The two "bods" whom I had completely forgotten about were down on the ground before me. They took up positions on either side of the glider while I went round to Paddy.

We got ready to beat a hasty retreat if another glider was coming in on top of us, but there was not a sign of anything in the sky. You have no doubt been at an appointed place at the right time, waited for someone to arrive, and had to go away in disgust. We felt like that at first. Then a feeling of loneliness came over us; even the Germans didn't greet us. Where were the independent parachutists who had put the "T" out? Not a soul, not a noise, nothing. Paddy looked at me, and I said "Let's get the tail off". We went inside the glider and began to undo the nuts holding the tail on. We had them off within a quarter of an hour, but the tail wouldn't budge. Even when Paddy jumped on the top it still wouldn't budge. We called the two drivers over, and then began the oddest tug-of-war I have ever competed in. One Horsa Mark 1 and four tired and sweating airborne types. The glider won, and while we sat back exhausted for a moment it sank back quite contentedly, for all the world as if it was back in England. We thought of using the charge to blow the tail off, but apart from the noise, and the fact that at present we were undisturbed, the type of equipment we were carrying decided us against it. Then, just as we picked up the hand-saw, we heard the sound of approaching aircraft, and right above us the air seemed full of parachutes. It was a wonderful sight, and we didn't feel lonely any more. For the next five minutes we were busy dodging kit bags which dangled from the feet of heavily-loaded paratroopers. One even landed on the tail, but nothing happened, and when we asked for help to get the tail off he grinned and vanished. An Albermarle on our left lit up in flames brought us back to earth with a jolt.

There was nothing for it but to saw the tail off. My knuckles were already sore from the exertions inside the glider, and Paddy, who was as strong in the arms as anyone I knew, took first shift. We must have been sawing for forty-five minutes when the driver looking out on the left gave us warning. Silhouetted against the skyline were ten armed men coming towards us. We crouched on the ground and debated whether they were Germans or paratroopers. They moved up to within touching distance and then we heard them speak. They were ours. Thank goodness. The password, "Punch" and the answer "Judy", for the night was exchanged. But would they help us with our tail—not a bit of it. They moved on to Ranville, not a bit interested. We had already decided that the only way to get the tail off was to get more manpower. There could be nothing holding that tail on now except willpower. Then the comparative silence was disturbed by the hunting horn which we had read had been used in the African campaigns, and the paratroopers went in to the attack on Ranville. For fifteen minutes there was a great deal of small-arms fire and a house burst into flame about half a mile away. The fact that we now felt sure we were on "British" ground gave us confidence and we decided to make our way towards the village. We crossed the road, Paddy darting across and knocking my compass out of my hand. I had already taken a bearing, and we didn't need it any more anyhow. We crossed a small orchard when, in our tracks and with a very low trajectory, something which I judged to be an anti-tank gun fired twice. We decided that we had best make a detour and went back to the road. "Punch" came the challenge. "Judy" we breathed. It turned out to be two signallers, one of whom had injured his foot in a tree, together with a Canadian major from the R.E's who, screened by the hedge, was trying to pick up his bearings. He had already walked a long way, he said. It turned out he was one of Brigadier Hill's party. I told him where I thought we were and it agreed with his guess. I then suggested that the best plan would be to make for the rendezvous we were supposed to be at by dawn, as we expected that by then Brigadier Hill would be there to set up his H.Q. There were two possible routes. One towards the coast and turn right, or towards Ranville and turn left. We chose the latter, and learned later it was the right choice.

The glider hadn't been forgotten, and together our party of seven made our way towards the glider again. It was still standing in glorious dignity. Then the major went up to it and said "Is this the tail?" gave two little pushes and the thing fell off. Now the drivers sprang forward, adjusted the steering wheels and we were all ready to go. Once again our attention was distracted by the drone of aircraft. This time it was Hamilcars and Horsas. One landed not far away, the others went over the brow of a small rise towards Ranville. We walked over to the glider pilots who were having no trouble in unloading. We exchanged names, just in case, and then went back to our jeeps. When we got back we saw a group of men inspecting them. They turned out to be Captain Dodwell (without his second pilot, who had injured an ankle) in company with Taffy Lovett whose own second pilot, Tug Wilson, was staying with Dodwell's No. 2. This considerably strengthened our little party, and we made for the road once again. We decided that while Taffy and I went ahead on either side of the road the two jeeps were to follow behind, carrying the others at a safe distance. The orders to the drivers were to make for Ranville with the jeeps if we ran into any trouble, while we gave them covering fire. We soon came to the crossroads, and turning our back on Ranville headed east. After about fifteen minutes we came to a small hamlet. Taffy stayed on the outskirts with the jeeps drawn into the hedge about a hundred yards back, while I crept cautiously along the street. It was more difficult to walk quietly now, and I was relieved when I came out on the road again on the other side. In a few minutes the rest of the party were through and we continued along the road which now seemed to rise slightly. About ten minutes later as we approached another crossroads, which could now be seen as it was beginning to get light again, a sudden burst of firing came from a light automatic immediately to our front and a little to our left. We halted, and then decided as there was no further noise to make for the trees. They turned out to be the entrance to the drive of the house which was our destination, the dawn rendezvous. The jeeps backed cautiously into the bushes at the side and we hastily dug a few holes as a small defensive position. It was quite light now, and round the bend of the drive came the middle-aged lady of the house. She showed no surprise at seeing us, and said that over the road there was an injured soldier; she was taking some wine to him.

The holes dug, we decided to investigate the shooting, and a small patrol consisting of the major, Paddy and myself with one of the signallers cautiously approached the cross-roads. On reaching them we decided to turn left along what appeared to be the fence of the house which had been selected as the H.Q. The right-hand bank was quite high, with a hedge bordering it, and on the left a similar bank terminated in a wire fence which made it impossible to climb quickly. Through force of habit we walked on the left, at about arms-length intervals, and had proceeded about seventy-five yards down the road when a noise resembling the low note of a cow call attracted our attention on the other side of the road. We stopped, listened again; there was nothing further. Then after another two paces I turned round to the major and said "I believe it's groaning." He said, "Maybe, challenge." I still had my head turned in the direction from which we had come when I said in a fairly normal tone "Punch". A voice replied "Wie ist Das" and followed it up, before we could have answered, even if we had wanted to, with a burst of automatic fire. The bullets went up the road behind us by about ten yards and by the time the last one had bedded itself in the bank, we were all lying full-length in a ditch with a very sharp gravelly bottom, about 18 in. wide and 18 in. deep, and facing in the wrong direction. To make matters worse our rifles were useless even if we could have seen where the fire came from there didn't seem to be a target. I had a grenade in my pocket and seeing that the major had one arm free I passed it back to him. He removed the pin, waited for what seemed an eternity and then threw it. The explosion took place where we judged the firing had come from.

We waited for an answering burst but none came, and so very gingerly turned round and began to retrace our steps towards the cross-roads, one at a time, only this time crawling in the ditch. My hands and knees were sore for days afterwards, and when I stood up to run the last ten yards I fell over again with cramp. But we all got safely round the corner and back to our H.Q. We felt that next time we should make a pincer movement, one from either side of the road, but from the height of the bank. Having chosen another two men, but before we could start on this little war of our own, the lady of the house came back and we decided to question her as to the whereabouts of the Germans. She informed us that next door there was an H.Q. with about seventy-five Germans. That explained the sentry we must have disturbed, and it rather changed our plans. The major and one of the others went off to decide the best way to attack the house while the rest of us decided to have a "brew-up". Paddy started to prepare and I decided to go to the entrance of the drive and look down the road. I was observing from the cover of some bushes when along the road towards us came a party headed by two glider pilots, with what looked like their passengers. They hadn't seen me yet, and when they were almost opposite, they sat down on the side of the bank with their backs towards me. I could have touched them, but I said "Hullo" instead. Their faces were a picture of surprise. Nevertheless, we now had some more reinforcements, and they came back into our hide-out to rest.

The next to arrive on the scene were the R.A.M.C., a party of about forty strong together with a Polish prisoner, a youngster who a moment or two later nearly died of fright when the pattern bombing of the beaches started. Even at the distance we were inland the ground shook as though a miniature earthquake was in progress. The senior officers now took command and decided to send us, the glider pilots, back to Ranville with a report on the position. There we were to rejoin the glider pilot pool of reserves which had been formed.

We started out cautiously, walking parallel to the road. We passed a sentry, who only just recognized us in time, and later saw what we took to be our own paratroopers picking up supplies which had been dropped, only to find later that they were probably Jerries after all, as we had no troops in that position. We made our way through the village, which was looking a bit sorry for itself, and passed a badly damaged glider which had hit a stone wall. We met a couple of newspaper reporters in the street and they directed us to the divisional H.Q. which had been set up in the outhouses of a farm. The approaches were already under fire by snipers—we found that out after a near miss.

Having made our report to the general we found a small corner behind some bushes and had a really wonderful cup of tea made from provisions taken from our 48-hour ration pack. Then, much refreshed, we moved off to the glider pilot rendezvous where there were already twenty to thirty glider pilots. The main intention was that on arrival of the main lift at 2100 hours that evening, all pilots should be taken to England as quickly as possible to get ready for another trip. Meanwhile, all we had to do was to wait. We dug another hole, Paddy and I, and had some more to eat. There was spasmodic firing in the direction of Caen, and now and again patrols were sent out to contact the troops immediately on our front and flank. And so the day passed.

As the time for the main force of the gliders drew near, the firing from the Germans grew louder, and the perimeter appeared to be hard pressed. I learned later that the gliders were late, and that they arrived at a very critical time. Eventually, above the noise of the firing, we heard the approach of many aircraft, the engines became a roar, and the firing seemed to cease. Even the Germans were struck dumb by what they saw. A magnificent sight, the air full of gliders sweeping in towards the German lines and then turning lazily and making a left-hand circuit over our slit trenches. They seemed very low, and yet not one of them appeared to be hit from the ground fire. After that perfect silence from the enemy an absolute inferno of noise broke out. Our position, which up to that time had not come under fire, was plastered with mortars, as Jerry tried to get the range of the landing zone. This forced us to keep our heads down, but we could still hear the whistle of the gliders as they continued to land. Later, after the firing had died down, I crawled cautiously to the high ground overlooking the landing zones. The area was covered with gliders, a beautiful "Balbo", which earned for it the name of the "Milk Run". Out of curiosity I glanced over towards my own landing position a little to the right of the main body. I was surprised to see that what I had thought to be my brake binding had in reality been the wing of the glider knocking over an anti-invasion pole. My luck must have been terrific for the glider had only touched this one pole, and had steered a course between the others without my having known that they were there.

We decided to keep watch alternately during the night. Not because we were in any immediate danger, in our position, of being taken by surprise, but because we felt that we should keep up appearances for other wandering units who, not appreciating our exertions of the night before, might take a poor view if they found us asleep. I took a benzedrene, which is supposed to keep you awake. At least I thought so, but I was overcome with sleep in about five minutes and just had enough time to kick Paddy awake. The next thing I knew he was kicking me, and my first vision was of planes flying over and dropping parachutes. We had been warned that Jerry might try an immediate counter-attack with his own parachutists, and that managed to get through to me. For the rest of that night I kept awake, and found out with relief just before dawn that they were our own Dakotas dropping supplies.

The next morning, quite early, we had orders to prepare to march back to the beach-head.

This is the second account, by Staff-Sergeant Leslie Foster whose glider collided with another in the air:

As we approached the French coast we could see the vast force of ships pouring shells and rockets into the defences of the Germans. Smoke rose into the sky as the missiles landed, and through the haze a British plane dived down in flames. The scene was both exciting and terrifying, magnificent and yet appalling. However, I had no more time to gaze on this vivid drama as we were almost over the coast. As I took over the controls from Tom I searched for the church tower and the other landmarks which marked our turning and landing points. Suddenly, there it was—as clear as it had been shown in the briefing film. I called up the tug and thanked him for the ride. "O.K., Matchbox," the Canadian voice drawled, "The best of luck." My right hand reached out and pulled the tow-rope release; there was a check in the speed and we were alone over the fields of France. I put down half-flap and turned slowly to port, a full 180 degress, and there was our landing field stretched out before us. I increased to full flap and put the nose down. Everything seemed to be going extremely well, when a warning shout came from Tom: "Les—kite coming in from ——." It was too late to do anything but pull back hard on the stick as the other glider soared up under and across me. There was a terrible tearing, crashing sound and I saw the other cabin hang for a split second under me and then fall away. The speed dropped alarmingly as we overed with the nose up, and I quickly brought up the flaps and pushed hard on the stick to try to get up some speed. It was obvious that my undercarriage must have gone in the crash and I realized that it would have to be a "belly-landing" if we were fortunate enough to reach the ground in one piece.

There was no sound from the men inside, but the roaring of the air increased as the needle moved faster and faster. It was no use letting up: I would have no brakes, and my safest best was to hit the ground as soon as possible and pray that the good hard French soil would halt us before we hit the trees at the far end of the field. Ninety, ninety-five; the screaming of the air past the fuselage. One hundred—a hundred and ten—full flap on—up with the nose—and we were tearing through the high French corn, the red earth pouring through the broken floor—nothing but the long straight parting of the corn, and then, suddenly, the open patch before the trees. Hard kick on the right rudder—would it work?—and we slewed round in a great half-circle, the soil spuming high in the air. As we stopped, almost touching the trees, there was a tearing sound, and a very tired port wing fell to the ground. When we had extricated ourselves from the remains we found that one of our Thermos flasks was, miraculously, unbroken, and as we sat sipping the hot tea we examined ourselves. A few scratches on Tom. A few on me. No passenger casualties. Our luck had not deserted us this day!"

The third account is by Staff-Sergeant A. Proctor, who was the last of a flight of Horsas to arrive on the pole-strewn target.

After a smooth, uneventful journey we crossed the coast of France, and were mildly surprised to see a Stirling coming out with all four engines on fire. Looking ahead, the landing zone was in sight, purple smoke flares indicating the wind direction, the ground well littered with gliders, and streams of tracer curving up to the oncoming aircraft. It became increasingly apparent that it was time to release; a glance at the altimeter showed 2,500 feet, a message wishing us luck from the tug, and we were in free flight. Fate (in the shape of the marshalling officer at Brize Norton) had decreed that we should be the last of a flight of Horsas to arrive over the landing zone and, in consequence, we were at the end of a long queue of gliders on the approach. Perhaps for this reason we presented the best target and the German gunners gave us their undivided attention. Evasive action became essential, and as there was no room in the approach area, I dived away into-wind with the intention of pulling out at the last moment and making a cross-wind landing. The plan worked well until I pulled up about 100 feet from the ground and turned cross-wind. The area I had chosen to land in was heavily studded with anti-invasion poles, and there was no alternative but to land here. In a rapid survey of the ground, I made an interesting dis-covery: the methodical Germans had erected the poles in a distinct pattern, and it was this that saved us. I manoeuvred the glider until we were flying a few feet over the poles then ordered full-flap, and as the next gap appeared I thrust the stick forward. Both wings struck poles simultaneously, and with a great rending of wood we landed heavily, but still on a straight course, coming to a halt before reaching the next alternating row of poles. Five trembling artillery-men emerged from the cockpit, and assured us that they had never doubted our ability. It seemed kinder, at the time, to believe them.

The second pilot, Sgt. Wright, took charge of the unloading, and while this was taking place I thought it might be prudent to see what was going on outside. It was then that I heard the whine of bullets uncomfortably close, and realized with some alarm that they were probably being directed at me. I went to ground with speed, and observed that the fire was coming from a church tower about 500 yards away. I shouted a message to this effect to the glider, to which Sgt. Wright replied, "Come inside then you silly ——." Saving my rude remarks until later, I asked for the Bren gun, and worming my way round the glider, sited the gun and opened fire on the church tower; this silenced them. Unloading was then completed, farewells were exchanged, and the Royal Artillery departed at high speed.

Sgt. Wright and I took a compass bearing and set off in a direct line for our own rendezvous, coming upon another Horsa that in landing in the same area had struck a pole head on, killing both pilots in a horrible fashion. A few minutes later, the sporadic fire, which had been bursting over the landing zone since we landed, suddenly increased with such intensity that it was literally raining shrapnel. We raced to the nearest cover and leapt in, and in the excitement I broke my braces, thereby increasing my problems. We decided that a circular approach to the rendezvous was desirable and practical, and believing that all ground to the west of the landing zone must be in our hands, we proceeded in that direction. After a mile or so cross-country we came upon a village which seemed to be completely deserted, and making our way cautiously through, we found ourselves approaching a road junction with myself in the lead a few paces ahead. I heard and then saw a vehicle coming towards us, and in the half light I could see it was a tracked vehicle, full of armed men. "It's Germans," I gasped. We dropped into the ditch, armed ourselves with a grenade each and removed the pins. As the vehicle reached a point on the road opposite us it stopped and I was about to throw my grenade when a voice said, "I say, you chaps, can you tell me the name of this village?" It was a Bren carrier and the men were Commandos. Concealing the grenade behind me I stepped out and said I believed the village to be Ranville, whereupon the Commando captain thanked me and said that they were probing for elements of a Panzer division believed to be in or around this village. They moved on and we spent an anxious few minutes clutching our grenades and searching for the pins.

A little farther on we came upon the main body of the Commando unit, who advised us against proceeding any further, although we suspected that they were more interested in having the extra support of our Bren gun, which they carefully sited for us and which we subsequently put to good use. At first light we gathered up our traps and stole quietly away, determined to find our own unit, and about an hour later we were wearily trudging past an orchard, hopelessly lost, when a head appeared out of a slit trench and said, "Where the hell have you two been?" It was lieutenant Norton of

"B" Squadron. Never was a reprimand so happily received; we had found the squadron area.

We had a horrible breakfast of compressed food (I have never tasted anything quite like these concoctions), and set up the Bren again. Bob Wright was allowed two hours sleep while I stood watch. The immediate area seemed quiet, but there was a lot of activity going on elsewhere, and *our* main source of danger was from snipers in a near-by wood. These were eliminated by a patrol led by Squadron-Sergeant-Major Watts, who, failing to answer a challenge on return, almost got shot by an alert sentry. What the Sergeant-Major said is not recorded. One other incident worthy of note was the part played by that grand old lady H.M.S. *Warspite,* who was lying about half a mile off-shore in support. A target just ahead of our position was found for her and action called for, and she fired a broadside from her 16-in. guns. The noise from these shells passing overhead was frightening enough; the effect was tremendous. We were relieved at noon on the second day and ordered to return to U.K., rumour having it that another Op. was being planned.

A second major landing was also made on D-Day, 6th June. It was by far the largest operation, involving 250 gliders which carried the 6th Air Landing Brigade, consisting of some 7,000 men, and their equipment and artillery. With this group was the Armoured Reconnaissance Wing, which was carried in Hamilcar gliders.

The same situation arose and landing zones were cleared of obstructions by parachute engineers. The landing zone consisted of four lanes running north and south and divided between Horsa and Hamilcar gliders. This was the greatest number of gliders ever flown into any battle.

By now the weather was very much changed. Only a light wind was blowing from the north-west, and the clouds were well over 2,500 feet. Indeed, apart from history being made with such a vast number of gliders being landed, the most significant point was the Hamilcar squadron. For the first time an armoured formation was being flown into battle. The Light Armoured Reconnaissance Regiment, consisting of Tetrarch tanks and Bren-gun carriers, must have had a demoralizing effect on the Germans, for they had never seen anything like it before. It had been a closely-guarded secret, and although these tanks were not of a heavy type they caused the Germans some concern. It was interesting to think that this Armoured Reconnaissance Regiment had been carried 200 miles during the morning, to be landed a few hours later in the middle of France.

straight on to the battlefield where they made immediate contact with the Germans.

The following brief account by Staff-Sergeant T. W. Pearce gives a spotlight picture of the hazards each pilot ran in a mass landing of such a size:

> Crossing the coast of France on "D" Day, 1,500 feet up, and "according to plan", it all seemed too peaceful—rather like an exercise, even though the "area" had received and was receiving a plastering from the Navy.
>
> Casting off, the air was crowded with other gliders, parachutes and discarded tow ropes, and we went down steeply on full flap, turning through 180 degrees. Without warning there came a tremendous jolting crash and the glider was partially stalled by colliding with another glider we hadn't seen, and we had only 600 feet to regain control.
>
> Control was regained just in time to "round out", but there was no time to do anything else. We landed sideways, rushing through the tall French corn to a juddering halt.
>
> My first pilot, Les, turned to me and said: "Time for a cup of char, Tom!" (We had two flasks strapped above our heads; one was still intact—as were the "pin-ups" we had admired on the way over!)
>
> Chopping our way out of the wreckage we dashed over to the other glider, or rather what was left of it. In the mid-air crash the tail unit had been destroyed and it had dived vertically from 600 feet. We had lost two of our own flight, for all in Z glider had perished.
>
> We could no longer use the term "according to plan".

Lieutenant-Colonel Iain Murray's own report of his experiences on D-Day ran as follows:

> As we approached the coast visibility improved greatly, and when over the Channel we could see the outline of the immense armada that was on its way. Our route took us to the east of our objective, which was all part of the plan to mislead the Germans as to which part of the coast had been chosen for the main landing. On reaching the French coast we turned west until we struck the waterways, which were the most prominent features to guide us.
>
> My own glider carried a full complement, including Brigadier the Hon. Hugh Kindersley, Commanding 6th Air Landing Brigade, some of his staff and the late Chester Wilmot, who subsequently wrote that great book *Struggle for Europe*,—who was doing a running commentary into a recording machine.

Turning in from the coast the visibility became very poor. A combination of cloud, smoke and dust caused by bombing obscured the ground completely. This may have been a godsend as the ack-ack fire, although considerable, seemed very inaccurate. Nearing our objective the visibility improved and soon the flares put out by the Independent Parachute Company could be seen, and gliders casting off from their tugs. We managed to make a good landing with plenty of speed so as to avoid action with the posts. In the last few yards one post tore a wing-tip and one collapsed when hit head-on by the cockpit. I always think this one must have been loosely placed by some patriotic Frenchman employed by the Germans.

Soon after landing I found that Chester Wilmot's recorder had been smashed by a piece of shell from an ack-ack gun, which was most unfortunate. However, he had a good picture in his mind and his description, which was later published, gave a very clear account of events up to the time of landing.

Apart from occasional rifle and machine-gun fire there was no great opposition, and we soon foregathered at the rendezvous to await the dawn. As soon as daylight came we went down to the bridge (later known as Pegasus Bridge) to find that one glider had landed within a hundred feet of it. This was a remarkable feat on the part of the glider pilot concerned, and it had enabled the troops carried to rush the bridge and capture it before it could be blown. This was a very vital task, and the use of the bridge was of great assistance to the Commandos and main body of troops in crossing over the river.

It was on this bridge that General Gale waited at midday to hand over to Lord Lovat's Commandos, having made a bet of a case of champagne that Lord Lovat would not be there at the appointed time. As the hour approached, there was no sign of him, but as the clock struck a piper seemed to appear from nowhere and led Lord Lovat and his Commandos to relieve us, and win his bet.

Things were now beginning to hot up, and mortar and shell fire became more frequent. Glider pilots were all allotted various tasks in defending divisional and brigade headquarters and other vital points.

As the light was fading the second lift came in, comprising several hundred gliders, some landing west of the River Orne and the others on the same landing zone as we had used. The ack-ack fire had greatly increased and it was an alarming spectacle to see the bursts all round the gliders as they came in to land. Many must have been hit, and those with inflammable loads caught fire, but it was remarkable how few casualties were suffered. The second lift came under considerable mortar and shell fire during unloading operations, which caused some casualties and delayed the rapid dispersal which is so important in an operation of this sort.

From now onwards the opposition became stronger and the whole division was hard-pressed to keep the enemy at bay until the main forces could lend support. Until word was received that the glider pilots could be withdrawn they were used in various tasks in holding the bridgehead, and during this time fully justified the military training to which they had been subjected in addition to their flying duties.

It had always been the intention to withdraw the glider pilots as soon as possible, as further airborne operations were in prospect, and word came through on D-Day plus 2 that we should make our way back to the beaches. This was an uneventful withdrawal, but it was heartening to see the amount of heavy equipment already landed in spite of the weather. One spectacle reminded us of the complete supremacy of the Royal Air Force. Just as we were approaching the beaches five enemy aircraft made an attack on the landing aircraft. In next to no time our fighters appeared and in less than five minutes every enemy plane had been shot down in flames. The need for air supremacy was soon evident when we saw the mass of equipment piling up; a few bombs could have thrown everything into chaos.

Our journey back was made in a small vessel manned by R.N.R. officers and men, who did everything to make us comfortable and showed their usual hospitality in every way.

We received a great welcome on arrival at Fargo Camp, where many who had been unable to take part for one reason or another greeted us. Our only sorrow was for those who had not come back and for their relations and friends. Considering all things our casualties were comparatively small and we felt that our first operation had not been as costly as expected.

And so the second glider operation of airborne forces came to an end, the glider pilots being immediately withdrawn to the depot in England where they were redistributed to their squadrons to await the planning of the second operation.

On the ground, the plan for this second operation was for the 51st Highland Division to pass through the 6th Airborne Division area, link up with an armoured division, and thus complete the encirclement of Caen. To forge this link it had been decided that the 1st Airborne Division, which had just returned from North Africa, would be dropped east of Caen to provide the second arm of pincers that would completely enclose that city.

For some time there had been difficulty in moving the Germans at all, and a stalemate ensued. I flew over to Normandy and went into conference with some senior officers in that area. For some time nobody knew quite what to do, but finally it was decided that it was imperative that the 1st Airborne Division should be dropped. I therefore flew back to England where a very high-level conference took place with the Air Commander-in-Chief Allied Air Force, Air Chief Marshal Sir Trafford Leigh-Mallory, in the chair. It was a most interesting experience, for I was by far the most junior officer there. It was thought that, at first, it might be possible for the 1st Airborne Division to be ferried over at first light, but this was finally decided to be too dangerous, and after much argument the whole thing was cancelled.

Thus came the end of the first phase of the liberation of Europe. The Glider Pilot Regiment had carried out the duties required of it, ninety-five per cent of the plan had succeeded, and I felt deeply satisfied with the result.

9

INDEPENDENT OPERATIONS

IN THE next few months many operations were planned but most of them, for varying reasons, had to be cancelled. Some of those that were carried out didn't make headlines, but nevertheless they are of interest, and to the men who took part in them they were important and deserve recording here.

The first (by an unknown narrator) deals with the invasion of the South of France from an Italian base:

The Independent Squadron, late No. 3 Squadron, left Italy before the 1st Airborne Division embarked for home. This may have been Authority being thoughtful or it might have meant that the squadron was destined for an operation that never materialized, a practice all too common in airborne planning. Be that as it may, the squadron embarked in American C47s at Guala del Coole in Southern Italy en route for Oudja in French Morocco.

Oudja at that time was the American Airborne Forces Training Centre. Here the squadron established itself and was engaged upon training and ferrying newly-constructed gliders (Waco C.G.4A) from Casablanca to Oudja. The squadron remained there for about a month, during which time it settled down very well. The members of the unit managed to get the "going home" feeling out of their systems and became resigned to the fact that they would be away from the U.K. for at least another year. Oudja was a friendly station, it was in fact a veritable United Nations. There were South Africans, French, Americans and ourselves. This regular allied organization got along very well together, and its camp permanent staff did their utmost to ensure that we had everything that we required for our comfort. While there, the unit was visited by Major-General E. E. Down, C.B.E., who was on his way to India, to take command of the Indian Airborne Division. Soon after American Thanksgiving Day the unit was ordered to return to Sicily as the whole of the American Airborne training centre was moving into that island. The American commander, Colonel E. Ready, a personality remembered by the whole unit, gave the officers a small party and wished us Godspeed for our journey.

On 4th December, 1943, the first gliders left Oudja for Camiso in Sicily which was to be our H.Q. for the next five months. Ten gliders left each day and it was proposed that the squadron should take three days to clear Oudja. That move was not too successful, but approximately a week later all gliders had arrived at Camiso.

Camiso, a pleasantly situated airport in the south of Sicily, had been very heavily bombed during the invasion of Sicily, and in consequence the buildings were pretty badly damaged. The squadron was given a barrack block near the main gate which, with the normal glider pilot make-do-and-mend methods, soon changed into a comfortable sergeants mess which was to become the envy of our American friends—who used it as if it were their own.

Flying at Camiso was the best that the squadron ever experienced. The American 54 Troop Carrier Group made five C47s daily available to the squadron and soon every pilot was thoroughly enjoying himself. The American group commander was determined that the squadron pilots should get as much gliding as possible, he therefore decided that the squadron should be divided among the other stations of his command. Accordingly a flight was sent to Girbini, another to Ponto Alevo, while the H.Q. and the third flight remained at Camiso. These conditions prevailed for about four months, in which time the squadron's flying skill increased until moonlight landings became a routine affair. In fact the squadron's flying ability was such that it ranked equal with any in the Glider Pilot Regiment. During this period we were joined by the 22nd Independent Parachute Platoon, the pathfinder unit of the 22nd Parachute Brigade. Training therefore proceeded with the unit which was destined to lay out the landing zones the squadron was to use in the invasion of the south of France. This co-operation was to pay big dividends as the pilots got to know and trust those who were charged with the clearance and organization of their landing zones. Every pilot in the squadron felt more confident in his personal ability as a flier after this training in Sicily, which was one of the main factors in the successful completion of the glider pilot job in the south of France.

About April 1944 authority realized that the American G.C.4A was not suitable for carrying the British 6-pounder anti-tank gun because it could only lift about 3,000 lb. which meant that a gun and towing vehicle required two aircraft to lift them. Although this limitation of the C.G.4A became apparent during the invasion of Sicily it was still employed operationally up to the end of the war. However, it was agreed that the 3rd Glider Pilot Squadron should re-equip with British Horsas, a glider which was considered in every way more suitable for operations.

The first problem was, where were the Horsas to come from? It was known that some were still in North Africa where they had been left since the invasion of Sicily in the summer of 1943. With the help of the Americans a search party set out to locate those which remained in the theatre and to bring them to Sicily where training on them could begin. The search party located some fourteen Horsas in all, twelve of them on "E" strip, by the old salt lake in the El Djem area, where they had been left when the regiment had returned home at the end of 1943. Not only were these aircraft in good condition, but it was discovered that they were maintained by a party of R.A.F. "erks" who must have been forgotten by their squadron. These men had done a wonderful job and the Horsas were ready for their trip to Sicily within twenty-four hours of the arrival of the search party. The R.A.F. men were taken to Sicily in the Horsas they had looked after and they became the nucleus of the squadron maintenance flight which was to serve the unit so well. Two more Horsas were collected from Blida. How they got to Blida the squadron never discovered in spite of a considerable amount of research into their movements. Perhaps one of our readers may be able to answer this mystery?

These sixteen Horsas were now employed on training and everyone was extremely pleased to fly them again. There was one famous mishap when the rope came out of the tug on take-off and the glider was forced to land in an olive grove. It turned out that the American tow-ship squadron commander had been persuaded to be a passenger, a duty that was not appreciated by the powered pilots. This officer had only flown in a glider once before and on that occasion he had been involved in a "prang". This experience, he admitted, ended his gliding career.

Training with the Horsas proceeded satisfactorily while they were lightly laden, but when fully loaded, the tow-ship (tug) captains complained that their aircraft were underpowered. This factor limited the scope of training, but light-load flying continued without interruption.

During this period the new Horsas began to arrive. They were shipped in packing cases to Catania, where they were assembled at the R.A.F.M.U. Although not Mark IIs, they were a considerable improvement on the old weather-beaten veterans that we were using for training. By the beginning of June 1944 the squadron moved from Sicily to Guido in Italy and began to train seriously with the units it was to take to France.

In July 1943 the 2nd Parachute Brigade moved forward to the Rome area which was to be the base from which the Allied airborne troops were to invade the south coast of France. The squadron first moved to an aerodrome known as Marsigliarne, but this proved unsatisfactory and during the last days of July, it moved farther north, to Tarquina. Tarquina was a good aerodrome, ideally situated on the west coast of Italy, with a runway that pointed out to sea and had no obstructions that might prove dangerous to heavily-laden gliders and tugs during take off.

On arrival at Tarquina the squadron was joined by a new C47 group. This group had taken part in the invasion of Normandy where it had pulled heavily-laden Horsas. There is no doubt that this C47 group was the best that the squadron ever co-operated with, and to them should go the major part of the credit for the success that was achieved. Nothing was too difficult for them, and any suggestions that were put forward were readily agreed to. It was a great loss to the squadron when at the end of the operation the group returned to the U.K., where it was employed on the airborne operations in Holland in the autumn of that year.

At the beginning of August the first briefing was given to the combined tug and glider crews; our objective was to be the south of France in the area of San Raphael. Briefing was carried out by the normal means, but the prize briefing feat was a sand model built on the floor of the briefing tent. This model was constructed by the brigade intelligence officer and it proved to be extremely accurate, giving a good bird's-eye view of the landing zone. The I.O. only had a map and an air photo of the area, yet he managed to create a first-rate model. In glider-pilot briefing a good model of the L.Z. was often of great value, for it allowed the pilot to get an impression of the ground he would fly over before the day of the assault.

The Americans agreed that there should be one complete dress rehearsal. This dress rehearsal was to be used to iron out faults in glider marshalling and take-off procedure. Yet when everyone was airborne, a three-hour flight was undertaken in order to practise the "loose pair" formation. This rehearsal proved that the squadron was in excellent condition, and the smoothness with which everything went boded well for the future.

During the spring and summer of 1944 the squadron's main problem was glider maintenance and repair. The establishment of a glider pilot squadron allowed for no personnel for ground duties except those employed on the actual towpath. When the squadron was re-equipped with Horsas, no real servicing unit was attached to the squadron. Servicing during the period when the Squadron had only C.G.4As was the responsibility of the Americans, but when the Horsas arrived the Americans were not equipped to undertake their maintenance. At the beginning the Horsas were maintained by the "erks" from North Africa, but as the number of Horsas increased with the arrival of new aircraft from the M.U. at Catania they were unable to cope with the job. It was then decided to create a maintenance flight from squadron resources, allowing the pilots to do the daily inspections and minor repairs to the airframes. This system proved very satisfactory and kept the squadron flying during the training. However, as the operation approached, all the pilots were required for briefing and consequently the servicing became a major problem. In this case the problem was solved by the local M.U. in the Rome area loaning the squadron some thirty "erks" of various trades until after the invasion of the south of France. Servicing was the worst difficulty the squadron had to face throughout its stay in the Mediterranean, and it did considerable harm to the efficiency of the unit. It is hoped that establishment committees have since learnt wisdom and that now all Army flying units possess their own integrated maintenance flights.

At 0400 hours on 14th August, 1944, reveille was ordered for the squadron. Breakfast was served from 0400 hours and by 0430 hours the aircrews were assembling at their aircraft. The aircraft were already marshalled the night before so that all would be ready for take off at the first signs of dawn. Dead on 0530 hours the first tow-ship started to move out on to the runway and the gliders' part in the invasion of southern France had begun. The take off went perfectly, and within thirty minutes the formation was heading out into the Mediterranean.

This take off, however, was not destined to be the actual assault. After one hour's flying the formation turned slowly and returned to Tarquina. The reason given was that the landing zone was covered with mist and that it would have been impossible to land. The marshalling of the ground formation for the mass take off of gliders was always a long and tricky job. In this case both pilots and ground crews set to work, and the gliders and tow-ships were marshalled ready within an hour and a half of the last glider returning. This was undoubtedly one of the major achievements of 3 Squadron The Glider Pilot Regiment.

The second take off for the invasion began at 1400 hours. This time everything went satisfactorily, and the squadron reached the landing zone on time. The zone was situated in a valley with relatively steep sides, about 400 yards square, and with boundaries well defined by stone fences and woods. The leading glider was flown by squadron commander Major. R. Coulthard, who missed the landing zone and ended up on the edge of the wood. Although he was badly wounded, his load was intact and it was delivered to the anti-tank battery. The squadron-commander was not the only pilot who made an unfortunate landing; indeed the valley, which had been studded with anti-invasion poles, was covered with bady damaged Horsas and Waco C.G.4As. It was surprising how few casualties there were, but it must be remembered that the Horsa was a dear old friend to the Glider Pilot Regiment and often protected the crews and passengers by breaking up itself without breaking up the inmates. Thanks to them, the troops were safely delivered and the invasion a success.

About this operation I will say no more than that it was not one of the spectacular efforts of the regiment. However, it was successful and it demanded the highest flying skill. It proved also that one of the most important factors in the success of any airborne operation is co-operation between the aircrews of the transportation aircraft and the airborne troops.

The second narrative describes a military mission to Yugoslavia and is told by Captain Cornelius Turner:

Bunghole, the glider operation into Yugoslavia, was a truly Allied undertaking. The towing aircraft were C47s of 64th Troop Carrier Group U.S.A.A.F., the glider pilots British, flying American Waco gliders. It was mounted at very short notice at the request of 133 Force, War Office Intelligence, and the human cargo consisted of a high-ranking Russian general and staff officers, under command of General Korneyev.

The first intimation to the Independent Glider Squadron, stationed at Comiso airfield in Sicily, that anything was afoot came in the form of instructions to fetch immediately from one of the airstrips near Kairouan in Tunisia three Horsa gliders that were said to be lying there. We flew over with the American troop carrier squadron to which we were attached and landed at dusk on the desolate abandoned strip. There the gliders were, looking utterly lonely and dejected, the last remnants, but for the wrecks and the rusty tin cans, of the masses of men and machines that had packed these air-strips, roads and olive groves when this area was the first Airborne Div. HQ and the base for the Sicily landings. These Horsas had been at the mercy of wind, rain and the Arabs for six months, but there was no question of a proper inspection, nor indeed anyone who was qualified to carry one out; in the morning the pilots got in, tentatively checked the creaking controls, patted the woodwork trustingly and flew them 250 miles across the Mediterranean to Sicily.

Their immediate orders were to carry straight on to Bari in Italy, with each glider loaded with a jeep and anything else that would make up a 7,000-lb. load. We tested the loading—for we never had any loading charts—by arranging the load so that a body swinging from the tail could just raise the front wheels clear of the ground. Our well-attested experience was that this simple method is always satisfactory. The flight to Bari, with the tow-ships barely clearing the high hills, through heavy snow and a north-east gale, was an unpleasant experience for all concerned.

The towing pilots on arrival immediately insisted that a C47-Horsa combination over the Dinaric Alps of Yugoslavia was out of the question, and this was indeed self-evident. The Horsa plan was shelved, but though cheated on this occasion of their rightful destiny, these gliders died honourably in the end, for their remains now lie in a vineyard twenty miles north-west of Cannes. The following day, therefore, three Waco gliders, on which all our overseas glider training up to then had been carried out, were flown up by the squadron, loading was carried out up to 4,500 lb. apiece and test flights made; the Russian commanding general insisted that all his staff should take part in these test flights in their appointed position. They went off without incident, if one excepts the sporting decision of Staff-Sergeant McCulloch to execute a 360 degree turn over the town from about 300 feet on his landing approach.

The aim of the flight was to land the Russian officers inside occupied Yugoslavia in a valley called Medenapolu (the honey field) two miles north of the small town of Bosan Petrovac, about midway between Zagreb and Sarajevo in the eastern foothills of the Dinaric Alps, which rise at this point to 8,000 feet. The L.Z. was about 100 miles inland from the Dalmatian coast and 250 miles north from Bari. A diversion raid was to be carried out by the 15th U.S. Air Force with fifty Fortresses on Zagreb to the north. Thirty-six American and British fighters, Mustangs, Thunderbolts, and Spitfires, truly a regal entourage, were the escort detailed for the three gliders. The time of take off was 1100 hours; it was to be the first daylight glider operation. After two days of wintry weather the skies cleared and the take off went forward as planned. The gliders were piloted by myself and Staff-Sergeant Newman, Staff-Sergeant McCulloch and Staff-Sergeant Hill, and Staff-Sergeant Morrison and Staff-Sergeant McMillen. Incidentally the C47s of the U.S.A.A.F., under command of Lieutenant-Colonel Duden, were navigated respectively by an Australian, a South African, and a New Zealander of the Royal Dominions Air Forces. The escort was met at the rendezvous fifty miles to the northwards off the coast opposite the 8th Army forward positions, and the train headed north-east across the Adriatic at 8,000 feet in an absolutely cloudless sky and unlimited visibility.

It was bitterly cold, and though the far-flung escort fighters were occasionally glimpsed wheeling and banking high overhead and far below, most of the time the gliders and tow-ships seemed quite alone and defenceless in the midday sun. When landfall was made dead on track over the island of Zirje, the Balkan coast was seen to be blanketed with snow. The sharp outline of the towering range ahead was discerned when we were still over fifty miles away, and below there was not the slightest sign of civilization in the tortuous foothills, ribbed and ridged with ravines and patched with forest under the deep white carpet. The air was by now very turbulent, and this steadily increased during the next half-hour until at length the flight rocked and swayed thankfully over the last saddle with 500 or so feet to spare and peaks towering on either hand. As the hinterland opened up before us we knew we were nearing our destination and in a few minutes, after getting a fix on a large river, the tow-ships turned about and, estimating my position about four or five miles from the L.Z., I let go the rope of my lead glider and headed for the landing, being anxious not to by-pass it a second time. As the gliders circled to land, thin wisps of smoke from straw fires were seen below, the first welcome indication that a correct pin-point had been made. Within seconds, and within a few yards of each other, the gliders touched down, or rather flopped with a sickening jolt into the snow, reared vertically on to their noses, and slowly settled back. The "landing run" was about twenty feet and the ground snow about three feet deep. We were about 4,000 feet above sea level. We were the first Allied aircraft to land inside the country since the Occupation. After being forcibly embraced by incredibly filthy and bearded natives we were all hurried to a hut in the forest which verged on the valley in which we found ourselves.

The Russians were very cheerful, laughing and shaking our hands; the general was avuncular, and even the colonel who had sat immediately behind me throughout the flight, nursing a tommy-gun, grinned broadly for the first time in our acquaintance. After a short meal and suitable speeches in various languages, all unintelligible to us, and my own no less mysterious reply, we set out by sleigh for Petrovac, the only delay being the insistence of the Russian general that two large cases out of the baggage should accompany us instead of being brought along behind by the "Drugs" —Serbo-Croat for "Comrades". We assumed that these were too important to be let out of his sight as he had sat on them all the way over. Arrived at

Petrovac, a village of about 4,000 inhabitants, we were escorted to a large, bare, upstairs room already filled to overflowing by picturesque brigands whose presence intrigued the nasal senses no less than the eyes. There we all sat down to a veritable banquet, and it was then that the studied forethought of the general bore fruit, for his two fine cases turned out to be full of vodka and caviare. It may here be mentioned that under their greatcoats the Russian officers turned out to be wearing their smartest uniforms with full decorations, and this was an adroit psychological move, for the Drugs were obviously far more impressed by these than by the somewhat individualistic sartorial affectations currently fashionable among British forces in this theatre. For three weary hours we ate course after course and drank tot after tot. But it was hail and farewell to banquets in Yugoslavia, for during our four weeks incarceration inside that desperately poverty-stricken country we never saw any tea, coffee, cocoa, salt, milk (only for children), sugar or any sweet things, yeast, butter or cheese, or other things which make food pleasant to eat. Our diet consisted exclusively of meat of every imaginable variety (except it seemed, beef, mutton or pork) and potatoes, water, and unleavened rye and maize bread.

There were some half-dozen British and American intelligence officers under command of Brigadier Fitzroy Maclean, already in the town when we arrived, together with some Signals N.C.Os who operated the whimsical wireless set that should have kept us in touch with Cairo. Our valley, a hundred miles from the sea, was temporarily isolated by elements of the German army. Everybody knew that when the snow and the bitter cold were gone, rifle fire was the town's only defence, and in fact, within a day or two of the snow's departure, the Germans landed—a few weeks after we were back in Italy—in the gliders we already knew were assembled at Zagreb for that purpose. Marshal Tito's mountain stronghold was at Drvar some ten miles away; it fell in a few minutes when the Germans came and Tito made a hairsbreadth escape into Italy.

Each night we would be out in the valley, ready to kindle straw fires arranged to form a code on the ground, for the guidance of aircraft detailed to drop blankets, boots, rifles and ammunition, and sometimes men, from bases in Italy. These were comfortless vigils with no means of warmth but the straw and a hole in the snow with a temperature of twenty degrees or more of frost. Only two or three drops were made successfully during our stay, though we often heard aircraft. Naturally the enemy also lighted fires, and a code of that nature is most difficult to interpret from an aircraft whose pilot is certain to hit a mountainside if he comes lower than three or four thousand feet above our heads. Once or twice officers dropped out of the dark sky, stayed for a night and then were off about their fascinating business elsewhere in the country, or to Austria, Bulgaria, Hungary, Germany, or heaven knows where; a pony was ready for them in the morning and with their guides they disappeared into the forest.

The Drugs were passionately devoted to their Leader but were not impressive as soldiers. We were told that there was a high moral code in the ranks where men out-numbered girls by perhaps four to one. With commendable efficiency they brought in accurate reports of all movements of the occupation forces and expeditiously wiped out any small patrol rash enough to enter their forests and mountain fastnesses. They thought the world of themselves, for, they reminded us, London radio told them nightly that they were well-nigh perfect. The fact is that after seeing the Yugoslav and Greek partisans, one must form the conclusion that under suitable conditions guerilla warfare is the easiest of all forms of war, and tends to attract the most shiftless no less than the most idealistic of recruits. It requires a very tough constitution and a marked ability to play hide-and-seek, touch-and-run, or what-have-you, and in a terrain of roadless mountain and forest nothing really could be easier. Food when required was to be obtained on demand from any half-starved terrified woman called to her hut's doorway in the dark of the night at the rifle-butt knock of the Drug. (In Greece we were later to know fine people who had carried out their day-to-day work throughout the Occupation, some of them the salt of the earth, but their guerillas were generally the scum.) The women were the heroes, for they could not run far even if they had wished. The good ladies who lodged us knew they could be called to account when we had gone and the Others arrived, but they gave us every possible comfort and service in their poor but spotlessly clean log houses. The ground floors were often devoted to domestic animals, the living quarters being on the first floor under the high roofs with broad eaves after the Swiss or Austrian fashion. There were no shops, for there was nothing whatever to sell; most of the houses were detached with a few orchard trees about them: we never saw the ground underneath the snow but most of the streets seemed to consist of beaten dirt and rubble roads. Surprisingly, a pair of minaret-like towers reminded us that many of the people were Moslems, and that for centuries past this had been Turkish soil. There was no sign of any calling but agriculture, and we saw no men at work except feeding hay to the animals and cutting logs for fuel. The countryside in general appeared much like a picture postcard of the Tyrol, or perhaps the Rocky Mountains, a white blanket of snow, the coniferous forests, and the naked white peaks above, sharp in the clear air.

Patrolling J.U.88s sprayed the town with a burst or two for luck as they passed over daily. About one third of the houses had been gutted by fire either by the Germans or the Chetniks of Mihailovitch of the Ustachi of Pavelitch. The two latter, the rival civil factions, were far more feared than the Germans, for civil war is the least civilized of conflicts; no quarter was expected or given between these parties, it being tacitly understood that if there are any accepted rules in war these do not apply to civil warfare.

But, war apart, the people were of a very good-natured disposition. Lovers of music, they would take up quite spontaneously the song of some packhorse driver entering the street, and soon a hundred voices, young and old, would be joined in harmony, the women singing at their work and the children at their play. One evening a dance was held and we all went and enjoyed ourselves immensely, for a country dance in Yugoslavia, Greece, Ireland or Kentucky is much the same and easy to get the hang of. Yes, war apart, they were a happy people, but should one wander towards the exists of the town a cross-bandoliered, bomb-belted pirate or amazon barring the way reminded us that there was little room for happiness in their lives now.

After three weeks there were signs of the coming of the spring thaw and at last the snow grew thin enough to consider the possibility of a landing on our L.Z., for it was judged impossible yet to get through to the coast and away by sea. No Allied plane had previously landed and taken off but intelligence officers were due to report at their headquarters at Bari; the details of Allied policy towards Tito had recently been fixed at Jajce, and new plans for opening up the country (new support for Tito) were afoot. So one night, a month after we had arrived, two Dakotas groped their way into our forbidden valley, circled and winked in recognition of our fires, and finally cut their throttles and bumped to a standstill, to the accompaniment of gasps of amazement from the inhabitants and of relief from ourselves.

The R.A.F. pilots jumped cheerfully out but after inspecting the snow, still a good nine inches deep on the field, they grimly set about cutting down weight. They threw the doors away and the seats, the parachutes and the dinghies, and all personal kit; no time was lost and the engines had been ticking over no more than ten minutes when we scrambled aboard and sat on the floor along with some seriously wounded Drugs and a couple of fortunate German prisoners. As the engines opened up and the Dakotas' leaps grew longer and the wheels came clear, one waited tensely, recalling the little hill at the end of the take-off track. But we saw it flash below through the dark void where the doors had been and that was the last we saw of Yugoslavia.

The third story tells of Sergeant G. Beezum's adventures with the French Resistance movement:

Exercise "Dingson" was a small and kind of personal operation. Just ten Wacos or, as they are now called, Hadrian gliders took off one Saturday night in 1944; August 5th was the exact date, 2000 hours the time, the destination St. Helene, about four miles south of Lorient, the big port in Brittany.

The light was just beginning to fail when we touched down in France roughly 170 miles behind the German lines. Our briefing officer had told us to watch out for a small fire and purple smoke indicators, but Jerry was more co-operative and had set light to a big country house. The landing was almost without incident, save for one glider flown by Staff-Sergeant Rossdale and Sergeant Newton, which crashed into a small orchard. The pilots, badly cut and shaken, were cared for by the Maquis. We didn't set eyes on them again until the G.P. reunion at the Queensberry Club a few years later.

By the time we had sorted out the injured in the crashed glider, our load and passengers—which consisted of high-powered jeeps and French S.A.S. troops—were ready to whip us away through the dusty lanes to a big lake, where we waited until the tide was up, before being towed across to the Maquis H.Q. This consisted of a farm, just like any farm in England but with one difference, it was a painful thorn in the Jerries' side.

The Frenchmen at the H.Q., all wearing the armband of the Resistance movement, were heavily armed but not half as terrifying as our passengers, the S.A.S. chaps. A more motley crew I have yet to see. Tough individuals, with bronze, scarred, leathery skin, armed with tommy-guns, knives and grenades. A few sported phosphorous bombs in their pockets. They gave no quarter nor expected any in fighting, and away some of them used to go, in their special jeep armed with twin Vickers-18 guns in front and a third one on a mounting in rear, and attack a heavily-armed pill-box defended by twenty-five Jerries. How they managed to win *and* live is beyond me, but repeatedly they came back with a few prisoners (the remainder were shot). These chaps had a total disregard for danger. One chap came in with thirteen pieces of shrapnel from an explosive bullet in his shoulder; the Maquis doctor was out somewhere with his tommy-gun, so my first pilot, Johnny Batley, D.F.M., cut the pieces out with a knife. No anaesthetic was used, just a little drop of iodine when the job was done and away went the chap, chewing a piece of dark brown bread, collected some ammo and off on the prowl with his comrades.

We G.Ps saw little action because the chief of the Maquis had forbidden us to go out, owing to language difficulties. Occasionally we did manage to slide away, but when we got back we were carpeted by Captain "Peggy" Clarke, the officer in charge of the little band of G.Ps. Staff-Sergeant Bill May and I wandered off one afternoon and ended up nearly in Lorient. Only luck saved us from walking into a patrol of White Russians who were fighting for the Germans. The villagers indicated that the patrol was in the village and ushered us into a small house while they fetched somebody who could speak English. It turned out to be an old man, complete with beard and spectacles. We nicknamed him "Professor". He led us back to the H.Q. where a very long strip was torn off us.

While we had been away some French women collaborators had been brought in and were in the process of being toughly handled by their captors. Another chap was happily cutting off all their hair, leaving a small tuft in the front. These women were put with the other prisoners in the pig sty which, still serving its original occupants, was far from pleasant. The duty of guarding these prisoners had fallen to the G.Ps, and a more smelly guard I have never performed. The sty was split into three sections, women in one, pigs in the centre and the male species in the remaining section. Our orders were, if attacked at night to toss a few grenades into the sty just to cheer them up.

One afternoon the pigs had a guest in their little abode. A sullen-looking chap in civilian clothes was dumped into their midst. This individual was an alleged Gestapo spy who had been living in Lorient for some considerable time. Later that night he was stripped of all his clothes and hung upside down. For the next couple of hours he was subjected to some hot treatment: cigarettes and lighters were applied to his body, a sword with the tip of its blade heated was poked into him repeatedly and finally one bloodthirsty S.A.S. chap carved a Cross of Lorraine on the Jerry's chest. The man from the Gestapo was left with the blood trickling down him, his nose almost in the muck from the pigs. Feeling sick inside but too scared to say or do anything, we crept away to the barn to try to sleep.

Life in this community was raw and hard. Skinny and sorry looking cows were killed in the morning and eaten at night, with a coarse, gritty brown bread. To drink there was rough cider and some sort of whisky made from potatoes. Sanitary arrangements were almost nil. An old open quarry was used by everyone for personal hygiene, and many a G.P. was embarrassed when performing his toilet requirements when along came a woman to do the self-same thing a few feet away. So, when the news came that Yankee tanks were approaching Aurai, a few miles away, we were not sorry.

The next day, after many farewells, we crossed the lake, this time on a raft, and were quickly transported to Aurai, just as the first American tanks were entering. To get away from the Maquis H.Q. was a relief because we had learned that there was a reward of 20,000 francs for the G.Ps, dead or alive. We also learned that the White Russian troops of Germany had broken the arms and legs of fifty people in a near-by village just after we had landed, as a reprisal. The amount of truth in these stories I cannot vouch for.

In Aurai a few of us stood on the corner taking a synopsis of the popsies when a big American came up to us, his battle bowler under his arm, and asked us how long we had been there. We asked him where he had been for a week, and why it had taken him so long. Suddenly he turned to speak to an officer at his side and we saw on his steel helmet the insignia of a two-star general. He took all our jibes in good part and offered cigarettes all round. After a couple of hours in Aurai we were taken to Varnes. There we spent the night helping to guard 400 prisoners. The next day these prisoners were bundled and packed into four American G.S. wagons. A fifth contained a few German officers and 18 G.Ps. Our destination from Varnes was Rennes.

As the five wagons sped through the numerous towns and villages, people threw stones at the prisoners, which included us, I am unhappy to say. I guess we looked a sorry sight, as we had set off from England in just shirt sleeves—without pay books or means of identification. A few people recognized the red beret and there were cheers and shouts of "Vive l'Anglais".

Finally Rennes was reached, and the prisoners handed over to a big cage. We were left in the hands of two English intelligence majors, who were under the impression that we were every bit as terrifying as the French compatriots we had flown in. Tales of fantastic deeds had reached the ears of these gentlemen and they couldn't do enough for us. They gave us money, cigarettes and accommodation in the best hotels. We enjoyed dinner in the American officers messes and the freedom of all Rennes, where nearly all places were "off limits" to the American troops.

Eventually we went to the aerodrome at Rennes and lived like lords, in a disused hut. This was a front-line drome providing a twenty-four-hour fighter cover of Thunderbolts and Mustangs. American Dakotas were flying their personnel to London for forty-eight-hour passes in Piccadilly. Finally, we could wait no longer so we gave a note to a Dak pilot to give to Brigadier Chatterton, asking for means of transport home. Two days later a lone Dakota joined the circuit. The back door was open; we knew it was ours.

We picked up the two R.A.F. pilots who were keen on souvenirs and gave them a short conducted tour of the drome. They bagged sign posts, speed limits, and numerous odds and ends, to decorate their mess.

Late in the afternoon we landed at Netheravon, eleven days after leaving England, eighteen G.Ps plus one Royal Marine Commando who was an escaped P.O.W. A quick meal and then off to the inevitable.

10

ARNHEM

IT WAS now decided that the Allied Airborne Army of one British airborne division and two American airborne divisions should be dropped at three points in front of the 2nd British Army, which was making a spectacular advance, led by 30 Corps under their commander, Lieutenant-General Brian Horrocks. This huge mass drop was to lay a carpet through Eindhoven to Arnhem. In addition there was to be one Air Portable Division held in reserve. The commander of this force was General Louis N. Berreton, U.S. Air Force. The main airborne task was commanded by Lieutenant-General F.A.M. Browning, C.B., D.S.O.

The allotment was: 1st Airborne Division to Arnhem, 101st American Airborne Division to open a corridor from Eindhoven Grave, and 82nd Airborne Division to establish its central section at Grave-Nijmegen, and to capture the high ground south of Nijmegen.

To the 1st Airborne Division (under the command of Major-General R. E. Urquhart, C.B., D.S.O.), fell the duty of capturing the bridge at Arnhem. Perhaps one of the major problems of this operation was the fact that the Royal Air Force could not carry the whole force in one lift. It would involve at least two—and as it eventually turned out, three—lifts. The whole division was to be used, together with the Polish Parachute Brigade.

Another major problem was flak. The town of Arnhem was very well protected by anti-aircraft guns from the German airfield at Deelan, just north of Arnhem, and slow-flying aircraft stood little chance when approaching the city by daylight. It was therefore necessary for the dropping and landing zones to be well beyond the range of the guns at Deelan, but the country around Arnhem is for the most part well wooded and the number of suitable open fields very limited.

The total number of officers and men who were to be airborne was 8,969 plus 1,126 glider pilots. It is not the intention here to go into a detailed description of the plan of the battle of Arnhem. This, again, belongs to the soldiers; and this book is the story of the Glider Pilot Regiment.

In this particular case the Glider Pilot Regiment was to be used as a whole and one important feature of the plan was to retain the glider crews in a defensive rôle in order that there might not be costly casualties. This was considered essential, for every available air-crew was to be used. In fact, ninety per cent of the regiment was committed to the action and, in effect, there were no reserves.

The landing zones were such that the rendezvous for the troops, after landing, was one and a half to two miles from the landing area. It was considered that it would take something like two hours for them to get to the rendezvous, allowing half an hour for unloading the glider.

One of the complications was that the British airborne division was to be at the farthermost point from the three other areas where the American divisions were to be dropped. In fact, no one knew whether the supporting forces would be able to conquer Eindhoven and Nijmegen or be in a position to relieve the 1st Airborne Division at Arnhem. It was because they were chiefly airborne that the regiment was armed mainly for defensive fighting, and had to be regarded as a unit within the 1st Airborne Division. The divisional commander controlled the regiment on the ground, but he was limited to a proviso that the fighting potential of the Glider Pilot Regiment must be used solely in a defensive rôle.

I therefore detailed the pilots on landing to form into squadrons and come under the command of their respective wing headquarters. No. 1 Wing would be under the orders of Headquarters 1st Airborne Division and No. 2 Wing under the 1st Air Landing Brigade, whom they were respectively carrying. They would carry out such defensive tasks as would be allotted by the divisional commander and would withdraw as soon as the situation allowed.

This was to be one of the greatest mass landings of glider and parachute troops: 588 Horsas and 4 Waco gliders—carrying elements of the British 1st Airborne Division, the Polish Parachute Brigade and the 878 U.S. Aviation Engineering Battalion Airfield Control Unit—had to be put down on four landing zones in the area of Arnhem. Apart from the problems of getting such a large force into the air, the landing itself was comparatively easy, particularly as the whole thing was to be done by day. However, the weather element did have to be considered, and therefore a reasonable cloud base had to be available. It was believed that a fifteen-knot down-wind would be apparent on the landing zone. Pilots were to be helped by certain aids such as smoke panels and lights.

By now the 1st Airborne Corps had its headquarters at Moor Park, and it was here that all the planning and the discussions took place. The lift being so complicated called for much discussion, and it was not surprising that there was a certain amount of disagreement among the planners. I had my headquarters moved nearer to the east coast, for we were stretched to the limits of our range by now.

The date of the first lift was to be the 17th September, 1944, and I was permitted to take an active part in this operation because I was to fly General Browning, his batman, his doctor and his cook, together with his jeep and his tent. The H.Q. Airborne Corps had decided to be dropped with the American 81st Airborne Division at Nijmegen, therefore I had to study my own landing zone in that area, and we did everything possible to brief the glider pilots in order that they should make no mistake on landing. Our landing zone was near the Reichswald Forest, where General Browning had decided to make his headquarters. So far as the enemy was concerned, there were 4,000 S.S. Cadets in the Nijmegen area, which was their training centre.

September 17th blossomed fine, and I shall always remember walking down to Harwell Airfield to gather up my belongings to climb into my glider. The airfield was a mass of gliders and soldiers and parachutists and tug-aircraft and Royal Air Force personnel. There was a great air of "business", but little solemnity, and it did not seem possible that we were taking off for one of the greatest battles in history.

On the first day there were to be 359 gliders in the first lift. It was a great day for General Browning, because it was the first opportunity he had had to go into operations and take part in all that he had prepared. He came to the glider immaculately dressed in a barathea battle-dress with a highly polished Sam Browne belt, knife-edge creased trousers, leather revolver holster, all gleaming like glass, a swagger cane in one hand and wearing kid gloves. He was in tremendous form because he realized that he had reached one of the climaxes of his career. There was immense gaiety everywhere.

General Browning entered the aircraft and I took my place on the port side, with Andy Andrews on the starboard side. General Browning had an old Worthington crate put down at the pilots door and sat down between us. Soon the signal to take off was given, and as the great Stirling moved forward and the rope tautened I could feel the surge forward of the glider as we hurtled down the runway We veered a bit, and round came the tail of the Stirling, but I checked this and soon we were both in the air, climbing up, up, until finally we turned towards the coast.

It was a fantastic sight, thousands of gliders and tugs seemed to be everywhere, above us, in front of us, below us, and behind us. Soon we were over the sea, which was like glass, with ships dotted here and there—obviously marker ships in case we came down. At last we were over the Dutch coast and moving inland. Spitfires and Tempests whizzed past us. We could see them shooting up flak positions as we flew on.

Soon Andy told me that we were nearing the landing zone and I took over. I had decided to land by the funnel system, so Andy was to give me the position as we came in. I was tense as we flew along the line and I can still hear Andy's shout: "Point A coming up", then "Point B" and then, "Point C." And my own hoarse voice shouting. "Let her go!"

The tow-rope coiled away like a great snake and we were alone in the air. The Stirling bomber rose and turned away, and we knew we were going down—there was no going back now. I saw flak bursting all round us, I heard Andy calling out the height: "1,500, 1,000," and then I did my turn and straightened up. I felt a great calm come over me as I turned in; I suppose that is always the way.

We landed in a small allotment garden behind some cottages. I had picked out my patch and realized as I did so that it contained row upon row of cabbages. Immediately in front of it was an electric cable that I had forgotten all about. Down went the glider and bang, bang, the front wheel came off. The glider settled herself among the cabbages, and we stepped on to Dutch soil. Gliders landed round me everywhere and I saw Billy Griffith away to the left. It seemed extraordinary that we were received so calmly; a few old Dutch peasants came and looked at us, but there was no military action whatever. It was strange and rather eerie; it didn't seem right.

Up the road the 1st British Airborne Division also had the same reception, and they were able to load and start on the road to their objective unmolested. Captured German documents have shown that the Germans were completely bewildered and didn't know what to do next. But we then had a dreadful stroke of bad luck. The German commander-in-chief in the west, Model, happened to arrive in Arnhem itself at this time. He was one of their most outstanding tacticians of the war, and it was his being on the spot that made the Germans react so efficiently.

Although the glider landings at Arnhem were successful, the airborne troops were put down too far away from the objective and as a result got badly split up. Nevertheless, the Parachute Regiment was able to seize the bridge, which they found had not been fused for demolition.

To continue with my story, we moved away from the landing zone and up into the great forest. As we did so, some Messerschmitts came over and started firing at the group of gliders. It was then that a very sad thing happened. A photographic expert of the Royal Air Force, who had been one of the passengers in my glider, had gone back to get his camera just as the Messerschmitts arrived, and he was killed. I must say I was beginning to feel a bit nervous because I knew the twenty-eight gliders in that field were the only ones in the Nijmegen area other than the American parachutists who had dropped farther out. The Germans began to react. Shells began to fall in the area where we were standing. We knew that 500 Waco gliders were due to land near us, and we waited with keen anticipation for their arrival. Soon the Germans were pressing us hard, and a few we could see gathering in the valley started to fire at us, so we got down under cover.

Then, in the distance, we heard a great roaring sound, like a waterfall, and ran out into the open, regardless of being shot at. There coming towards us was a vast armada of Dakotas and Waco gliders—two per aircraft. They flew straight on over our heads and then, unlike the system we used, the gliders released and landed anywhere. It was a fantastic sight. The Germans were even more staggered than we were, and all firing ceased.

One of the most amazing things about this landing was that it consisted, in part, of an artillery unit, and before one could say "Jack Robinson" the Americans had hauled their guns out of one glider, the jeeps out of another, connected the two together, run them into the woods and were shelling the German batteries. I must say I felt a great deal safer with those guns around than I did with a number of distant parachutists.

General Browning chose the site for his headquarters and we put up the airborne tents which had been packed in the jeeps. The fighting now became hot and the Americans were fairly laying into the Germans as they tried to push us out of the woods. We went down with the Americans to Nijmegen, but the Germans were fighting fantastically and the Americans could not get near the bridge. Indeed they suffered a great many casualties in trying to do so.

The division had now distributed itself over a wide area, and it was determined to keep what it had captured of Nijmegen, especially the road leading back south to the 2nd Army. Soon we heard that the Guards Armoured Division had arrived at the Grave bridge, and General Browning instructed me to drive him down in a jeep to meet them. I drove flat-out down the road with the knowledge that the Germans were on either side of the road and that we were the "carpet" in between. Every now and then we would be stopped by a formation which had been intercepted by or was intercepting Germans. "Drive on," Boy Browning would say ruthlessly. I must say I drove with my heart in my mouth.

Soon we came to the Headquarters of General Maxwell Taylor, the commander of the 101st Airborne Division, with whom General Browning had a long conversation. It was clear that General Browning was worried about the situation at Arnhem, and one reason for this was that he could not maintain contact by radio. It was revealed afterwards that radio communication could only be had via London.

It wasn't long before the leading elements of the Guards Armoured Division caught up with us at Nijmegen, and with them came General Horrocks, commanding 30 Corps. He was tremendously impressed and interested by the whole of the airborne achievement, and I remember being surprised that he had never before seen a parachutist drop.

The Guards went on towards Arnhem but first they had to winkle out the Germans from Nijmegen bridge. They made two attacks but were strongly repulsed by entrenched 88-mm. guns, whereupon a conference was called, as it was imperative that the Guards Armoured Division should cross the river to get on up the

Arnhem road. I was present at the conference which General Browning called with the general commanding the American 82nd Airborne Division, and the brigade commander of the advance elements of the Guards Armoured Division, and Colonel Tuck, commander of the American 82nd Assault Regiment. It was an extraordinary meeting and I have never seen men so contrasted in all my life: General Browning, standing, in his immaculate uniform; the brigade commander of the Guards Armoured Brigade, with clipped moustache, in battle-dress with the insignia of the D.S.O. and M.C. on it, and wearing suède shoes, sitting on a shooting stick; and on either side of him three colonels whose black berets were adorned with the badges of the Irish Guards, the Grenadier Guards and the Scots Guards respectively. Their faces were covered in dust and mud thrown up at them as they stood up in their armoured cars or tanks as they dashed down the road. Each of them had an old school scarf—I noticed Eton, Harrow and Winchester above the collars of their battledress tops, and each had a pair of faded corduroy trousers and suède Chukka boots. They wore a most amazing air of nonchalance and gave the impression that this was not a battle but an exercise near Caterham Barracks.

In contrast to them, Colonel Tuck, the American commander, had a tin hat on which covered his whole face, a jumping jacket on which there were several decorations (including our D.S.O.), a pistol strapped under his arm, a knife on the right-hand side, long trousers and lace-up boots. He chewed a fat cigar, and every now and then spat. Each time he did this a faint look of surprise flickered over the faces of the Guards officers.

The two generals quickly agreed that a combined Anglo-American assault must be made on the bridge as soon as possible. It was agreed that Colonel Tuck would take his assault regiment down to the river and swim across in rubber dinghies. In the meantime one of the Guards commanders would make a rush at the bridge and attempt to break through at this end. I think that both of them had a pretty tough assignment in front of them.

Colonel Tuck took his regiment and marched down to the river where they stood to, waiting to cross. In the meantime the Guards again attempted to break through the Germans guarding the entrance to the bridge. The Guards undoubtedly were getting bloody noses, and several tanks had been put out of action, but at last they managed to overwhelm the fanatical Germans on the defences.

Colonel Tuck's men pumped up the rubber dinghies and pushed them out into the river. It was a most heroic action because the Germans on the other side had a complete view of them. I don't know how many hundreds went over but not many reached the other side. Nevertheless some did, and they drove the Germans out, moved over, and got round to the other side of the bridge where they put up the Union Jack and the Stars and Stripes. In the meantime the Guards had broken through, and as the two met on the other side a great cheer went up.

Now came the crux of the matter. Over the bridge streamed the Guards Armoured Division in their Sherman tanks, but what had been overlooked by intelligence was a village called Elst, where there were four 88-mm. guns, anti-tank and anti-aircraft guns in concrete emplacements. The road leading from the Nijmegen bridge through Elst was mounted road over flat, boggy country. It was only just wide enough to take a Sherman tank, and as the Sherman tanks debouched from over the bridge they were sitting ducks for the 88-mm. guns at Elst.

In the meantime the battle of Arnhem was becoming desperate. Parachutists were still holding the bridge, but under the greatest difficulties. General Urquhart was missing, and Brigadier Hicks was in command of the Division. What was more, panzer armour was appearing. Apparently, north of Arnhem a panzer division had been "refitting," or so it was thought, but actually it was only resting, and as soon as Model realized that he was up against an airborne division with little protection against armour, he brought it in. And now the 1st Airborne Division, split up and fighting to the death, were faced with a whole Panzer division.

The remainder of the first lift had now landed with part of the 1st Battalion the Border Regiment and the 2nd Battalion of the King's Own Scottish Borderers. It was their duty to seize and hold the landing grounds and dropping zones so that the second lift, due to land on the next day, might do so in safety. The latter had a misty take-off and rather a rough crossing and some came down in the sea, to be rescued by the Air-Sea-Rescue.

Throughout the afternoon and night the Borderers held the dropping zones, being thrice unsuccessfully attacked by the Germans. The same thing happened to the Border Regiment holding the dropping zones to the south. They suffered a great deal from mortar fire.

The following narratives give some idea of these landings: The first narrative is by Staff-Sergeant Gordon Jenks:

"All operational crews report for breakfast at 0730 hours," the voice on the Tannoy kept repeating over and over again. I sat up in bed and promptly lay down again. My head was aching like hell and my mouth tasted like something out of a dustbin. I lit a cigarette and sat up more slowly this time. My second pilot was showing signs of activity so I spoke to him, "They're not kidding this time! This is for keeps, we're really going." Dressing slowly I thought about the night before.

We had been confined to camp, the usual procedure after being briefed for an operation, and had settled down for a drinking session in the mess with our Halifax tug crew. Prior to this briefing we had been briefed for about sixteen ops. since D-Day, and they had all been cancelled for some reason or other. Most of us thought this one would be "scrubbed" as well, so we were rather surprised when no cancellation had been announced by midnight. The mess had been crowded with glider pilots and tug crews having a steady few pints. In one corner a big "school" was playing "shoot", and at one time there was over ninety quid in the kitty.

By ten o'clock blokes started to drift off to their various billets, and by midnight there were only a few of us left. I'd had a gutful of beer by then so called it a day and went to bed.

Now, as I dressed, I was beginning to wish I hadn't had so much to drink. After a wash and shave, I stuck my head under the cold water tap for a couple of minutes, and felt a whole lot better. Back in the billet I finished dressing, grabbed my flying helmet, weapons and equipment, and made tracks for the mess dining hall, along with several other glider pilots and R.A.F. air-crew.

That breakfast! It was to haunt me in the months to come when I was starving in a P.O.W. camp. Sausages, eggs, bacon, and coffee. All I could do was drink the coffee and turn my nose up at the grub.

Into waiting trucks and down to a magnificent sight. Halifaxes, Hamilcar gliders, more Halifaxes, Horsa gliders. They looked absolutely terrific, lined up ready for take off. I soon spotted my Hamilcar. It was third in line and had "Bun House" chalked on it in large white letters. You've guessed it! The "Bun House" was the name of my local pub where I had spent many a happy hour on leave.

Hamilcar glider - tank transporter, from the *Illustrated London News*.

Troops leaving a glider after landing in North Africa. 1943.

Glider pilots ready to fight as a platoon.

After checking the controls, I climbed down to have another look over the load which the "Bun House" had to carry that day, and deposit safely in a field somewhere in Europe and about sixty odd miles behind the German lines.

It was a pretty formidable load by any standards, consisting of a 17-pounder anti-tank gun and trailer, 8 men, a 3-ton lorry and some high explosive shells. The "Bun House" was going to need every inch of runway to get this lot off the deck.

Time for take off, and we all climbed aboard. I made myself as comfortable as possible and fastened my safety belt tightly. The Hamilcar in front of me started to move as the tow-master waved his flags. My turn! . . .

Ninety, ninety-five, and now she was fairly eating up the runway. One hundred m.p.h. on the clock and I eased back the control column. The "Bun House" came off like a bird and I held her just above the slipstream of the tug. The end of the runway was getting far too near for my liking before the Halifax got off the deck, but at last we were airborne and beginning to climb. As we climbed slowly I called up the tug to test the intercom. "Matchbox to Zero, Matchbox to Zero. Testing. Over." The reply soon came. "Zero to Matchbox. Zero to Matchbox. How's things, Lofty?" I answered, "All right, Cock! Just make sure you keep your ruddy finger pulled out!"

I called up the boys down below.

"Everybody O.K. down there?" Somebody answered, "O.K. Lofty." "Right, well make yourselves at home, we've got a long way to go."

I didn't see a lot of other aircraft around at this stage. There seemed to be a few combinations of tugs and gliders dotted about haphazardly. The two Hamilcars that had taken off before me were just ahead and slightly to starboard. Flying the leading one was Major Alec "Dicky" Dale, D.F.C., the squadron commander. He was only a little man but he had tremendous courage and we all admired and respected him.

After we'd been stooging along for an hour or so, I decided to give the boys below a shaking up by taking the "Bun House" down through the slipstream and flying below the tug. It's a perfectly harmless procedure really and a practice adopted by glider pilots when flying through cloud. To the uninitiated, however, it could be rather an alarming experience the first time.

I eased the control column forward and the "Bun House" trembled violently as she was caught in the slipstream from four powerful engines. I held her in it for about thirty seconds, pushed the control column farther forward and we went through into the relatively calm air below. We were now flying behind and below the tug and could see its belly.

A voice called up on the intercom. from below. It was "Taffy", a young Welsh boy, not yet nineteen, and as tough as they come.

"Hullo, Lofty man! What on earth is going on?"

I said, "It's all right Taffy Bach" and explained what was happening.

We would soon be approaching the East coast, so I gently coaxed the "Bug House" back through the slipstream to her more normal flying station behind and above the tug.

I looked around me and was very impressed with what I saw. Where before I had just noticed odd combinations dotted about, there were now literally hundreds of aircraft converging into one solid mass.

As we flew across the coast the sight was fantastic. A brilliant blue sky with not a cloud to be seen. Below us the North Sea looked as calm as a mill pond. To starboard of the "Bun House", I could seen more aircraft than I had ever seen in the sky at one time. They were all there—Halifaxes, Hamilcars, Stirlings, Horsas, Dakotas, Waco gliders, and squadron after squadron of Dakotas carrying paratroopers.

Below me I saw a Horsa going down to ditch in the North Sea, having broken the tow rope. I spotted an Air-Sea Rescue launch speeding out to pick up the occupants.

Off my port side, I couldn't see a single aircraft, as we were flying just to the left of the main stream.

The coastline loomed up, and when we'd crossed it things warmed up a bit. Ahead I could see our fighter escort doing their stuff. Whenever German ack-ack guns dared to open up, rocket-firing Typhoons were diving on them and making life generally unpleasant.

We were getting near to our target now and a few puffs of white smoke suddenly appeared around the "Bun House". I felt a couple of slight bumps. A voice called up from down below.

"Hey Lofty! The ——ing glider's on fire!"

I replied with as much sarcasm as I could muster.

"Well —— on it and put the —— thing out then!"

I could see a fairish amount of smoke coming from the port wing just near the fuselage but decided it was only a piece of shrapnel that had lodged in there and was smouldering. Later I learned that another piece of shrapnel had gone through the fuselage, hit one of the gunners a glancing blow on the hand and had then lain smouldering on the floor. It caused a lot of smoke and it was this that made the gunners think that the "Bun House" was on fire.

Another stray piece of shrapnel had apparently damaged the controls as neither the air-speed indicator nor the altimeter was working.

We were almost at the release point now and the scene below looked exactly as it had appeared on the photographs at briefing the previous day. To starboard I could see the main reason for our trip—the bridge across the Rhine.

Below and just ahead were the river and a railway embankment. Just beyond them I could clearly see the two fields divided by a hedge or stone fence which had been allocated to the Hamilcars as a landing zone.

The Hamilcars in front of me had now released and were going in. The tug skipper called me on the intercom.

"All right, Lofty, you can release whenever you like."

I said, "O.K., Arthur, thanks for the ride. See you soon!"

With that I "pulled the tit", and eased the control column back to gain a bit more height while I appraised the landing situation.

The sky was chaotic now. Worse than a traffic jam at Piccadilly Circus in the rush hour, only these were aircraft instead of cars.

I decided to get on the tail of the Hamilcar in front and follow it into the first field. I had to guess my height and speed for reasons previously mentioned.

Below me and to my left another Hamilcar appeared, going in much too fast and too low. It hit the railway embankment at a terrific speed and somersaulted with a vivid flash. I wondered which of my pals was in that one.

Over the railway embankment now I could see "Dicky" Dale had touched down in the first field. He seemed to be making pretty heavy going of it and his Hamilcar appeared to be careering all over the place and breaking up.

The "Bun House" was positioned nicely for a landing now and behaving very well. I called my second pilot.

"Keep your eyes open for any gliders coming too near us, Harry. I want to concentrate on the landing." There was no reply and I didn't know whether he'd heard me or not.

At this point the Hamilcar in front of me touched down, going very fast. The ground must have been very soft and the pilot must have slammed his brakes on as soon as he touched down because the Hamilcar promptly dug its wheels in and flipped over on to its back. Again there was a terrific flash.

That decided me against this particular field. I reckoned that if I put the "Bun House" into a dive now she would have enough speed for me to hold her off the deck until we had cleared the fence and get safely into the farthest of the two fields.

I pushed the control column forward and we went into a dive. We must have been halfway across the first field when I levelled out a few feet off the ground. The "Bun House" responded beautifully to my every action. What a gem of an aircraft she was!

We were still doing about ninety miles per hour, when I eased her gently over the fence and put her down in the next field as light as a feather. I let her run on for perhaps thirty or forty yards before applying the brakes and she came to a halt.

The "Bun House" had made her last majestic flight. The day? Sunday. The date? September 17th, 1944. The place? ARNHEM!

This is Lieutenant-Colonel John Place's account of his flight to Arnhem.

We took off from Broadwell, near Brize Norton, on Sunday, September 17th, and as my glider, No. 161, started to roll behind the tug, I looked at my watch which registered 09.45 hours. The weather was reasonably bright but overcast, and in a few moments after take off we were climbing through cloud, and as I was never any good with the "angle of dangle" I had to concentrate hard on keeping position. However, in a moment or two we were in a clear sky above the overcast and all around stretched a rolling sea of white, dazzlingly bright in the clear sunlight of the morning. Then we headed towards Aldeburgh on the Suffolk coast, which was our forming-up point before heading out across the sea for Holland.

My co-pilot was Ralph Maltby, our number two wing intelligence officer, and on board we had twenty-eight men of the Border Regiment, together with a handcart loaded with paraphernalia of the airborne platoon which we carried, including mortar bombs. I shall never forget the incredibly wonderful sight of scores of tug-and-glider combinations stretching in what seemed almost unending lines to the horizon, and all converging towards our forming-up point.

My tug and glider arrived at our forming-up point, and we were number one in the vast line, and so turned out to sea. I remember looking down and noticing that the cloud had broken up very considerably from below us. The sea looked like beaten bronze with a few small warships, or what looked like warships, and possibly R.A.F. Air-Sea Rescue craft, scattered here and there. We had scarcely been on our way for more than a few minutes when Wing-Commander "Jeff" Jefferson, our tug pilot, rang up on the intercom. to say that his C.47 lacked power and he found he couldn't maintain sufficient cruising speed to stay in front of the stream of tugs and gliders, and suggested that the only way we could stay in front was to cut out the "dog-leg" which we were scheduled to make over the sea. This dog-leg should have taken us on a north-easterly course from Aldeburgh and then over the sea we should have altered course in a south-easterly direction and passed over the island of Schouen in Holland.

Jeff asked whether we should cut the dog-leg and I agreed, and so we flew off on our own and watched the main stream angling away to our port side. I think both Jeff and I were a little apprehensive in case a wandering enemy fighter should spot us, but we felt reasonably secure as there seemed to be a large number of our own fighter screen all over the sky.

It was not very long, however, before the Dutch coast came into view and as we approached we were relieved to notice the main glider stream coming in fairly fast on our left. As we crossed the flooded island of Schouen we were in our correct position as number one.

It was not long after crossing the Dutch coast that we got our first lot of light flak thrown up at us—luckily very inaccurately—and the only effect it had was to cause a somewhat startling rattle or vibration throughout the glider.

It was just about this time that Ralph and I saw something which puzzled us for a moment or two, and that was a wavy white streak shoot up from the ground and continue curving up into the bright sky until it finally disappeared, leaving a thin trail of smoke which disappeared very high up. It was only after a few moments that we realized that we had watched a V.2 take off on its way to England!

Our first sight of Holland was depressing. Schouen was almost completely inundated. Here and there a lonely roof and a few trees showed above the flood waters, and now and again we saw the steeples of churches and a few more house roofs to mark where villages had been partially submerged. There did not appear to be a sign of life anywhere.

Shortly after the first rattle of flak when Ralph and I were engaged in reassuring ourselves that it was a long way off, we were startled out of our wits by shouts from our passengers of: "Sir, Sir, the tail is coming off!" For a second or two Ralph and I looked at each other and then I very gingerly tested my elevators and rudder by pitching and yawing the glider as quickly as possible. Everything seemed all right but I told Ralph to go back and find out what the trouble was. He undid his safety belt and got up from his seat and disappeared through the dividing doors from the cockpit. About two or three minutes later he came back grinning all over his face, and told me that he had had a look out of both doors and, so far as he could see, there was nothing wrong with our tail or any other part of the glider. He also said that he thought that the passengers had heard and felt the vibrations of the flak explosions and had momentarily been a bit worried!

We were flying in the low-tow position at this time and we still had about half an hour to go before reaching the L.Z.

Ralph had just strapped himself back into his seat when I told him to take over as I wanted to check up on the map. I had barely got my map out in front of me and was bending over, tracing our course, when I heard a sudden very rapid and curious swish-swish sound which was quite loud. I couldn't make out, for a fraction of a second, what was causing it, but when I looked out of my window I saw a lot of little red sparks shooting upwards from beneath the cockpit and past my port window. Next second there was a tremendous bang right in the cockpit and a thin wisp of greyish smoke. I automatically grasped the control column and as I did so I could smell high explosive; then poor Ralph rolled sideways in his seat as far as his straps would let him. I shouted for somebody to come forward and see what could be done for Ralph, and the platoon sergeant poked a startled head into the cockpit. I told him to try to get Ralph back on to the floor of the cockpit, but before he could do so Ralph was dead, so I told him to leave him in his seat and to shut the door.

By this time I was considerably frightened because I realized that if I was incapacitated, nobody else knew how to get the glider on to the ground in one piece, and I was terribly sad about poor Ralph, who was a grand boy and a personal friend. I remember ringing up Jeff, the tug pilot, and asking him if he could possibly weave about a bit as we had been hit by flak and Ralph was dead. Jeff apologized and said he was very sorry but that he had not enough boost to jink around—in fact I think he was rather worried to think that he would not get us to the L.Z. However, a few minutes later he rang up to say that the L.Z. was in sight and asked me if I could see it. The L.Z. was absolutely plain and I recognized it immediately and began to make preparations for casting off and going down. By this time, another glider combination or two came almost level with us, as we were still not cruising quite as fast as the rest of the stream. As we turned northwards towards the L.Z. from the line of the River Rijn, which we had followed more or less from the coast past the small town of Shertogenbosch, I looked to see if we were still at our operational height of 2,500 feet. It was only then that I noticed that most of my instrument panel was in bits and I began to have serious doubts about whether we had any air in the flap bottles, as the flak had obviously come into the cockpit from below on the right-hand side.

I thought the best thing to do was to do a steep climb after pull-off, stall, try the flaps as I approached the stall, and if I had any air, go straight down. If not then I would try a series of pancakes down to the ground. As we arrived at the L.Z. Jeff rang up and wished us good luck and said to pull off when we were ready, and this we did. Fortunately there was air in the flaps and I went straight down almost vertically. I think we must have been shot at from somewhere on the ground as, after landing, I discovered that we had two other casualties in the back, though neither was fatal.

Having got on to the ground the men of the Border Regiment carried out a copybook "de-bussing", surrounding the aircraft in a defensive position on the ground. They unloaded the hand-cart, and as soon as they were ready they got out their two casualties and then we got Ralph out and laid him under the glider wing and moved off to the rendezvous.

As I moved off to my own rendezvous, I was very deeply touched by a young private of the Borders who came up to me, stood smartly to attention, and said: "Sir, I just want to thank you."

The dividing of the 1st Airborne Division into three lifts could possibly be the reason for the situation becoming critical in the battle, for the fact that Major-General Urquhart had two battalions of the Air Landing Brigade held down protecting the landing zones must have caused embarrassment. The lightly armed parachute battalions battling on the high ground west and north of Arnhem found the German resistance too strong for them—armed as they were. If they had had the assistance of the more heavily armed air-landing battlions, would the positions have been altered? It is more than likely.

The general commanding the 1st Airborne Division had to protect the landing zones at all costs, for to be defeated there would have led to a hopeless situation. As it was, at a crucial moment on September 17th, 1944, the necessary punch was not there. Had the whole division been available at the moment, carried in one lift, it is possible the position would have been very different.

The failure of the second lift to arrive on time undoubtedly made matters worse. It was due to arrive at 10 a.m. on 18th September, but all the air-strips in England were enveloped in fog and the second lift could not leave the ground. To add to the trouble, it was a beautiful day in the Arnhem area, and everyone there waited in despair as time passed and the lift failed to appear. Alas, it was unable to leave for some hours and did not land until about four in the afternoon. Those six hours made all the difference. It is tragic to realize how much has to be learned by mistakes of this kind.

I was aware of the great difficulty that the commander had in obtaining sufficient aircraft, and the constant battle put up by both Air Vice Marshal Hollinghurst and General "Boy" Browning. It was a battle of request for aircraft—and more aircraft. How can one sum up this situation? The aircraft were needed for other operations, but I often ask myself—was it, possibly, also prejudice? Was it that strange "dead hand" which had so often handicapped us in earlier campaigns.

The airborne effort was regarded as an expensive luxury by many of the more orthodox officers of the R.A.F., the glider almost a nuisance and farce. In fact, I know some considered it was nothing short of an insult to tie another aircraft to the tail of a bomber! Imagine what might have happened if the 1st Airborne Division had arrived in one lift on the morning of September 17th? Had this happened and tipped the balance, had the Arnhem bridge been captured and held, Monty's dream might have come true, the Siegfried Line might have been turned by the autumn of 1944, and the advance on Berlin might have been made much earlier by the Allies. Perhaps this is too much to have hoped for, but it was a possibility, and I feel sure there are many who share my view.

Brigadier Hicks, who was temporarily commanding the division in General Urquhart's absence, was determined to try to reinforce the men holding the Arnhem bridge—elements of the 1st Parachute Brigade. He therefore dispatched units of the South Staffordshire Regiment who had come by glider to aid them, but after bitter fighting, they were unable to reach the bridge, for the Germans had reacted and brought in reinforcements, which included elements of a Panzer division.

It was at this stage that Major-General Urquhart, who had himself been cut off by the battle, faced a critical decision, whether to abandon the force at the bridge under Lieutenant-Colonel Frost, D.S.O., M.C. He decided to do so and form a perimeter round the sub-town of Oosterbeek and hold out there until the 2nd Army arrived. It was in this perimeter that the formations of Nos. 1 and 2 Wings, The Glider Pilot Regiment, fought.

During this defence, Brigadier J. W. Hackett, D.S.O., M.B.E., was wounded, and his command of the 4th Parachute Brigade came under Lieutenant-Colonel Iain Murray, D.S.O., the Glider Pilot Regiment.

This is an extraordinary example of the flexibility of the Glider Pilot Regiment, for Murray had flown the glider which carried Major-General Urquhart. He commanded this brigade with distinction and courage.

Another example of this flexibility was the fact that Regimental Sergeant-Major Tilley took over the command of the 7th Battalion, the King's Own Scottish Borderers, in which he fought with such distinction that he was later decorated with the Distinguished Conduct Medal.

Some idea of the actual conditions of this battle is graphically described by Staff-Sergeant Leslie Gibbons of D Squadron, as related here:

SUNDAY, SEPT. 17th

The first lift, watched by the whole aerodrome, took off this morning in perfect weather without a hitch. We had bade goodbye to them and promised to see them the next morning at Arnhem. The trip across to Holland will take approximately four hours. We went back to our billets to prepare for our trip on the morrow and to await the return of the tug-planes.

We watched the tug-planes returning and counted them to find if any were missing. Listened in on the radio and heard that the landings had been announced by 21st Army Group and that opposition was light. This is good news, but all the same we are wondering what sort of reception we shall get on the morrow when the Huns realize they are being attacked and are wondering who will get there first, their reinforcements or us.

We get our final briefing, and our course is to be different from that of the first lifts; instead of flying in over the Dutch Islands we are to cross over the Belgian Coast and then fly up over the 21st Group battle. Nobody seems very keen on this as we expect flak from the enemy ack-ack guns.

Have a bit of party in the mess that night. Several of the chaps get under the weather but for once I remain a T.T. Want to have a clear head in the morning.

MONDAY, SEPT. 18th

Weather does not look too good. We have just finished a breakfast of egg and bacon and are awaiting further orders. This waiting is the worst part of any operation; looking around, everyone seems calm enough, but you can't help noticing the air of expectancy hanging over the place. The chaps are just the same: one fellow is taking bets as to how many of us will get the chop; wonder if he'll come back to collect his debts or maybe pay out. My second pilot, Sergeant Knapman, is as always calm, cool and collected; we were together on D-Day and now consider ourselves a battle-hardened crew. Anyway we both have confidence in each other.

We are now on the towpath and have just heard that our take off has been postponed due to bad weather. Have just checked up on our glider and its load. Our load consists of a 6-pounder anti-tank gun, a jeep and four bods. Our own personal armament is as follows: Knappy has a rifle and a hundred rounds of ammunition, four hand-grenades and a fighting knife. Myself I have a sten gun and six magazines of ammunition, four hand-grenades and a fighting knife.

Have just heard that take off starts at 1030 hrs.; our turn will be at approximately 1045 hrs.

Five minutes to go, we are all strapped in and awaiting our turn. Our glider has been named "Isle of Jersey".

Knappy is now flying the thing. We had a good take off, one of the best I've made, must be, as even Knappy complimented me. The weather is pretty lousy; plenty of cloud and slight rain but not bumpy.

The English coast is now behind us, weather is still lousy and one or two gliders have come down in the drink; should be picked up all right as we have seen one or two boats hanging around.

In another fifteen minutes we should be over our landing zone. Weather has cleared up and it is really quite fine. Can at this moment see some of our fighter escort flying around; they are Typhoons. One of them has just done a good job of work. Just after we had crossed the Dutch coast an enemy flak barge opened up but hadn't time to do any damage before the Typhy shot it up and silenced it for good.

Will be over our landing zone in another five minutes; am getting ready to take over from Knappy. Have just had a bit of flak at us, believe some went through the wing.

We are now safely on the deck; made a good landing and unloaded in fifteen minutes. We are sheltering in a wood, forming-up and waiting to advance on Arnhem. Have joined up with the rest of our flight; everyone seems to have got here safely. Our captain is away getting instructions. Was a good job that our take off was postponed this morning, as enemy fighters were over here the time that we were due to arrive.

Our orders are to join in the advance on Arnhem and to provide infantry support for the anti-tank guns.

Am writing this in the dark; we are somewhere on the road to Arnhem; our leading columns have run into trouble and there is a bit of a battle going on a few hundred yards ahead. We are guarding the flanks. Enemy fighter is now overhead; has just strafed the column a few hundred yards down.

TUESDAY, SEPT. 19th

Column is still halted, and fighting is still going on forward. Spent a miserable night; no sleep and intensely cold. Knappy is now cooking our breakfast on his tommy cooker. Consists of porridge blocks, dry biscuits and the indispensable tea.

Breakfast went down well and word has gone round that we will be advancing in a very short while; also heard that things aren't going to plan. Have cleaned our weapons and checked our ammo.

It is now lunch-time and am writing this at the side of the road just outside the village of Osterbeek somewhere to the west of Arnhem. Things can't be going to plan as we should have been in Arnhem by now. Got involved in a battle this morning and quite a number of the chaps got the chop. Also had a strafing attack by German fighters; had to abandon our jeep and dive for cover. Counted fifty of the fighters: didn't seem to do much damage; good job they didn't carry bombs. Wonder where our Air Force is, supply planes are due in this afternoon. As we are not in control of our intended dropping zone I wonder if they have been informed of the fact by wireless. Our flight has got somewhat split up after the battle this morning; at least two thirds are missing, including our captain. This afternoon we are going to try to contact glider pilot headquarters.

Evening is here and many things have happened. I am now in the grounds of a large house which is being used as divisional head-quarters, and have joined up with some of the squadrons. There are still quite a number missing. The re-supply came in this afternoon, also a few gliders. They had a very hostile reception and quite a number got shot down; have never seen so much flak in all my life. After the re-supply we got orders to withdraw to our present position with the Boche following up on our tails. We are now well dug in and things are fairly quiet. Have managed to get a meal. Also had a wash and shave.

The time is almost midnight and things are still fairly quiet, though we have had slight mortaring with a few casualties. Every one is standing-to, as I believe they are expecting an attack to develop. Too cold in any case to attempt to sleep.

WEDNESDAY, SEPT. 20th

Dawn was heralded by an intense mortar barrage, quite a frightening experience when one has just to sit there and take it, quite unable to hit back. Managed to brew up a cup of tea, which went down well; also had an oatmeal cube for breakfast. Camouflaged our position with branches of trees blown down by the mortar barrage.

Once again I find myself in a new position. Late this morning the Boche broke through almost into our positions; we counterattacked and drove them back. My sten gun jammed when I needed it most. We are now dug-in at the side of the road with the Boche in a wood about a hundred yards in front of us. Mortaring is getting rather annoying and becoming more intense. Casualties mounting up. No news reached us of 2nd Army; rumour is that they are held up at Nijmegen. According to plan they should have reached us by now. Hear that there is a small party isolated down at the bridge. It appears that we are split up into small groups and fighting is completely disorganized.

I am sharing a trench with a young fellow called Tyler. We have made it comfortable by lining it with an eiderdown and blankets from a neighbouring house.

Contacted Knappy who is quite well but he informed me that our section leader, Lieutenant Chittleburgher, has been killed.

Guard duties have been arranged but we must all be prepared for immediate action. Have checked over my sten gun and am certain that the thing won't jam again.

Mortaring is still continuing. One has just burst a few yards away and we are both crouched down in the trench. Praying that the 2nd Army will arrive on the morrow. Morale is high but casualties are mounting up.

THURSDAY, SEPT. 21st

No fresh news of 2nd Army, though plenty of rumours flying around.

Mortaring once again heralded the dawn—pretty intense, too. We are having trouble with a sniper; he has already killed a couple of chaps. It is a case of running the gauntlet to fetch water and supplies. Fell in the sanitary trench this morning to take cover from mortars; feel a bit lousy.

Re-supply is due in this afternoon. Looks as though they will get another good reception. Plenty of 88 m.m. flying around, hope they know that we are in different positions.

It is now evening. Re-supply came in under murderous fire. Counted at least twelve shot down. Doubt if twenty per cent of the supplies fell into our hands. One container fell near us. Rushed for it, hoping to find food, only to find that it contained two 17-pounder shells, absolutely useless to us as all our 17-pounders are out of action.

Mortaring is still our main source of trouble, but food is also running short.

News of the 2nd Army is that elements have reached the bank of the river and should attempt a crossing tonight. Let us hope that they make it. We can't possibly hold out much longer. Casualties are heavy; there can't be a quarter of the division left. Food is short and ammunition low.

Closing this tonight to the accompaniment of the blasted mortars. Counted eighteen in a minute at one time.

FRIDAY, SEPT. 22nd

Glad to find myself still alive. Hope and the will to carry on rises up and down. We can see in one another what wrecks we really are. Our nerves have not cracked, but the intense bombardment, lack of food and washing and hygienic conditions is beginning to show its mark. Rumours are still flying around but nobody seems to believe them as we have already had too many false hopes.

Breakfast this morning consisted of a couple of pieces of biscuit and some tea we managed to scrounge from a dead man's pack. Mortaring started a few minutes ago. At the moment they are falling roughly fifty yards away but close enough to make us keep our heads down. A sniper is still active and a chap in the next trench was killed by him last night.

I am now in the regimental aid post feeling very lucky to be alive. Have a shrapnel wound in the left hand and a bruise over the heart. Was coming out of the door of a house after collecting some food when a shell (it must have been a shell as I didn't hear it coming) landed a few feet away. I was knocked out and on coming to found that, apart from entering my hand, a piece of shrapnel had torn through my wings on my jacket and yet had failed to penetrate my skin.

The regimental aid post looks a sorry sight. The roof has been blown in, as have the doors and windows. The carnage of war has certainly left its scar on this once beautiful and picturesque countryside. Roads are torn up, houses blown down, the once green wooded area is splashed with the blood of friend and foe alike.

On going back to my trench this evening I found that it had received a direct hit and can find no trace of my companion. The next trench is also deserted. Have moved to the shelter of a house. Only food today has been apples and the few scraps of biscuits I had for breakfast.

Rumour has just come through that a brigade of infantry is to assault the river tonight. We are all going to pray that it is true and that it succeeds.

SATURDAY, SEPT. 23rd

Haven't felt like writing until now that it is evening and a lull has set in.

Still fighting on, on our own. No sign of 2nd Army, and that brigade rumour of yesterday is a washout. Would like to find who started it.

The day has been like yesterday and the day before, just staying put and being plastered with shells and mortars. Never believed that anybody could stand that much. Have often seen and ridiculed war on the films, but no studio effect could ever exaggerate this.

A few American Thunderbolts flew over us today and expended a few of their rockets on the Boche. A sight for sore eyes.

SUNDAY, SEPT. 24th

The daily mortar barrage seems heavier than usual—or is it because our resistance is weakening! Rumours, and still more rumours—only a few more hours—hang on, chaps—when you're stuck in a trench being blasted to hell—tired, hungry and filthy—the hardest part is not knowing what you're really there for and what's going on. Have been out on a patrol searching a row of houses for a sniper. Must have heard us coming as we saw no trace of him, though a few odd bullets came a little too close. In one house was a piano which I managed to strum a few notes on until shouted at to shut up else the whole —— Germans would be at our door—spoil sports. Hand was throbbing but had it dressed at R.A.P. The patrol was a welcome break from sitting around in a trench.

MONDAY, SEPT. 25th

Beginning to despair of ever getting out of here in one piece. Still being mortared and still more rumours.

It's late afternoon, and we've just heard the news we're pulling out tonight across the river. 2nd Army can't reach us. Our time for withdrawal is 12.30. Also told our artillery from over the river is firing in support, and what a welcome sound. Their shells are pretty close at the moment; they appear to be falling only a few hundred yards ahead.

I'm now over the river and lucky to be here. Must have fallen asleep in the trench as I awoke to find the chaps from the neighbouring trenches had already evacuated without me. Made my way towards the river and was lucky to join up with a group of paratroopers. Not much trouble getting to the river, but while on the bank awaiting a boat those blasted mortars caught up with us and plastered the immediate area. A boat came to the bank with a Canadian in charge—what a welcome sight! And when we saw the flat helmets of the British Tommy—different from the airbornes— we knew help was at hand. I was lucky. A voice shouted: "Any wounded?" and a para private, seeing my bloodstained bandaged hand, pushed me forward. There was no panic, the others held back. Once the boat was full—only a handful aboard—we were away. All around the boats chaps were swimming—a last fanfare from those —— mortars—a muddy crawl up a bank—a helping hand—a long march down a country lane—and safety!"

Other aspects of the fighting in and around the woods and on the Osterbeek-Arnhem road are given in the following accounts. Staff-Sergeant Maurice Willoughby writes:

During the Arnhem battle I saw a party of officers crossing a garden and disappearing over a high brick wall. One of them was General Urquhart, whose first attempt at climbing the wall was unsuccessful. Glider pilot Major John Hemmings suddenly appeared behind him, and, placing both hands firmly under the general's bottom, heaved him over. As the great man disappeared from view, the boyish-looking glider pilot grinned and said: "I'll be able to dine out on this one for months."

Some days later I saw him with other glider pilots inside Osterbeek church. They were a motley of very tired, wet and dirty men, but somehow Major Hemmings had managed to keep himself shaven. He eventually moved off with Major Cain of the South Staffordshire Regiment, to take up position along the Arnhem-Osterbeek Road, and I did not see him again until 1946, in the Holy Land. He was then lying severely wounded, the victim of a terrorist attack. When I visited him in hospital some time later, his first remark was, "Golly, what an anti-climax." He remained in hospital for three years.

Staff-Sergeant Carling recalls two incidents which show that even in the heat of battle the human touch was never far away in the company of these very tough young men.

The kid with the Schmeiser opened up on us from seventy yards and I saw a splinter fly off the stock of McDonald's rifle, just as he started to fall. I side-stepped behind one of the big trees on the verge, and Wicks, who had the Bren, dived into the scrub oak just ahead of me.

Our patrol had run into an ambush, about twenty yards from the crossing where we were supposed to set up the machine-gun. When I looked out, the German boy had just started up the track towards me. He stopped to fire a long burst when he saw me aim at him, which was his fatal error. One carefully aimed shot is always better than a scatter from the hip, unless you're at point-blank range.

My .303, however, brought answering fire from an M.G. 34, and as I joined Wicks in the scrub, I could hear the bursts cutting into the tree-trunks. There was no way of seeing where they came from, but I wanted to have a bash at them with the Bren. I gave my rifle to Wicks, to cover me for the run up.

What an abortive effort! As I was moving forward, I seemed to pass through the next burst. One shot struck the barrel locking-lever just by my left hand, and put the gun and my hand out of action. By some act of grace, I was not hit and had time to get close behind a big tree while I recovered my composure.

I could see McDonald lying face down, with a big hole in the back of his smock, all bloody and ragged. He looked very dead, and I needed a rifle. Heaven forgive me, but it seemed the only thing to do at the time.

I heard orders being shouted in German. Their commander was urging them to move in, so I lobbed a grenade in the general direction of his voice. Somebody shouted in English, "Who the hell's chucking bloody grenades about?" just a split second before the real hate got going.

McDonald wasn't breathing enough for me to detect it, and when I turned him over I saw that he had a nasty little hole in the middle of his chest.

I met him in Chelsea seven or eight years later. He told me about his escape from the ambulance train, and his long session with the

All these weapons have been used in action by glider pilots.

H.M. the King inspecting pilots of the Glider Pilot Regiment, April, 1943.

H.M. the Queen talking to glider pilots, 1944.

Dutch underground. He asked me to stay with him, after we'd swopped a few yarns in The Bunch of Grapes.

As I greeted his father back at his house he said, "Carl has just been telling me how he saved my life."

I'll always remember that hooded, sideways glance and quiet half smile of his.

A bullet had ricocheted off his rifle into his chest and had somehow been deflected round the outside of his ribs. Although badly hurt, he was able, as soon as he was bandaged up a bit, to jump from the moving train and make a run for freedom.

But that's his story, and I hope he takes time to write it for us.

I left him there in the scrub oak and the Jerry Red Cross types picked him up later, by God's mercy.

I often wonder whether they picked up the kid with the Schmeiser, as well. I'd like to have a yarn with him if they did. Maybe he's with the others, of course. If he's getting old and weary, I've no doubt he's shed most of the hate nonsense by now, and is hoping, like me, for a nice peaceful old age—and some grandsons to listen to his line-shooting.

Within this fatal perimeter immense courage was shown. The elements of the 1st Airborne Division all fought with astonishing tenacity. They suffered under an intensive bombardment, and it is said that fifteen mortar bombs rained down a minute; it was these bombs which caused more casualties than any other weapon.

The wonderful work of the R.A.M.C. dealing with the ever-increasing number of wounded is today a legend. Casualties were placed in St. Elizabeth Hospital on the evening of the first day, but the Germans re-occupied the buildings, taking everybody prisoner, and a full-scale battle raged round the chief medical station and even in it. Here is one poignant story about the hospital:

TONY MURRY AT ARNHEM

During the battle I had received written instructions to send a squadron (Tony Murry's) to occupy a position away on our right. The remnants of Number 2 Wing of the Glider Pilot Regiment was holding the left-hand corner of the perimeter farthest from the river. At this time Peter Jackson was trying to cover a thickly wooded area with his now depleted squadron.

It was not long after we had parted with Tony Murry's squadron that he was heavily attacked and lost 25 per cent of his remaining strength, and was compelled to withdraw, having been very nearly cut off. Tony got back to divisional headquarters and I requested that he be returned at once to my command, as I was very short of man power. We had been fortunate enough to acquire a Vickers gun and its crew of parachutists, together with a 6-pounder anti-tank gun, and things began to seem a little better. The machine-gunners did tremendous work from a corner of the wood which we were holding, and the anti-tank gun blew up a German tank at short range, while Peter Jackson and his men held off repeated attempts by the enemy to drive them out of the wood with flame-throwers and armoured vehicles, including self-propelled guns.

It was just about this time that Tony Murry walked somewhat shakily into wing H.Q. and remarked: "I think the so-and-so's have got me." We sat him on a couch and began to examine him for the damage. At first we couldn't see anything, then Tony said something about his neck feeling funny, and we spotted the trouble. An enemy bullet had passed clean through his neck from one side to the other, just about level with his collar!

There was very little bleeding, but we couldn't tell what damage had been done inside, and as Tony was obviously not feeling very good, we despatched him on a jeep to the hospital which by that time was being operated by both German and British personnel and was inside the German lines. We later heard Tony's own story which I think exemplifies the spirit of the glider pilots.

Having arrived at the hospital, Tony had to wait his turn and was eventually patched up and told to take it easy. He was, of course, by then ostensibly a prisoner. The doctor, I believe, told him that he was very lucky, as he, the doctor, would have found it quite difficult to push a sharp instrument from one side of his throat to the other without doing any material damage.

Tony hung around the hospital for a couple of days and finally, getting fed up with doing nothing, walked out and spent most of the day dodging the enemy. He finally got back to us, explaining when he arrived that he had been a little bored in hospital, so thought he would come back!

It was at this time that we lost poor Tony Plowman, who had taken over Tony Murry's squadron when he was wounded. The Germans were, as usual, extremely aggressive, and shortly afterwards put in an attack on our hard-pressed corner of the wood. They came in yelling under a hail of mortar fire, and actually got into the thinly held line, where they were stopped by Tony Plowman, who—gathering his few weary men together, and with a revolver in one hand and a walking stick in the other—led an immediate counter-attack which drove the Germans out. Then as a final insult to Hitler's men, Tony led his men in the derisive singing of "Lilli Marlene", the Germans' own song. Having completed the first verse or two, Tony Plowman, in a voice which carried to the farthest corners of the wood—now strewn with the dead of both sides—roared out to the enemy: "Come on you bastards, and get her." There were roars of delight from his men, quickly followed by frightened yells from the enemy, who began to shout: "Don't shoot, don't shoot," as a number came in with their hands up.

Not long afterwards a jeep rolled up to our headquarters, flying a Red Cross flag, and on it lay poor Tony Plowman. As the jeep drove away, I heard him call out: "Tell John (myself) I'm sorry." It was with very great sorrow that I heard later that he had died in hospital.

Soon food and ammunition started to go down, and the defenders of the perimeter had to forage for food in the houses of Arnhem. The battles and skirmishes in and around the houses is well illustrated in the following narratives.

Staff-Sergeant Les Foster's story:

It was the morning of the third or fourth day of the Arnhem operation and we had taken a row of houses on the extreme left flank facing towards the river. I say the extreme flank because the house next to ours across the width of the road was occupied by Jerry and we felt that this was "extreme" in any one's book! Lieutenant Smith, myself, two other staff-sergeants and another sergeant were the first to move in, and we were trying to find positions which would command views on three sides, the other side being covered by the chaps in the next house along the row.

How to defend the house was a tricky problem as some parts were already missing, which made us feel exposed, and there were, for a start, only the five of us for "all round" cover. Personally I was all for "Heads down in the cellar and no one breathe a word", but I was outvoted! One staff-sergeant—I can't remember his name so I'll call him Charlie—insisted on reconnoitring the rooms with a Meerschaum pipe going full blast and sending up what must have seemed to the Germans to be smoke signals. I had just returned from one of the upstairs rooms when I heard a shout from Charlie, who staggered out into the hall with his face covered in blood. I wiped away what I could and found that a bullet had scoured a deep furrow right across the top of his forehead taking a good part of the bone with it. As I bound this ghastly wound with my first-aid dressing, I kept thinking that half-an-inch lower and he would no longer have been with us!

Although his courage was amazing and an example to all of us, it was obvious that the five of us, so far as any fighting was concerned, were now reduced to four. The lower part of the house contained only one room which was not exposed on the sides covered by Jerry, and this we used as our H.Q., and first-aid room. Fortunately this room contained a bed, an enormous thing with three great mattresses, and into this we put Charlie, where he lay propped up with several pillows, the inevitable smokescreen pouring from his pipe.

By this time we had been reinforced by another three pilots and were waiting to see what Jerry intended to do. We weren't left wondering very long, for at about five o'clock we heard the ominous sound of tanks, and from our look-out in the bathroom saw the ugly hull of a "Tiger" come to rest outside the house across the road. This was too good an opportunity to miss, so we dashed downstairs for our Piat* and set it up on a small table in the bathroom. I pushed the first bomb into the Piat and Lieutenant Smith sighted and then fired. The bomb exploded just in front of the tank and our second hit the same spot. At this, the hatch was thrown up and the head of a German officer popped up. He looked somewhat surprised and seemed to be asking the German infantry men in the house what all the noise was about! I immediately let fly with my rifle but missed an absolute sitter by about a foot. The bullet ricocheted off the hull of the tank and the head shot down. This, I regret to say, was not taken very kindly by the tank crew, for a couple of hours after this incident Jerry decided to move us out of our temporary accommodation, and to this end put in a fairly heavy attack. Our great advantage must have been that he didn't know our actual strength, and although in vocal output the Germans proved far superior we were dashing about firing and throwing grenades like a group of instructors on a refresher course, and this must have been extremely confusing for the enemy.

It was during this rather warm period, and just as the light was beginning to fail, that one of the sergeants in the next house down the road hearing Germanic war cries round our house and thinking that we had been overwhelmed, decided to give a helping hand by tossing three grenades from an upper window of his house into our H.Q. This was happening just as I had dashed across to his house

* *Projectile Infantry Anti-Tank.*

to report to the captain that for the moment we were holding our own. While I was talking the sergeant came into the room in a terribly agitated state indicating that he had realized too late that, from the Anglo-Saxon oaths that had fallen on his ears, "he had done a terrible thing by throwing grenades, etc., etc." Hearing this I hurried back expecting to see a gory mess, only to find that two of the three grenades had been quickly snapped up and hurled out again and the third had exploded under Charlie's bed. This had lifted him almost to the ceiling, but by the grace of God and the Dutch housewife's love of mattresses he was still, more or less, in one piece. He had in fact taken the whole thing, including our contretemps with the enemy, quite calmly and was again in full blast with the old Meerschaum!

The following morning we were attacked in greater strength, after a rather hectic night. A self-propelled gun joined in for good measure and 20 m.m. cannon shells were whipping through the house at an extremely rapid rate. Although Jerry failed again in this attempt to become the new occupant of our by now not very desirable residence, we decided that it was time to shift Charlie farther down the row where it might be just a little quieter. So out through the window Charlie went, heavily bandaged and very pale, to run the gauntlet down the back of the house for about thirty yards. Several of us had already been farther than this the previous day to scrounge more ammunition and we had received no injuries in the process. However, Charlie was not to be so fortunate, for he had almost reached his destination when he was shot in the backside. This was enough to make any man give up his Meerschaum, but not Charlie.

It was his staff, his emblem of strength, of courage and of fortitude. When at last I reached the other side of the river I enquired whether Charlie had made it. I found that he had, although he had been shot yet again—this time in the arm. When I asked whether he was smoking when crossing the river I received the inevitable reply: "That Meerschaum—it was going like a bloody camp fire!"

Sergeant N. J. Read's story:

My first pilot, Staff-Sergeant Atkins, and I took part in a patrol on the fifth morning, its object being to secure and hold houses at the north-east corner of the perimeter. Our section, commanded by Lieutenant Palmer, held a house overlooking a cross-roads. After settling in, we awaited the usual hectic night, but it did not develop. The nights from then on were almost deathly quiet, only patrol skir-

mishes breaking the silence.   We heard that many of the enemy troops
were withdrawn for resting after dark.

On the sixth afternoon, an enemy supply lorry took the wrong
turning, and drove straight towards us.   A Piat bomb damaged it
and knocked out the crew.   The lorry was later towed to divisional
headquarters and its contents distributed among the troops.   Included
were German cigarettes, unpleasant but nevertheless welcome.

That night the glider pilots on our right went house clearing and
we could hear their opponents calling for stretcher-bearers.

Later I had some sleep but was awakened on the seventh morning
by the noise of firing.   German infantry were attacking but we held
them off, our section hitting several who walked within yards of
our concealed trench.   Then they brought up a self-propelled gun.
Our Piat struck the chassis but the undamaged gun retaliated by
shelling us out of our good position.   All of our section hit by shrapnel
were sent to the R.A.P., the more serious cases having to go to the
C.C.S. in German hands.

Leaving the R.A.P. I joined a group of glider pilots setting up
positions in the woods with the remnants of the 4th Parachute Brigade.

Sunday, September 24th, our eighth day was my birthday.   I had
a birthday present that morning—three hours of constant mortar fire!

On the ninth day we received orders to move out that night.   White
lead tapes were set up and boots were wrapped.   During the day we
watched Bostons and Mitchells bombing to the north.

At zero hour we moved off, and after some incidents, including
being shelled by our own 25-pounders, we reached the river.   Waiting
for a boat at the water's edge was even more uncomfortable than a
day at Fargo!   (The Glider Pilot Regimental Depot.)   It was pitch
black and raining.   The puzzled Germans used flares, mortar bombs
and machine-guns with little effect except for one unlucky salvo
which sank a boat loaded with wounded.   After several hours, I was
ferried across by a British R.A.S.C. boat-man.   Safely over, military
policemen directed us down a muddy slide on to the road and off we
tramped to Elst.

A tot of rum and a bite to eat at Elst, and we were transported
to C.C.S. to have our complaints attended to.   Then a convoy across
the bridge to Nijmegen, where we were surprised to see our administrative troopers awaiting us with evident concern in spite of their
own hazardous journey.

Staff-Sergeant Vic Wade's story:

On the third day after landing the situation was becoming serious.

"Jerry" had captured the landing ground only after a costly resistance by our forces, and was piercing the outer perimeter at Oosterbeek. We had withdrawn towards the centre of the perimeter, and part of the force was dug-in on the edge of a wood. Soon, a German tank was seen advancing from the wood across our front and trundling determinedly across the open ground. Suddenly, to our amazement, two men appeared running out of the woods in close pursuit of the tank. One was armed with a Piat which although a comparatively light weapon becomes extremely heavy when at the double. The other was carrying the bombs which seem equally as heavy in such circumstances. In a matter of seconds the tank was enveloped in smoke effected by a smoke-grenade. With speed and efficiency the Piat was brought into action and two bombs were effectively fired into the rear of the tank, which was completely disabled. Through the haze the crew appeared out of the turret and I assure you they had a very warm welcome! Whether these deeds were recognized I don't know, but such courage should be lauded, for no one can estimate the number of lives saved by their action.

The day when my colleagues were obsessed with the fear of becoming casualties was on Monday, 26th September, when news came through of the proposed withdrawal. I shared these feelings and wished only for zero hour when I would be "away" from it all. That our sector ever knew of such a plan was due to the heorism of three men.

For two days our sector, which comprised a row of houses, by this time shell-shattered, had been cut off from the remainder of the division. The Germans had gradually encircled us and we were kept well occupied twenty-four hours a day. There was no wireless communication, and the suggestion that we were still part of an Allied plan came only from the sound of 2nd Army shells, shrieking through the air Jerry-wards, and this indeed was a source of comfort.

On this Monday two captains and a staff-sergeant, Louis Hagen—(later decorated with the M.M.)—volunteered to go through the enemy lines to contact brigade H.Q. They were successful in their mission and returned about 1600 hours with the news that we had to withdraw at 2200 hours. Instructions were that we should hold on to our particular houses, engaging only in sporadic fire so that when the time to withdraw came there would be no marked cessation of fire to arouse suspicion. During the hours of light we prepared the material; from carpets and other household goods, which would be tied round our boots to muffle the sound when we withdrew.

At stand-to the tension was great. The period of waiting was a nightmare. The hopeless situation had suddenly been transformed into one of hope and in consequence each one was terrified that something would happen to prevent his taking part in the withdrawal.

My allotted position was by the wall of a house, covering the side approach with a Bren-gun. Kneeling behind me was my friend, with whom I had flown for over a year, and he was laden with grenades. Both of us were excited and we exchanged at intervals, "O.K., Vic", —"O.K., Dido". The horror of the situation was that a sniper, positioned in a ruined house across the road had our post well taped, despite the darkness. He would fire tracer intermittently, hitting the wall not more than three feet above our heads. You can well imagine our thoughts, but on no account could we leave our posts. With joy we received the order to withdraw one by one and take up our appointed place at the rear of the houses beneath the cover of a friendly hedgerow.

Many never survived the two-hour crawl and march through the enemy lines to the bank of the lower Rhine; it is an experience I never wish to have repeated. I count it an honour to have been associated with such men and to have served in the Airborne Division.

All through the battle wireless communication failed and Major-General Urquhart was never in touch with General Browning: Because of this the information passed on to the R.A.F. was very meagre. As the battle developed and the airborne force was reduced in numbers, it was forced away from the original dropping zones because these could not be wrested from enemy hands. This being so, a new zone had to be chosen. Through the breakdown in communication this detail never got through to the R.A.F. and, as a result, the vital supplies they dropped fell into German hands and not into those of the airborne division.

In order to carry out this operation the 38 and 46 Group aircraft had to fly through highly concentrated flak, an immensely hazardous feat because of the low speed and height at which the aircraft had to fly. Nothing daunted, on flew the Royal Air Force into this hail of bullets and shrapnel, trying to bring sustenance to the beleaguered garrison. It is a terrible thought that those strained and desperate men of the 1st Airborne Division had to watch the whole of these parachuted supplies drop into enemy hands, and that the R.A.F. suffered so many casualties in a fruitless journey. The sight of burning aircraft circling the zone, with no hope of survival, was terrible to see. Yet the operation was carried out in the finest traditions of inter-service co-operation.

The 1st Airborne Division war diary shows that on the fifth day the situation was desperate. They had had no news of the elements fighting in Arnhem or on the bridge for twenty-four hours. Their casualties were extremely heavy and the ammunition was running out, but still no relief was at hand. There were still another four terrible days to go, while this gallant force remained there.

It now became imperative that full communication of the situation be sent to General Browning at Airborne Corps H.Q. Major-General Urquhart selected his G.S.O.1., Lieutenant-Colonel C. B. Mackenzie, and Lieutenant-Colonel E. C. Myers, C.B.E., D.S.O., to carry the information of the state of the division. They managed to inflate a rubber boat and to cross the Lower Rhine, with great courage, and although fatigued they got through and discussed plans for evacuation, which they got back to their divisional commander.

The evacuation was arranged for the night of September 25th/26th and was to start at 10 p.m., and it was imperative that the withdrawal should be done in silence and at night. It was arranged that the division should move down to the bank of the Lower Rhine, near Oosterbeek. Thus, the airborne division prepared itself for withdrawal, leaving both enemy and friends. The Dutch people had shown immense patience and fortitude in frightful circumstances. How can it be described, the feeling which must have been theirs? For they had seen this wonderful force drop from the skies to liberate them from German occupation. Yet as the battle developed they had to witness their town being reduced to rubble and ashes. Despite the most terrible ordeal, they gave every assistance. The Resistance Groups had fought with tenacious courage, the Dutch women had nursed and tended the wounded, and they had supplied food and water. Yet now they were to be left—to face who knew what reprisals.

Indeed the 1st Airborne Division were leaving friends: the wounded lying in their hundreds, unable to cross the Lower Rhine, and knowing that they had to face prisoner-of-war camps. The doctors and chaplains cheerfully stayed with them, knowing that their only fate was to be prisoners-of-war too. It is with much pride that the Glider Pilot Regiment can claim that they were selected to be guide posts on the night of the withdrawal. Such was their discipline that these men stood all through that night helping others to free-

dom. It was here that the men must have been tested to the limit—
yet they did not fail.

A heavy bombardment had been arranged by the 2nd Army to
cover the withdrawal, and the Germans, who were also tired, but
wary of any movement, mistook this bombardment for cover for
reinforcements.

The crossing was extremely hazardous and there were too many
men for the boats. Many were drowned, killed and wounded in this
crossing, yet it went relentlessly on.

By noon of September 27th the ordeal had come to its end, and
the epic of the Battle of Arnhem was over.

Out of 10,095 men of the 1st Airborne Division, 7,605 officers
and men were killed, wounded and missing. The Glider Pilot Regiment emerged tremendously proud but desperately reduced. Their
casualties in this operation were: 23 officers and 124 staff-sergeants
and sergeants killed; 31 officers and 438 staff-sergeants and sergeants wounded and prisoners-of-war. A total of 615 glider pilots.
For the regiment this was all but a death blow, for to make up the
replacements, to train this number to fly and give them the necessary experience would be truly impossible.

This was to be the cause of extraordinary action being taken, as
will be told later.

The result of the operations in Holland proved to me that everything had been done to perfect the fighting abilities of the Glider
Pilot Regiment. They had flown some 600 gliders into this battle
and in doing so had brought to the battle many thousands of men
and jeeps and guns. Their fighting ability, spirit and adaptability had
been tested to the limit, and had not been found wanting.

One further interesting point is that Lieutenant-General Browning found that he had, after the glider landings of the 82nd and
101st Airborne Divisions, over 1,000 U.S. glider pilots who could
have been used with tremendous impact in the Arnhem battle, but
for the fact that they had no formation on the ground—no military
training in the fullest sense. Had this been so he might have used
this force to release an American battalion of infantry holding the
twenty-five mile perimeter round Nijmegen, and this might have
relieved the pressure on Arnhem. He could not do so. In fact he
had no reserve at the most critical of moments. Even when the
battle was in its third day, and the Guards Armoured Division was
battling for the bridge of Nijmegen, it was impossible to get infantry

up from the Eindhoven-Grave road owing to congestion and the continuous cutting of the road itself.

However, so far as I was concerned, Arnhem fully satisfied me on one count—that the formation, training and equipment of the Glider Pilot Regiment had been fully vindicated.

11

AFTERMATH OF ARNHEM

THE REGIMENT (or what was left of it) now returned to its bases and we had time to think again. We had been badly mauled, and I was at a loss to know how to reorganize, for it was almost impossible to recreate the regiment because of the long preparation needed in the R.A.F. training schools. It looked very much as if we had come to a standstill.

It was then that I was sent for to attend a conference at the War Office. I arrived to find myself sitting at a table surrounded by British and American officers. In the chair was General Brereton, the commander-in-chief of the Allied Airborne Army.

This was the latest Allied force and consisted of the 1st and 6th Airborne Divisions, British Army, and the 82nd and 17th Airborne Divisions, United States Army. A formidable force indeed, with a carrier fleet of two groups of R.A.F. bombers and Dakotas and a wing of the United States Air Force. It represented a total of some 40,000 parachutists and glider-borne troops and 30,000 R.A.F. personnel. It was the last word in planning, training and equipment, and I do not think that the people of either Great Britain or the United States have ever fully appreciated quite what was achieved in assembling this great army, for this immense force of aircraft, men and equipment was capable of operating over a range of 300 miles at 130 miles per hour, and landing behind or on the battlefield. It was an extraordinary achievement.

At this momentous meeting I was told of the projected invasion of the Rhine by this great force. Two airborne divisions were to be dropped simultaneously on top of the defences, this time within the range of the supporting armies and artillery, to swamp and overwhelm the enemy, the Allied armies following up immediately to speed through into Germany.

My instructions were to prepare a glider force large enough to fly, if required, 2,000 gliders. But with what? I had a casualty list of well over 500 men and no reinforcements. Clearly rapid improvisation would be needed. The only recourse was to turn to the Royal Air Force, with whom a meeting was arranged at the Air Ministry—I shall never forget it!

This time I took the Director Air, War Office, Major-General Sir Leonard Crawford with me and, sitting among the R.A.F. officers, we explained our requirements. To say they were difficult is to put it mildly. They stolidly refused to budge. They did not like the idea of mixing R.A.F. personnel with the Army. I was amazed at their attitude, hidebound and obsessed by inter-Service rivalry, and waited impatiently for the frustrating meeting to end, sick at heart and despising them all.

After it was over I walked down the stairs to the entrance leading to Whitehall, where I turned to Major-General Crawford and said: "Sir, would you come with me to Bush House now, for I think I can find the answer to our problems there."

"What is that?" enquired the general, obviously very annoyed with the situation.

"Sir," I continued, "I have a friend there, the Director of Training, Air Chief Marshal Sir Peter Drummond. He will help us, I know."

"All right, lead the way," answered the general.

I hailed a taxi and we departed for Bush House. At the enquiry desk I asked: "Can I have the Director of Training, Air Chief Marshal Sir Peter Drummond?" The man hesitated but then gave me a telephone line.

A voice answered curtly, "Yes?"

"Sir," I said, "it's George Chatterton speaking. Can I come up and see you for a moment? I have with me Sir Leonard Crawford, Director Air, of the War Office. I won't keep you long."

"By all means, old boy, come up!" said Sir Peter, and up we went in the lift.

There sat my old friend, that kind, courageous and brilliant man, with a continual twinkle in his eye, in spite of what was now a sad, serious expression.

"Good afternoon, George," he said, "so here you are again. You seem to have done quite a deal since you last came here. Which army are you in now?" For he remembered that I had come to his office as a colonel in the United States Army, before the Normandy invasion.

"It would seem that you took advantage of what I arranged for you, by all accounts."

He spoke to me as he had done fifteen years before when I was a pilot-officer in No. 1 Fighter Squadron, R.A.F.

"What is it this time?" he laughed. His eyes twinkled and he looked at me.

I explained the position, what had happened at Arnhem, the demand by the Allied airborne army, and the result of the meeting at the Air Ministry.

"What, no men for your force! What utter nonsense!" said the Air Chief Marshal. He rang a bell and an air commodore came in.

"Bring me the list of R.A.F. flying personnel in the pool," the Air Marshal demanded. The air commodore disappeared and returned a few minutes later with a large file, which Sir Peter Drummond gazed at for some time before looking up.

"Well, there seems to be plenty of chaps in the pool of reserves—the overflow from the Empire Air Training Scheme.

"In Blackpool, Bournemouth and other camps there are 46,000 officers and N.C.O. pilots. Perhaps I could let you have some of these. How many do you need?"

"About 1,500, Sir," I answered.

"Is that all? I will arrange it, Sir Leonard. You say when!"

The general sat silent for a moment and then said: "Well it does seem the only answer, and the sooner we can get together and put it on a committee paper the better."

This was the usual procedure for the War Office, because everything, no matter how urgent, had to be minuted.

Thus, before long, 1,500 officers and N.C.O. pilots of the R.A.F. were made over, so to speak, to the Army, and were posted to the strength of the Glider Pilot Regiment.

Then, of course, the problems started, and I had to make a number of fateful decisions. Whatever I did was bound to be unpopular with one or other of the Services, so I finally decided to integrate the R.A.F. with the Army pilots, trying to match rank for rank.

Taking No. 1 Wing, I disposed the new intake so that the wing was commanded by Lieutenant-Colonel Murray. I then laid down that the squadrons should be commanded equally by majors and squadron-leaders of the Royal Air Force, the flight captains and flight-lieutenants of the Royal Air Force, and so on down through the ranks, even to the crews, for it was imperative that the Royal Air Force should be nursed in "affairs military" by Army personnel.

It was difficult to agree to all requests, and many of the R.A.F. personnel were thoroughly browned off. They had voluntered to fly powered aircraft, but had been frustrated by the state of the war. There were not enough duties for them, and in consequence many were bitterly disappointed because they had to be content to fly gliders, instead of Spitfires, Beaufighters, Mosquitoes and the Halifax and Stirling bombers.

Nevertheless, on the whole, they bore their disappointment with patience and goodwill, though there were a few occasions when I had to deal with what today might be called sit-down strikes, but these were few and far between.

The most difficult task was to raise the standard of *esprit de corps* and discipline of the R.A.F. glider pilots to the level of the Army pilots, most of whom were battle-trained, knew what was in store, and knew that their training had been a vital factor in the battles of Sicily, Normandy, and Arnhem. It was extraordinary how desperately the R.A.F. glider pilots tried to follow the Glider Pilot Regiment example. I had great trouble, for the officers and N.C.O.s felt that they should have some distinguishing mark to show the world what they were doing.

I attempted to obtain special recognition from the Air Ministry for these men, and asked that they might have a special badge, rather like the Pathfinder Force, since, after all, they were completely different from most of the men serving in the R.A.F. The Air Ministry, however, would not hear of it. Nevertheless, the pilots of the R.A.F. contravened Air Ministry orders and piped the rings which were the officers' chevron, and the sergeant-pilots whitened their stripes. They even wore red berets with their R.A.F. blue. This caused a dreadful to-do, and I was constantly being rung up and told that the men were not to be allowed to do this, it was desecrating their uniforms.

While all this was going on the plans for the Rhine operation were developing, and I began trying to devise a new technique for landing the gliders into battle. Air Vice Marshal Hollinghurst, at this time, had been relieved by Air Vice Marshal Scarlett-Streatfeild, and by good fortune we had known each other in the old days in the R.A.F. Yet again that past paid its dividend, for we at once saw eye to eye—in planning, in operations, and in training. It was because of this that the difficulties that had arisen over the R.A.F. glider pilots were dealt with with understanding and sympathy. But I had to make a new plan for the coming offensive, and get him to agree to it; this is how it evolved.

12

THE RHINE CROSSING

THE HUGE ARMADA of aircraft was now at the ready. It was immense: 1,795 troop-carriers were available for the parachutist element and 1,305 for the glider element.

Two divisions, the British 6th and the American 17th, were to assault the Rhine crossings.

This time it was decided to give the airborne force the fullest protection from the outset. In the plan the 6th Airborne Division would always be within the range of the 21st Army Group artillery. In fact, the system to be used was entirely different from anything tried before.

Zero hour would see the van of the 21st Army Group over the Rhine, lying close-up to the main landing zones of the airborne force, and the parachute force and glider-borne troops would fly in over the top of this leading army. In this way it was hoped to achieve complete tactical surprise.

It was now known that the enemy had their anti-airborne troops ready, but they were waiting for mass landings in one area. They were to learn a rude lesson.

It was accepted, as I have already said, that the airborne force must land on top of the objective, but in tactical formation. All agreed that the tragedy of Arnhem was that the landings had been made too far from the main target. In fact, the Arnhem bridge was eight miles from the dropping and landing zones.

The soldiers, therefore, were more or less asking for the gliders to be put down where they wanted them—back gardens included.

Another point of great importance was that General Brereton, commanding the 1st Allied Airborne Army, insisted that there should be only one lift, and that the maximum number of aircraft must be available for this operation. He made no bones about this. He also demanded the complete crushing of anti-aircraft defences, which was to be carried out by bombardment and bombing.

It was known that the Germans were weak on the ground in the

P

area chosen for the assault, and it was also clear that they had few reinforcements.

The Allied airborne army was commanded in the field by Major-General Ridgway, one of the veterans of France and Holland, with General Gale as deputy-commander.

The main object of the operation was to capture the high ground forming the western edge of the Diesfordten Wald. Its capture was vital to the main forces of the army group crossing the Rhine, otherwise enemy troops ensconced there would inflict heavy casualties.

Farther inland the River Ijssel was crossed by three bridges in the area to the front of the airborne attack and, again, it was of vital importance that these should be captured intact to allow the main army to break through into Germany with great speed.

The 6th Airborne Division's task was to capture the northern flank of the front and this was to be done by the 3rd and 5th Parachute Brigades. The 6th Air Landing Brigade's task was the capturing of the bridges and to contain the village of Hammelkehn. The artillery and other divisional troops would be landed in the centre of the entire drop.

Four hundred and forty Horsas and Hamilcars were allotted to the operation, the glider pilots of No. 1 Wing being the air crews. Yet again Lieutenant-Colonel Iain Murray, D.S.O., was to be in command of the Glider Pilot Regiment on the ground. On March 24th, 1945, this great formation of aircraft rose into the air and headed for Brussels, and thence to the target—the Rhine and Germany.

At 9.45 a.m. the great air fleet approached the area at a height of approximately 2,500 feet. It was here that a strange situation faced the pilots of both the R.A.F. and the Glider Pilot Regiment. In the major plan there had been a demand for the intensive shelling and bombing of Wesel, and by some freak of fate the smoke and dust which arose from this bombardment was blown right over the landing zones. This made dead accuracy most difficult, particularly near the ground, but in spite of these extremely difficult conditions many gliders reached their objectives, though few gliders landed unscathed, and many passengers were hit by flak and small arms fire as the gliders descended on the target. Some gliders exploded and some that carried petrol supplies went up in flames.

The R.A.F. glider pilots more than proved themselves and fought on the ground with courage and distinction. Here are the accounts of some of the glider pilots who took part in the operation.

Staff-Sergeant Clifford Tuppen's story:

After detailed briefing, I was confidently expecting to lead a flight of three gliders to take a farmhouse and secure divisional head-quarters! I knew every tree and field and the concentration of German artillery, etc. After a fitful sleep (no reveille was needed) I met the airborne troops I was taking, and their officer, who was unfortunately superior in rank, and the battle for command took place at zero minus one hour!

After the long tow, we approached the dropping zone, to find smoke from the barrage had covered all landmarks. We flew a few more miles into Germany, and after scraping over H.T. cables, which cut the bottom of the cockpit out like a cheese wire, we made a landing which filled us full of good earth!

Now "rank" took over! I had managed to unload the jeep, etc., by pulling off the glider front with the aid of a small tank—our nose wheel was no doubt still in the H.T. wires, plus my small kit.

I suggested the route we should take, to the div. H.Q., but no! it was the *other* way and no arguments! We boarded the jeep, and it was obvious to my second dicky and I that the front line was near, by reason of the noise, flames and casualties.

On a command, we made a right turn from our cart track, and we were then actually driving through no-man's land, with a German regiment commanding all the houses, etc., on one side, and the American paratroops on the other—throwing everything they had at each other.

The jeep stopped (no glider pilot driving!) and I had the most horrible experience of sitting in the middle of this inferno without cover, until I was shot at, which brought me to my senses and enabled me to do the 100 yards in battle order in about six seconds (unconfirmed).

After many eventful encounters, my second dicky and I managed to get back to H.Q., where we were admonished for being late and told to get out on patrol duties, which lasted until relieved by the army boys next morning.

I was evacuated at night, with some wounded, by "Duck" across the Rhine and we were dive-bombed. By now I was sure my time was running out—luck couldn't hold much longer. Then we were put in the back of an ambulance en route to a convent in Holland, the convoy being shot up for about twenty minutes by night fighters, at the end of which the ambulance resembled a colander. Being shut in was the frightening part. The noise at about 2 a.m. was fantastic—but the luck held.

After about six weeks in hospital in Belgium—I reported to the regiment and I was greeted with the words: "You're for Japan." I felt it was nice to be home!

Captain Boucher-Giles, D.F.C., gives another graphic description, this time on the Rhine crossing:

The trip to the Rhine was almost entirely uneventful. For the first two hours or so we cruised around in the calm early morning air, so as to give time for other aircraft from other stations to rendezvous. There were 440 British Horsa gliders in this operation, and some 865 of the much smaller American Hadrian gliders. I remember a thrill of excitement as we swept over Brighton in the van of what must have been a most impressive spectacle and looked down at the crowds who had assembled to stare at us. The weather was perfect for flying, and we did the whole of the journey in the low-tow position (the best petrol-saver for the tug) so that we pilots could see the black form of the bomber like a gigantic crow in the perspex window just above the level of our heads. There was no rough air, and as we were in front we fouled no one else's slip-stream and indeed saw very few other aircraft at all—either gliders, bombers or fighters. At Dunkirk (still in enemy hands) we were fired on, but were well out of range of even the heaviest ack-ack guns.

It was only after we had flown quite low over the roofs of Brussels and had left the field of Waterloo behind us that we began to join up with other tug-and-glider formations (quite a number of them in front of us by now) and to see, twenty miles ahead over perfectly flat country, a little of what lay in store for us.

A dense haze of smoke hung over the Rhine, above which could be seen the bursts of ack-ack shells as the first aircraft flew over the river. I saw one aircraft go down in flames, but when our turn came to cross we could see little of the river, and indeed the smoke haze (from the very heavy bombing and shelling which had taken place earlier) was so great as to cause confusion. I glimpsed a few parachutes open on the ground and a minute or so afterwards came the signal to release. We were at three thousand two hundred feet. At the same moment I saw the river Ijssel and the nearby autobahn through the smoke-haze down below and knew we must have come a little too far. A steep turn to the right was considerably accelerated by a vicious burst of machine-gun fire which came up through the floor of the glider just between where Sergeant Garland I and were sitting. I put on half-flap, but this refused to work, obviously having been damaged by flak. In fact, the glider had been fairly peppered, but luckily no one had been hit.

Visibility was almost nil, and we could not see Hamminkeln at all, so the only thing to do was to make a long snaking turn down to where I thought the landing-ground must be underneath the smoke-haze. We could not see the ground properly, until we reached a height of five hundred feet, so the landing we made about sixty yards to the east of the woods and about six hundred yards due south of our proper L.Z. was disappointing but perhaps not too bad under the circumstances.

We made quite a soft landing on a ploughed field and everyone was able to get out unhurt. We did not take long about it either, because we were under mortar and small-arms fire from the moment we touched down.

We were evidently on the northern side of the L.Z. of the gliders belonging to the American 17th Airborne Division. There was a large building about eighty yards to our right (evidently a school) and another set of buildings about one hundred yards in front—both unfortunately occupied, with sniping coming from the wood behind us. No other gliders were near.

Luckily the flaps on the glider belatedly started to work and the cover was very welcome. There were only seven of us, but most of us had automatic weapons with which we heatedly peppered every door and window in the offending building. We were rewarded after a few minutes with the gratifying sight of some German soldiers running away.

Now seemed the time to unload the glider, and get away to the R.V. near Hamminkeln in the jeep and trailer. Unfortunately no one seemed to be able to find the key to undo the tail-unit, and after a few minutes of rather frustrating slashing with an axe at wires which refused to part I decided to try the alternative of blowing the tail off. We had been provided with some special explosive cord for this purpose, but to wrap it around the tail unit from the outside of the glider meant exposing oneself rather obviously to any Hun sniper who might be around. However, this was obviously the pilot's job, so Garland and I proceeded, the others taking up firing positions to cover us.

The job was nearly completed, when there came a burst of fire from the flank, and I felt a blow like a kick from a mule high up on my right thigh and a sensation of a red-hot poker passing through my leg. I tried to rush for cover, but must have passed out, because when I came to, Sergeant Garland had very gallantly got me in a little slit trench which he had dug in the ploughland and had fixed a field dressing over the wound. He also doped me with morphia.

Major Rogers had been hit in the arm, one of the Devon privates killed, another wounded, and the C.S.M. who had been such a tower of strength with his Bren gun, shot to pieces. Poor fellow, I remember how a few minutes before we went into our run-in, he came into the cockpit and chatted with me. "Sir," he said, "I'm not a bit worried about what happens when we get down, I can cope with that. It's this landing that worries me!" I assured him that it was just the other way round with me, and we parted the best of friends.

Help was now at hand, as several gliders came in to land near us. Staff-Sergeant Nigel Brown, my troop staff-sergeant, stepped out of a Mark II Horsa elegantly adjusting a silk scarf after a perfect landing, for all the world as if he were on an exercise. Brown was a first-rate soldier who had, I believe, served on every major glider operation and had never been even slightly wounded. His comrades believed he bore a charmed life, and it is told of him that later that morning the heavy machine-gun of a Tiger tank shot the Bren gun out of his hands and reduced it to twisted wreckage—still without either injuring him or even disturbing his morale.

Flight-Lieutenant Tom Parsons, one of the "G" squadron troop commanders, brought in another Mark II Horsa, and although neither of these aircraft was carrying much besides stores and ammunition, the few men who were with them proved useful reinforcements. After clearing both sets of buildings, Major Rogers, in spite of his wound, led them all into the wood to clear it, as the sniping and mortaring from that direction was getting worse.

As for me, I wish I could relate some gallant story of bravery and adventure, but I was (presumably from shock and loss of blood) unconscious half the time, and only half-conscious for the rest of it. The others said they would come back for me, though this understandably they never managed to do, and meanwhile I could not move, and seemed to be drifting in a kind of dream world, in which I could not always see properly. A sniper paid me unwelcome attention for a time, but he did not hit me, and after a time the fighting drew away, and I remained in a sort of no-man's land between the American and British L.Zs.

As the sun began to get low in the sky I heard muttered voices and footsteps the other side of the glider. I cocked my pistol and challenged them in what I hoped was a strong firm voice, only to be answered by a cheery "Hiya, Bud!" It was a recce patrol of American airborne troops.

These boys undoubtedly saved my life. After showering me with cigars, candy, and chewing-gum which I was in no position to enjoy, they returned to their H.Q. for a stretcher for me.

Adventures in various American casualty clearing stations, where I received a blood-transfusion and more morphia, were fantastic. Twice the whole C.C.S. had to be evacuated owing to heavy shelling and mortar fire, and one night we were subjected to a direct attack by German infantry. Mortar bombs and bullets were coming through the tents. I can remember lying across my stretcher and emptying my pistol into the wood from which the enemy fire was coming. After that they took my ammo. away from me, but I clung to that pistol— I had grown very fond of it by now!

Flying-Officer John Love, D.F.C., R.A.F.:

In October 1944, along with a few hundred R.A.F. pilots, I arrived back from training in Canada, and was stationed at a transit camp at Harrogate.

One morning we were all assembled in a lecture hall for a talk by someone from the War Office, who explained that the war was entering its final phase, and that due to heavy losses sustained at the battle of Arnhem the Army did not have time to train replacements in time for the next push, that is, the crossing of the Rhine. He suggested that if we wanted to see a bit of action this might be the chance to do so. He ended up by asking for volunteers.

Those of us who did so, had to take some leg pulling from the "wise guys". We had the last laugh when we reported to Fargo for training and found that most of the wise guys had been "press-ganged" into service, as the number of volunteers had been insufficient. However, I am pleased to say that there were no hard feelings, and everyone settled in and eventually took a great pride in his connection with the airborne forces, so much so, in fact, that there was great controversy as to whether we wore red berets or blue with our R.A.F. uniforms. The powers that be decreed that it should be blue, but I do know some of us acquired red berets and stuffed them in our smocks or small packs, for wearing when we got over the Rhine.

Our military training consisted of a fortnight on small arms at Fargo, and a week of assault course and field training at Bridgenorth. Our flying training meant conversion to Hotspurs at Croughton, and a few hours on Horsas at Seighford, Staffordshire, before being posted to our Squadron. We settled in very quickly at Tarrant Rushton, and struck up a fine relationship with all the pukka glider pilots. We, who were posted to "C" Squadron, felt that we had got the plum posting, and could be pardoned for being a bit big-headed for flying Hamilcars and not Horsas.

On the operation itself my second pilot was an R.A.F. man, Sergeant-Pilot McEwan, my load a Tetrarch tank, and eight soldiers under a Lieutenant Starkey.

Everything went smoothly from take-off, in Essex, and we crossed the Rhine. Just after we pulled off we were hit by flak, and I was hit in the legs, and a few seconds later, gliding down through the smoke which had drifted across the landing zone, we were hit again. This time we lost bits of the glider, and the hydraulics were smashed. We careered across a field with no brakes or flaps and ended up with our nose in a ditch. One or two of the chaps were hurt, but not many—and they scrambled out and began to dig in. Mac had joined them, and shouted for me to join them. I tried but my legs were jammed and I told him that I would just stay put.

Just at that moment some Germans opened up with a machine-gun, and bullets spattered across the glass of the cockpit. I was out of that cockpit and found myself lying waist deep in the water in the ditch, along with the others.

As all the officers were wounded, Sergeant McEwan took charge and all the troops followed him. He had had only three weeks army training—so it says a great deal for his leadership. On one occasion he was put on to guard a collection of German prisoners in a house, when along came American parachutists who attacked the house and eventually McEwan had to "surrender" to the Americans!

Nevertheless, we of the R.A.F. were immensely proud of the fact that we took part in the battle.

Squadron-leader V. H. Reynolds made his approach to the landing under intense ack-ack fire. The colonel of the Oxford and Bucks Light Infantry was his chief passenger and he had requested that Reynolds should put him down near a railway station. As they descended they found there was a flak emplacement near this railway station, and they landed between the flak battery and the station itself. Nevertheless he, like many others, managed to bring his glider down in a perfect position, and immediately took part in the attack on the ack-ack battery, which was captured. He fought on, like many other soldiers, with courage and distinction.

Some of the gliders landed within only 200 yards of their objective, despite the conditions. Some of course were smashed to pieces by ack-ack fire, or crashed to the ground. The gliders of the bridge force landed with pin-point accuracy, and both bridges were captured intact.

The Hamilcars were carrying bulldozers and Morris trucks and petrol, and it was indeed a stupendous feat to land a Hamilcar glider with such a load. The glider itself weighs sixteen tons. In one case the bottom of a Hamilcar gave way and the tank it was carrying came tumbling through to the ground, with the crew following. This was the only known instance of a glider breaking up in the air.

The demoralization of the enemy was revealed by a strange incident. One of the gliders crashed on landing and both pilots were hurled through the perspex covering the cockpit. The remainder of the passengers were terribly injured. In the crash the glider pilots' rifles were bent like croquet hoops. One staggered to his feet and walked back in a daze to the wreck of the glider. Sitting on a wheel, holding his head, and with his bent rifle on his knee, he heard voices, and looking up, saw about twenty German soldiers surrendering to him, despite the fact that he was alone, surrounded by dead, and his rifle was bent in half!

Brigadier G. K. Bourne, O.B.E., described his sensation as he came down in a glider as a passenger: "I wanted to see what was happening. I could see the Rhine as a silver streak and beyond it a black haze, for all the world like Manchester or Birmingham as seen from the air. For a moment I wondered if the bombing of Wesel had been out of time and had preceded the attack. If so the whole zone would be covered in smoke."

His glider landed 200 yards from his briefed spot. By one o'clock that afternoon all the objectives had been captured and by ten o'clock that evening General Ridgway had been able to pay the division a visit. At 10 a.m. the following morning, March 25th, the link between the airborne forces and the 2nd Army was strong and unbreakable.

Thus ended the airborne phase of the operation. The lessons of the earlier battles had been truly learned. This time nothing had been left to chance, everything was tied up completely. It resulted in an astounding victory.

It was not, however, carried out without cost, for the Glider Pilot Regiment suffered over 100 pilots killed, missing and wounded, but I had the great pleasure of writing out citations of a military kind for the R.A.F. glider pilots, and flying awards for the glider pilots of the regiment.

13

THE REGIMENT DISBANDS . . . BUT LIVES ON

THE PRECEDING CHAPTERS have told the fighting story of the Glider Pilot Regiment, and all that remains is to give a brief outline of its activities before it was finally disbanded in 1957. Before the cessation of hostilities, and for some time after, the regiment was kept together and used in various capacities in many sectors of the world.

INDIA

In accordance with the conditions agreed on when our "improvisation" scheme was adopted after the heavy losses at Arnhem, in India the regiment came under the command of the Royal Air Force, who employed it in a number of ways, not the least important being for the re-supply of China.

It had been planned to use gliders in an attack on Malaya, and I had been sent out to India to study the terrain, and had lectured there to both Mountbatten's and General Auchinleck's staffs. Little was known of airborne warfare in that sphere, but an Indian airborne division was in the process of being organized and finally took shape as the 44th Indian Airborne Division, commanded by Major-General E. Downes, C.B.E. It was very widely dispersed and must have been most difficult to command.

It was soon found that the wooden type of glider (such as the Horsa and Hamilcar) was unsuitable for operation in the Far East because of the climate, and the glider crews therefore changed over to the American Waco gliders. At about the same time the glider pilots learned that their passengers would be Indian troops and that, in the event of their officers becoming casualties, the glider pilots would have to take command. There was, of course, nothing new about this, since on many occasions in Europe pilots had taken over command in emergencies. Nevertheless, because of the different personnel involved and the new type of terrain, courses in leadership, on jungle survival, mountain warfare, trekking and skiing (the last-

222

named for action in the Himalayas or in Kashmir), were arranged for them and were enthusiastically attended by the pilots.

Three airfields were developed, at Bilanpur, Raipur, and Kiangi Road, and a great many Wacos were flown to these airfields from over 300 miles away. Here, unfortunately, a cyclone wrecked a large number of them and there was considerable delay in replacing them. While waiting for the replacements, however, training still went on. There were endurance trials of ten consecutive hours' flying, and of flying at a height of 10,000 feet, and the Indian troops, in preparation for the planned attack on the Japanese, were given lifts to acclimatize them to airborne operations. Then, just when tension had reached breaking point and the troops seemed in sight of going into action, hostilities against Japan ceased. The contribution of the Glider Pilot Regiment to the war of 1939-45 had come to an end.

PALESTINE : BERLIN AIRLIFT : KOREA : MALAYA

After the cessation of hostilities the Regiment ran down rapidly until only three squadrons remained in the United Kingdom and one in Palestine.

It was in the September of 1945 that the Glider Pilot Regiment was ordered to Palestine with the 6th Airborne Division, and by Christmas the personnel were making last preparations for the voyage. There is no need here to go into the rights and wrongs of the unhappy events that were then taking place in that country, but it must be said, that there are few forces in the world capable of exercising so much self-discipline, patience and control under provocation as the men who served in the British Army in Palestine in the period that preceded Britain's relinquishment of her mandate over Palestine. Among these men were members of the Glider Pilot Regiment whose main duties were the local defence of the airfields on which they were stationed, duties which included nightly patrols round the airfields and nearby villages and settlements, the guarding of arms and ammunition, security checks which sometimes involved house-to-house search, and divisional searches, which were serious affairs since they were often ordered with the object of finding terrorists and caches of ammunition. The men of the regiment acquitted themselves as they had done during the war, and I can offer no greater praise than that.

By 1948 the regiment found itself down to a headquarters and training squadron based at Aldershot, and two operational squadrons, A and B, which were based at Waterbeach and Netheravon respectively. A Hamilcar flight which was part of B squadron existed at Fairford. Fargo, by this time, was no longer the Glider Pilot Regimental Depot and, in fact, was soon to disappear completely from the face of Salisbury Plain.

With the closing down of various R.A.F. elementary flying training schools all potential glider pilots eventually became the charge of R.A.F., Booker, near High Wycombe, a pleasant little grass field station equipped with Tiger Moths and Austers, the latter for the use of trainee Air O.P. pilots who eventually finished their advanced training at the Air O.P. School at Middle Wallop. The glider pilots' advanced training was carried out at R.A.F., Upper Heyford, where a conversion was made straight from Tigers to Horsa II's without the intermediate stage on Hotspurs.

In late 1948 glider flying came to a standstill with the commandeering of nearly all tug-aircraft for the Berlin airlift. As much flying training as was possible was carried out with the few Tiger Moths in the squadron but it soon became obvious that the airlift was to be more than just a two-month affair and that it was therefore necessary to find some other means of occupying the crews. The C.O. of the regiment, Lieutenant-Colonel C. J. Deedes, managed to persuade the R.A.F. that a worth-while job the glider pilots could perform was to assist Transport Command crews flying in and out of Berlin. One flight of pilots drawn from both squadrons therefore attended an Air Quartermaster Course at R.A.F., Hartford, and on New Year's Day 1949 the flight reported to R.A.F., Wunsdorf, in Germany, ostensibly to help with the colossal loading problem which existed at all the airlift fields. It was soon apparent, however, that the rear airfield supply officers had the situation well under control and that these keen new air quartermasters were not needed. In no time, however, each York crew short of a second pilot found itself with a "Red Beret" in the right-hand seat, and after convincing the captains that they did know something about flying, the glider pilots were warmly accepted as members of the respective squadrons. The glider pilots found that they were able to get a great deal of instrument flying which, apart from being useful to themselves, was of considerable help to the aircraft captains. A second glider pilot flight existed at R.A.F., Schleswig, where most of the pilots were able to join Hastings crews, many of whom had only recently been tug crews on Halifaxes back in U.K. A friendly rivalry ensued between Schleswig and Wunsdorf flights—particularly between the respective flight commanders.

All types of weather were encountered and only the very worst of conditions ever brought the "lift" to a stop. The York aircraft landed at Gatow in Berlin while the Hastings landed at the new airfield by the name of Tegel in the French sector.

Every conceivable commodity had to be lifted into the hard-pressed city, but after the initial difficulties had been overcome it was obvious that the "lift" could succeed even if it had to go on indefinitely. Besides food and clothing, large amounts of coal, and even petroleum and other liquid fuels, were transported by civil air tankers. Operation Plainfare, as the "lift" was more properly known, was a tremendous operation in which every glider pilot was proud to take part.

One unfortunate accident marred the glider pilots' memories of Operation Plainfare. This was the death of Staff-Sergeant Toal in a Hastings crash while taking off from Tegel. He was buried with the rest of the crew in the military cemetery near the Olympic Stadium in the British sector of Berlin.

It was not unusual for the empty aircraft flying out of Berlin to carry Service passengers. On one occasion, after off-loading a cargo of dehydrated vegetables, one aircraft captain was ordered to report to the tarmac in front of the tower where a V.I.P. was to be picked up. It was apparent from the size of the party accompanying the V.I.P. that he was a very senior officer. The aircraft was duly parked in the right place, passenger emplaning steps were pushed up to the door and the crew stood alongside the aircraft to receive their passenger.   From the entourage stepped Field-Marshal Lord Wavell, dressed as Colonel of the Black Watch. He was met by the aircraft captain, Flight Lieutenant White of 206 Squadron, R.A.F., who in turn introduced the crew, one of whom, the second pilot, was Captain Downward, the glider pilot flight commander at Wunsdorf. While the remainder of the crew set about preparing the aircraft for flight, the second pilot—whilst answering numerous questions on why he, as a soldier, was part of an aeroplane crew—attempted to brief the great man on normal safety precautions and emergency drills and finally to fit a parachute on him. An observer type 'shute had been provided, where only the harness needed to be worn during flight. Captain Downward fitted and adjusted the shoulder straps and then reached down to pull the leg straps from the back, through the passenger's legs and ultimately to the securing box in the centre of the body. Downward's sudden embarrassment had been anticipated by the numerous press photographers whose fusillade of flashes recorded a moment of horror when the harness fitting was brought to a halt by the realization that the Field-Marshal was not properly dressed for this part of the journey—he was wearing his kilt! The A.O.C., who was in the farewell party, came to the rescue by issuing a quick verbal amendment to Air Ministry Flying Orders by allowing V.I.P.s dressed in kilts to fly with only the shoulder straps adjusted until such time as the captain considered an emergency was imminent; leg straps would then be properly adjusted!

After the end of the airlift glider flying was resumed, and trainee pilots who had been waiting for over a year to go on to the heavy glider conversion stage were able to complete their training and to gain their wings. The courses were run at R.A.F., Upper Heyford, which was also the Parachute School. Since the days of the Central Landing Establishment at Ringway in 1940, the wheel of fortune appeared to have turned a full circle, for now both parts of airborne forces—gliders and parachutes—were back to small selective establishments and once again sharing the same school. Similarly, Netheravon became the joint user station for the continuation training of both regiments.

A land air warfare demonstration which was periodically staged at Netheravon was Exercise Mephisto. This was a display of parachute troop dropping, heavy equipment dropping, free dropping and a full display of glider equipment, including an exhibition of a glider "snatch" in the Waco glider by Staff-Sergeant Bell. This pilot could keep up an almost non-stop relay with the Waco. The tow rope, which was made of nylon to give extra elasticity, was looped at one end and the other end was plugged into the towing point on the glider. The loop was arranged so that a length of rope was suspended from the tops of two posts about thirty feet apart. The tug-aircraft, which had to be specially adapted for this rôle, then flew towards the loop which it aimed to engage with a rigid boom protruding downwards from the fuselage. As contact was made, the hook on the tip of the boom was allowed to pay out on the end of a steel cable which was wound round a winch inside the tug aircraft. By carefully braking the feed-out of the cable the whole tow-line between tug and glider would eventually become steady. The whole snatch operation required very skilful operation by the winch operator as well as precision flying by the pilots at either end of the combination. Too hasty a braking action of the winch while paying out usually resulted in the cable snapping and the glider being placed in difficulties while at low height.

The glider Pilot Regiment, however, was not the only unit to suffer embarrassment arising from the Mephisto demonstrations. The heavy equipment drops, arranged by the Army Air Transport Development Centre, frequently provided breathtaking spectacles as jeeps and field guns were released on clusters of outsize parachutes from transport aircraft. The occasional failure of one or more parachutes usually resulted in a rapid descent of the load with devastating consequences as it struck the ground. The free dropping of nonbreakable items such as bales of blankets, M.T. spares suitably padded, and vehicle tyres, all helped to keep the spectators on their toes; particularly if a large three-tonner tyre, recovering from its initial impact with the ground by bouncing to a height of about one hundred feet, then decided to change direction towards the crowd.

In 1950 the Glider Pilot Regiment suffered a further reduction by elimination of A and B Squadrons and the Training Squadron, becoming a single squadron as from 1st September. This squadron, known as the 1st Independent Squadron the Glider Pilot Regiment, was commanded by Major R. King Clark, M.C., who, pre-war, had achieved notoriety by being the first Army officer to "troop" himself overseas in his own private aircraft when he flew his Miles Whitney direct to Egypt in 1937 to join the 1st Battalion of the Manchester Regiment. The second-in-command of the new squadron was Major Stonor; and the three flight-commanders, Captains Johnson, Brown and Downward. The regiment—which for so long had worn the distinctive badge of the eagle surmounting the initials A.A.C., the whole surrounded by a laurel wreath—adopted a new badge which still retained the eagle but incorporated a scroll bearing the title of the regiment in place of the earlier wreath and A.A.C. The new badge was more appropriate, in that it gave the regiment its correct title; it had long been a favourite question by people outside the regiment, "Why does the Glider Pilot Regiment also call itself Army Air Corps?" The latter title had been the name given to airborne forces in general when they were first started in 1940 and then became a Record Office nomenclature which embraced Glider Pilot Regiment, Parachute Regiment and Special Air Service. The Glider Pilot Regiment, being the "first born", kept the Army Air Corps badge while the other regiments designed new emblems of their own. In 1950 the nomenclature Army Air Corps was dropped and was replaced by the Record Office title of Glider Pilot and Parachute Corps.

The occasion of the formation of the 1st Independent Squadron of the Glider Pilot Regiment (incidentally the second time in the life of the regiment that this title had been used) was marked by a small ceremony at Aldershot when, "in the presence of Brigadier Chatterton," the old flag was struck and the new one, bearing the new regimental badge, was hoisted in its place. The old squadrons marched off to disbandment followed by the new squadron whose task it was to keep alive the glider-flying technique as a form of cadre. The salute of the march past was taken by Lieutenant-Colonel Deedes, o.b.e., m.c. So departed the last of the wartime squadrons.

The 1st Independent Squadron continued to fly gliders, all Horsas, and the continuation training was carried out at Netheravon. No elementary flying courses were held and no new pilots joined the regiment. It was apparent that the rôle of gliders in modern warfare was disappearing fast, though the parachuting side of airborne forces still appeared to have a future. It was obvious that the slow-moving glider-tug combination was no match for modern weapons and fighter techniques. This point was brought home forcibly in an airborne exercise when, for the first time, jet fighters made short work of the glider formation.

About this time the new Hastings, of which we had heard so much, came into the airborne support rôle, and some towing was carried out behind this aircraft. The verdict of this trial was that it was damned hard work for the glider pilots who were finding themselves being tugged around the sky about forty knots faster than usual. The Horsa didn't appear to be very happy with either and the effects of the strain became apparent in increasing unserviceability. And so the towing continued as before, behind the faithful old Dakota which could cope happily with a lightly laden Horsa but was no match for the type of hauls seen during the war from U.K. to the Continent.

The training of the pilots of this lone squadron in normal ground tactics presented a further problem as there was no way of exercis-

A view of one of the fields where our gliders landed near Hammelkiln station.

Airborne troops engage the enemy on the outskirts of Arnhem with 75 mm. guns, September, 1944.

Austers now in use.

A Bristol helicopter in the Malayan jungle.

ing as a company of infantry; the scale of equipment wasn't designed for this rôle, and of course the number of men, both officers and other ranks, hardly made up a normal rifle platoon. It was decided, therefore, on the instigation of the commander of 16 Parachute Brigade Group, to attach one flight of glider pilots to each of the three parachute battalions for purposes of training when O.C. 1st Independent Squadron so desired. This arrangement worked very smoothly and the flights were looked after extremely well by the respective battalions. Besides gaining some valuable field training, some close friendships were built up in the officers' and sergeants' messes, and Aldershot—even if only for a short while—became the accepted home of both regiments. During this period quite a few glider pilots volunteered to do parachute courses, though unfortunately it was not possible to even up this exchange by offering any of the Parachute Regiment N.C.O.s a few hours' pilot training.

In 1951 the glider was officially doomed and it was clear there was little purpose in continuing with this expensive form of continuation training, even as a cadre. The problem of course was what was to happen to the thirty-odd pilots? Some could be taken back into their parent regiments though quite a few—particularly among the N.C.O.s—were not so well placed and the very suggestion that they should finish flying was strongly resented. However, an answer was not long in coming, for at this time the Commonwealth Division was forming in Korea and its G.O.C., Major-General Cassels, requested two flights of light aircraft. The first flight was made available almost straight away by the close proximity of 1903 Air O.P. Flight, R.A.F., in Hong-Kong. As a "Gunner" flight, their task was almost entirely devoted to supporting the Commonwealth Divisional Artillery, which comprised British, Canadian, and New Zealand field regiments. The second flight was not immediately available and in fact was not even formed. And so, in July 1951, a new type of flight was formed at Middle Wallop and was named 1913 Light Liaison Flight, R.A.F. This was entirely a glider pilot flight and basically was all infantry so far as the pilots were concerned. The flight was commanded by Captain P. A. Downward who had one officer, Capt. A. T. C. Brown, as second in charge and six staff-sergeants and sergeants.

1913 Flight went into immediate training in North Wales where it was felt that some value could be gained from flying around the mountainous areas which were the nearest approach to the Korean terrain. Having carried out as much training as time would allow, the flight returned to Middle Wallop and started the monotonous task of boxing all the kit, including the aircraft, for despatch by sea to Japan. The flight arrived in Japan in late September, and although very much on its own as an R.A.F. Unit it quickly got to work at R.A.A.F., Iwakuni, where the Australians could not have been more helpful; also eager to assist were the Royal Navy who had their reserve aircraft in store there.

By mid-October 1913 Flight was ready to move. The vehicles and ground personnel were loaded on to a ship in Kure, which by a piece of good fortune had on board as O.C. troops, one, Captain White, who had been in A Squadron up till 1949. The crossing to Pusan on the southern point of the Korean peninsula was smooth enough but a further sea passage was to follow in tank-landing-craft from Pusan to Inchon in order to save the party the rather hazardous journey up to the battle area. The aircraft meanwhile were able to cross the sea under escort of a Sunderland flying-boat, and eventually arrived at Seoul on the 8th Army air strip, which in former days had been the Seoul racecourse.

The move up to the battle area was delayed a couple of days while a new strip was being prepared to support the Commonwealth Division during its advance, but at last the flight was able to advance, the vehicles moving up through the shattered village of Uijongbu and arriving in a heavy drizzle on the site of the new strip on the edge of the Imjin River. The location, which was merely a patch of paddi, and pinpointed by latitude and longitude, was given the code name Fort George. As a strip it was quite the worst that the flight had ever seen; vehicles sank up to their axles in mud, and the moment an aircraft touched down it threw up a shower of muddy water which almost completely blinded the pilot, whose main concern was then to keep the aircraft on the strip. The landing run was no more than twenty yards and gave the pilot the feeling of having landed aboard a fleet carrier. Taxi-ing could be carried out only at full throttle, and after six aircraft had landed it was apparent they were not going to get off again until some very drastic action had been taken to improve the surface. The Canadian sappers proved their resourcefulness by obtaining some drums of napalm from an American air base and, after aircraft and vehicles had been removed to a safe distance, flooding the strip with this highly combustible mixture. A Very light was then fired at the strip which reluctantly began to burn and eventually baked into a hard surface on which aircraft were able to take off and land. Soon 1913 Flight was joined by 1903 Flight, which moved forward to support the advance. The flights occupied opposite ends of the strip and combined their respective messes, though both units were operationally entirely independent.

Much valuable experience had been gained by the gunner flight during its few weeks in the theatre, and this experience was handed on to the glider pilots who were keen to take on the recce rôle over the line. No definite rôle had been laid down for the Light Liaison Flight and the G.O.C. gave the flight-commander almost carte blanche to develop his task as he saw best. General running about of the staff was obviously a big requirement, and the flight set to with passenger-carrying to rear strips, despatch runs, and numerous other tasks that the staff suddenly found could be carried out by this new flight. Captain Downward, the flight commander, was keen to use his flight to more effect and gradually a recce rôle was built up in support of the infantry and armour. This had the effect of relieving the Air O.P. Flight of the task of taking up passengers during "shoots," many of which were of two and a half hours' duration. The glider pilots (as mentioned earlier) being basically infantrymen were able to give valuable assistance to the numerous infantry unit and patrol commanders who wished to see only one particular part of the front. The liaison and understanding of the forward units was further improved by two or three-day visits from the individual pilots. Pilots found that they were "adopted" by their own favoured units in the line and conversely pilots were keen to support those units when there was a call for air recce.

Flying over the Korean front was reminiscent of aerial warfare in the 1914-18 war. Sorties were carried out between five and seven thousand feet, and looking down from aircraft the perfect demarcation of the line could clearly be seen by the large amount of digging and earth works on both sides, the Communists favouring long communication trenches which stretched for miles back into the rear areas. Binoculars were invaluable for examining the ground, and with the help of aerial photographs much valuable information was collected by the pilots. Aerial recce for the untrained observer could be a complete waste of time unless he was fully briefed and constantly orientated throughout the sortie by the pilot. Normally, anyone taken up for the first time in a light aircraft had not the slightest idea of the direction he was facing or where to compare his map with the ground; aerial photographs again proved to be extremely helpful.

1913 Flight remained in Korea for some time after the armistice in 1953—under the command of Captain P. F. Wilson and, later, of Captain M. Hickey—until its return to U.K. With the armistice and the return of prisoners came Sergeant Cameron, who was shot down a few weeks earlier and who, together with his passenger, had managed to bale out. Happily one of the Air O. P. Flight also returned from a similar, though longer, experience as a P.O.W.

Of the number of officers and sergeants who were not absorbed into the 1st Independent Squadron of the Glider Pilot Regiment, a few were asked if they would like to assist the Air O.P. Squadron operating in Malaya, where terrorist activities in the jungle were hotting up and the call for light aircraft support for the security forces was increasing steadily. Two officers and four sergeants were diverted to Austers and duly dispatched to 656 Air O.P. Squadron R.A.F. in Malaya, where they were able to take on a valuable share of the task of searching the vast areas of jungle for the Communist terrorists hideouts. Captain D. T. Young (one of the two officers) was the first glider pilot after the war to win the D.F.C. and Sergeant J. Hutchings the first to win the D.F.M. Although it was not realized at the time, these few officers and N.C.O.s were the pioneers of a new flying unit in the British Army which was ultimately to play a big part in producing the present-day Army Air Corps.

In Malaya two flights of 656 Air O.P. Squadron R.A.F. had gradually been built up with the above-mentioned new pilots from the Glider Pilot Regiment. Eventually, with their own glider pilot flight commanders, they became so completely "red beret" that it was thought best to re-name the flights as Light Liaison Flights instead of Air O.P. And so, 1907 and 1911 Flights were re-named and the squadron itself became 656 Air O.P./Light Liaison Squadron R.A.F. The work this squadron did in the Malayan emergency was of immense value to the security forces, pilots flying a great many hours, sometimes up to 100 hours per month during intensive operations, the results of the searches and recces being proportionately rewarding. To spread the load as much as possible flights were "rotated" round the five strips every few months. This meant that no flight was banished for too long to an outlandish strip while another enjoyed a more comfortable station, such as the Royal Naval Air Station, H.M.S. *Simbang*, on Singapore. Although not actively engaged in an all-out shooting war as in Korea, the flying task was no less hazardous. A considerable amount of night flying was carried out, and pilots target-marked with flares suspected terrorist hide-outs in order that bomber aircraft could strike the enemy where he was most likely to be concentrated. Whether the bombing was effective in causing casualties to the terrorists was rarely discovered; nevertheless, it did cause the enemy discomfort and eventually forced the terrorists to abandon their hideouts and—most valuable of all —the cultivated plots which provided the main part of their daily food. Jungle flying unfortunately took its toll of two old glider pilots. Staff-Sergeant Gay was killed while flying in the Johore area and Sergeant Perry disappeared without trace over the jungle of Northern Malaya. Actually, the wreckage of Perry's aircraft was discovered purely by chance some six years later. To be forced down in the jungle is one of the biggest fears of pilots operating in this type of terrain, for the jungle reveals absolutely nothing of what is on the ground below it. Trees up to 200 feet high would merely close over a crashed aircraft as if nothing had happened, while from the ground the picture was little better, as patrols often passed within yards of wreckage that had been swallowed up by the incredibly thick foliage. One glider pilot N.C.O. who achieved local fame in the early days of the emergency was Sergeant Webb. Having crashed into the jungle after an engine failure, he set to with his passenger to build a raft on the bank of a main river, which they managed to reach, and then sailed down-stream until they reached civilization. This was an outstanding example of resourcefulness and cool thinking which undoubtedly saved their lives. Another walk-out from the jungle was made by Sergeant McConnel, who, having crashed and been partially injured, with an open wound in one of his legs, hacked his way out of the jungle until he came to a Dyak community some twenty-one days later. He could not have survived much longer for he was by then considerably weakened from the effect of his injuries and lack of food. McConnel's determination to survive was certainly what brought him through this very hazardous ordeal.

By late 1956 plans were afoot for the Army to own and operate its own aircraft and these were to include helicopters. It was appar-

ent that the days of the Glider Pilot Regiment were numbered. In
early 1957 Major Downward handed over command of the regiment
to its last C.O., Major M. W. Sutcliffe, who had the regrettable task
of closing the regiment down eight months later, on 31st August,
1957. The Light Liaison rôle joined forces with the Air O.P. rôle
and from this was born the new Army Air Corps which started its
existence on 1st September, 1957. The close down of the regiment
was marked by a farewell ceremony at Middle Wallop in rather
dismal weather conditions. The rain, however, failed to prevent the
last fly-past at the tail of which came the regimental flag towed by
a Skeeter helicopter flown by Major Furnivall.

The helicopter rose into the air and set course for the Military
College, Sandhurst. In front of me sat two officers of the Glider
Pilot Regiment—and beside me sat Major Peter Downward,
D.F.C.

As I looked at the three red berets, I realized that this was a
unique moment. The fact that these pilots were all helicopter pilots
but sported the regimental badge of the Glider Pilot Regiment was
significant. I had witnessed a full turn of fortune's wheel, and as
we sped through the sky I was deeply moved.

My mind sped back to a day fourteen-odd years before, when I
arrived at Tilshead Camp on Salisbury Plain. I was alone there, but
for my batman Alec Gaul. It was here that I was to form the
nucleus of the glider pilot Regiment. That was in January 1942,
nine months after the German airborne invasion of Crete in which
the Germans had used an insignificant number of gliders and, as a
result, had achieved nothing of any lasting merit. I was destined to
see the full development of airborne forces, and the crushing defeat
of the German Army at the Rhine crossing.

Now, the glider's life was ended and I was sitting in a helicopter
piloted by the last of the Glider Pilot Regiment. We circled the
Military College and down below I could see row upon row of cars
belonging to the generals, who were all attending the same ceremony
as I.

We landed on the cricket pitch and Peter Downward and I stepped
to the ground. "Surprise was complete", for I was mistaken for a
Royal personage—and when it was found I was not, there was Hell
to pay!

There is little to add. On 31st August, 1957, the Glider Pilot

Regiment was disbanded, merged with the Flying O.P. Royal Artillery, and the new Army Air Corps was born.

The experience had proved one thing to be true, that the wartime motto of the regiment was no exaggeration:

" Nothing is impossible."

*   *   *

People have often asked, "Why should we have an Army Air Corps? What was wrong with the old system where the Royal Air Force was responsible for the aircraft, the servicing and the pilot training?" Admittedly there might be some justification for thinking that this was just another air force that could do little to improve the doctrine administered by such an experienced service as the R.A.F. Prior to 1957, particularly in the 1939–45 war years, such a feeling might well have been true, but by 1957 it was outstandingly clear that the Royal Air Force's task was far removed from the days of fabric-covered light aircraft and operating from grass fields. The high performance jet aircraft presented an entirely new conception of aerial warfare.

Since the days of the 1914–18 war, when aircraft first made their appearance in support of the Army, it has been a common-sense point of view that the most intimate support came from pilots or observers experienced in ground rôle. To the sceptic mind this may appear superfluous, for all that is required is to teach an airman the principles of the soldier's task and let him get on with it. Here at last we come to the vital point. One may be able to teach the principles of soldiering but one can never substitute the experience of that trade. It must be remembered that the Army aircraft is in no way intended to be an offensive weapon requiring the highly skilled operation of a pilot trained to deliver a costly and highly lethal bomb or missile. To the Army, the light aircraft or helicopter is primarily a means of conveyance which provides the soldier with a further means of mobility or a platform from which to improve his observation. In this modern age, with the whole military concept a slave to automation and technical "know how", the task of the commander is now far too complicated for one man to perform without the advice of a team of experts. One of these must now be the army pilot.

The Air O.P. organization of the Royal Artillery proved from its early conception that the most efficient direction of the guns by aerial observation came, not unnaturally, from a gunner. Although this point is so obvious it was frequently ignored or forgotten when discussing the merits of airman versus soldier as pilot in support of the ground forces. With the start of Light Liaison in 1951 the advantage of the soldier as an aerial support to other arms outside the Royal Artillery became firmly established in Korea and Malaya. There is no mystery connected with the army pilot to enable him to do this. It is essential that he remains at all times primarily a soldier and secondly an aviator. He must be as much a part of the ground forces as the officer or N.C.O. in the forward observation post or the recee troop commander in the armoured car. He must be able to appreciate the ground situation, to advise the commander or even to guide the junior N.C.O. about to take out a patrol—or even to nurse him through his mission by keeping in contact from the air.

Do not feel that the flying side of the task is considered as unimportant or that the Army pays any less attention to the quality of its pilots than does the R.A.F. The pilots, who are all volunteers, are carefully selected in accordance with the R.A.F. standards for aircrew suitability and are further screened by an Army board for suitability as soldiers. The potential pilot is then trained in accordance with the Army Air Corps syllabus and after nine months training at Middle Wallop the fledgeling is then turned out fully qualified to operate from the shortest of strips, to low fly, navigate, establish communications and perform his task as a soldier. The Army aeroplane, whether a conventional aircraft or a helicopter, must be regarded purely as a vehicle from which the soldier performs his task.

Of the men that fly these aircraft, most are officers and the balance are N.C.O.s and, like the old Glider Pilot Regiment and the Air O.P. organization, all are volunteers. A large number of pilots come from the Royal Artillery, the Royal Armoured Corps and the infantry line regiments, besides many from the corps and services. The maintenance of the aircraft is the responsibility of the R.E.M.E., though it is not unusual to see sailors and airman working alongside the craftsmen in all Army Air Corps units world wide. This is purely a temporary measure to tide over the shortage of technicians.

Unlike modern air forces, the essence of army aviation must be simplicity of equipment and operating techniques. The Army pilot, as always, must be an individual prepared to fly, work and fight with the troops that he supports. There can be no reliance on black boxes, navigational devices and ground operated aids in time of war, particularly in the forward areas; and to this end the Army pilot is trained to fly his fixed wing aeroplane or helicopter relying on his own strength, intelligence and courage.

Because the requirements are exacting, the standard of man in the Army Air Corps is high. On visiting an Army Air Corps unit one cannot fail to notice the high morale and keenness that are always the "hall-mark" of any volunteer force. There is an air of efficiency and a professional approach to their very wide selection of tasks.

Any Glider Pilot Regiment veteran of the last war would see little change in the pilots in the blue berets of 1962 to the generation of twenty years earlier who built up the first Army Air Corps; the men who took in the gliders laden with troops, anti-tank guns, vehicles and ammunition to Sicily, Normandy, Arnhem and the Rhine. There is still that same pride in their unit which stems from one quality—unfortunately lacking in so many young men of to-day—a pride in oneself. They fly well but, as they will show you (they don't need to tell you) they are soldiers, and soldiers of the highest quality and integrity. The men of the old Glider Pilot Regiment and the old Air O.P. can be proud of their successors and can rest assured that their good name is in safe hands.

POSTSCRIPT

I AM writing the conclusion to this book in May 1962.

The world is now in a strange and terrible situation. Both sides of the Iron Curtain face each other stalemated—for the moment—by the terrible weapons to hand.

I was recently privileged to visit the H.Q. of our deterrent force. It was an awe-inspiring experience, but my most overwhelming impression was of the dedication of the flying and ground personnel. There is no let-up night and day, and the inspiration of this force is "The Preservation of Peace". This is the guiding principle. The entire force is fully aware that it has the means of world annihilation at its disposal—if that means were ever to be used—so that there is little to hope for once the die is cast. Yet, *because* of this knowledge, their spirit and discipline is of the very highest order.

It is the same spirit that prevailed in the Air Force 30 years ago—the spirit which is described in the opening to this book, and which is common to nearly all voluntary forces. (It is not often realized that all the flying personnel of the R.A.F. were volunteers throughout the war—as were the pilots of the Glider Pilot Regiment.)

The Glider Pilot Regiment is no more—for the Army Air Corps has now absorbed it, as it has the Flying O.P. Royal Artillery. Yet it was the Regiment that first made the Army "air minded", and paved the way for the present "A.A.C.", now complete with its own light aircraft and helicopters.

The Army of to-day has a new function, and needs a new outlook to go with it. It must be prepared to move as rapidly as is possible, to prevent *minor* campaigns from developing into a *major* war. Thus both the Army and the R.A.F. have vital rôles to play—not in the making of war, but in its localization and suppression. It is obvious that this new outlook will always require men of vision and courage.

238

Understandably and rightly, the coming generation is preoccupied with what is now the stark necessity of keeping the peace. But I know, through dealing with many youth organizations over a long period, that one of the most important things which young people *still* require is Adventure. I feel sure that such organizations as the Duke of Edinburgh's Award Scheme, which includes the Outward Bound and similar schemes, must be of the utmost importance to this country. The young men of the Glider Pilot Regiment stepped forward to volunteer, impelled by a craving for adventure. The young men of to-day feel this craving just as acutely. The art of flying, including sports such as sky diving by parachute, gliding and of course powered flight are among the most logical modern means of fulfilling that craving.

Perhaps I might end this postscript by quoting the words which are painted in platinum paint on the memorial to the Glider Pilot Regiment in St. Martin-in-the-Fields. This memorial is the head and shoulders of a young pilot, and beneath it is one of the last flags to fly at the mast:

"To the memory of a Regiment which died in name only, but left its spirit, Service, behind."

Appendix I

ACHIEVEMENTS AND PERSONALITIES

IT IS amazing to think back to August 1942 when I flew in a formation of 8-seater Hotspurs towed by 8 bi-planes, which were called Hectors, to land in front of Sir Winston Churchill (and to nearly run him down), while in a fury he watched a handful of parachutists land near by. Yet within the short space of three years 2,000-odd gliders had been landed all over Europe and in formations of 400 at a time. I do not know the exact number of men carried, but it must have been in the region of 20,000. These were landed by glider *into* the battlefield. Also some 3,000 tons of tanks, guns, jeeps and supplies were landed in support, and all of this in the immediate vicinity of the battle.

The coup-de-main night flights on to the bridges of Ponte Grande in Sicily were an epic, and provided a basis to work on. Also the landings on the bridges over the Caen Canal and the River Orne during the invasion of Normandy were among the finest pieces of flying that I have ever seen. It has not been surpassed by any nation.

The development of the Hamilcar glider was remarkable. Major Dickie Dale, D.F.C., was the magnificent leader of this force. How can one adequately describe the achievement? Can the hugeness of these gliders really be appreciated? Can it be truly believed that the cockpit was twenty-five feet from the ground, and that the pilots would have to climb down from that cockpit and release the oil from the oleo legs and let the air out of the tyres in order that the load of tanks, jeeps and trucks could emerge? And all of this done under fire in the middle of the battlefield?

The co-operation of the Royal Air Force was an example to all. The standard of training in the R.A.F. flying training schools showed nothing but the best and was able to stand every glider pilot in good stead, particularly when he was desperate for practice and had to take gliders into action without any practice whatsoever.

To Air Vice Marshal Leonard Hollinghurst is owed the virtual existence and success of the regiment, and he made it a reality. A less imaginative or more hidebound senior officer—and they did exist in the R.A.F.—would have caused a disaster. This attitude was maintained by Air Vice Marshal Scarlett-Streatfeild when he took over for the Rhine crossing.

Another officer who saw through the "smokescreen" was Air Commodore Fidderment, O.C. 46 Group. We owe him a great debt for his understanding and good humour.

And now let us turn to the Army.

Of course it was immense good fortune that Sir Alan Brooke became the Colonel Commandant of the Regiment. That he was there was enough. His kindness and consideration to me on my all-too-frequent visits to his office were an inspiration, and much that happened to the regiment to their advantage came through him. We were indeed lucky to have such an honour.

I enter here a cable that he sent to me on the day that we returned from Normandy after the invasion:

FROM C.I.G.S. WAR OFFICE 050922A
TO COMMANDER GLIDER PILOTS,
AIRBORNE CORPS REAR
QQX BT

SIGS/BM/22/8674/18 RESTRICTED FOR COLONEL CHATTERTON
FROM FIELD MARSHALL BROOKE. AS COLONEL COMMANDANT OF THE
GLIDER PILOT REGIMENT I WISH TO CONVEY TO THE REGIMENT MY
ADMIRATION FOR THE COURAGE AND DEVOTION TO DUTY SHOWN
BY ALL RANKS IN THE RECENT AIRBORNE OPERATIONS. THE SKILL
AND DARING DISPLAYED IN THE SUCCESSFUL LANDING OF THEIR
GLIDERS IN THE FACE OF OPPOSITION AND THEIR PART IN THE
SUBSEQUENT BITTER FIGHTING HAS FULLY JUSTIFIED THE
CONFIDENCE PLACED IN THE REGIMENT AND ADDS YET ANOTHER
FINE CONTRIBUTION TO THE TRADITIONS OF THE ARMY AIR CORPS.

BT 050922A

General "Boy" Browning was another source of inspiration. At the very beginning he saw the great possibilities of the regiment. It was he who obtained the instructors from the Brigade of Guards. He was visionary enough to see that if the finest training and standards could be instilled at the outset success would be the result in the end. His desire to fly was enough, and the fact that I was able to send him solo in the same time as a man much younger than he, is a great credit to him. I am of the opinion that he had the most incredibly difficult job in raising the first airborne division. I, too, had a taste of the frustrations inflicted by the impossible outlook of those who should have known better.

In the critical hours of the battles for Arnhem, Nijmegen and Eindhoven, he did everything possible, only to have the full fruits of victory snatched from his grasp.

It was no fault of his that the radio failed, or that there was armour near Arnhem, nor was the fact that 30 Corps was held up between Nijmegen and Arnhem and could not follow through in time. No one could have envisaged the fatal resistance to the Guards Armoured Division at Elst. I saw a colourful and congratulatory letter to him from Montgomery in the middle of the battle when all was going well. Surely that was enough. It was a sad day for me when he left to become Chief of Staff to Mountbatten in the Far East.

General Gale followed General Browning. Here was a real personality, with drive and ambition. Somehow I never really hit it off with him. But there is no doubt that his bluff character, humour and drive were vital to airborne affairs, and he succeeded in all he did.

General Hopkinson had been a good friend of mine. As I have said, he was tremendously enthusiastic for his gliders, because he was an amateur pilot before the war. He showed me great gererosity at Ponte Grande in Sicily by meeting me in his jeep. I know that he was fully aware of the disastrous effect the operation might have on me and others if he did not show his enthusiasm for the effort we had made. I was very friendly with him and deeply sad at his death.

Major-General Urquhart I also saw a great deal. Here was a real tough soldier, very much one of the "Monty" school. He wrote a very nice letter to me after the battle of Arnhem, which I think shows his generosity and brave character. Here is the letter.

Headquarters 1st Airborne Division,
A.P.O., England.   *21st October, 1944.*

Dear George,

As a humble chauffeur, I think you write a very good letter. Thank you so much for it and your remarks. You know that I, as well as you, regret the heavy losses that the Glider Pilot Regiment had in Holland. There is no doubt about their success, both as airmen and soldiers, for they have made a name for themselves which should help in providing a background during the reconstruction of the regiment.

I am delighted to see that Iain Murray has got the D.S.O. You might tell him quietly that I was going to put him in for it but was told not to under the circumstances.

Hope we shall meet again soon,

Yours ever,

Roy Urquhart.

Major-General Eric Bols, who commanded the 6th Airborne Division on the Rhine, was a dashing and brilliant officer. He again was one of the "Monty" school, and new to airborne warfare. I feel that he was a little unfortunate to encounter his first tactical landing by an airborne division in dense smoke. This made him a little critical of the gliders and their landings and he did not fail to say so afterwards. Nevertheless he had great courage and inspired leadership, and we all admired him very much.

The three air landing brigade commanders all varied in personality. Brigadier Pip Hicks was my immediate chief in the Sicilian operation. Big, bluff and humorous, he became my great friend. He did not know what fear was, and he was dearly loved by all. His distinguished courage at Arnhem is legendary. He was a very splendid type of Englishman and soldier, and very sympathetic to the Glider Pilot Regiment and to all the problems that it faced.

Brigadier Kindersley was a different type. He commanded the 6th Air Landing Brigade under General Gale. A distinguished man in his own right, he was an officer of the Brigade of Guards and set an immensely high standard in his own air landing brigade. He had been an amateur pilot before the war and therefore had

quite an eye for the Glider Pilot Regiment. He subsequently supported glider pilot flying wings. I had my own views on this, but
said nothing. I fought him on one point and that was the indepen-
dence of the Glider Pilot Regiment, which point, of course, I
eventually won!

Brigadier Ralph Bellamy, who commanded the 6th Air Landing
Brigade on the Rhine, was a charming man, full of gaiety and
laughter. He was immensely sympathetic to the Glider Pilot Regiment and as a result all problems put before him were quickly ironed
out—and success followed.

I came in contact with most of the parachute commanders. In
some way we seemed to live in a different world, despite the immense
importance of one to the other. Brigadiers Lathbury and Hackett
were outstanding men of courage and leadership, as were Hill and
Poett. They were all of a type which it is an honour to meet.
Lieutenant-Colonel John Frost was also outstanding as a character,
a man to whom there was no such word as fear. The result of
their leadership has been the mainstay of the whole airborne story.

Lieutenant-Colonel John Rock was the original commander. I
feel that the best tribute to him is the obituary already printed.
He was a man of steadfast courage and determination and the
regiment was never really able to recover from his loss.

Lieutenant-Colonel Iain Murray, D.S.O. and Bar, was one of the
outstanding characters in the regiment. He was one of the Guards
calibre—having been in the Grenadiers. His courage was legendary
and he was an example to us all.

Lieutenant-Colonel John Place was yet another who was inspired
to lead. He was with the regiment from the beginning and the
articles that he has supplied for this book are an example of his
character. He was loyalty personified to me.

Within the regiment one had the squadron commanders, on
whom fell so much responsibility. They were the backbone of the
whole affair, for it was up to them, isolated on the airfields, whether
the whole thing was a success or failure. Such men were Major
Ian Toler, D.F.C., whose diary of Arnhem has already been published; Major Peter Jackson, D.F.C., who joined the regiment at
its inception—a determined officer with a great sense of humour,
who showed great courage and leadership throughout.

Majors Bill Griffith, D.F.C., and Hugh Bartlett, D.F.C., who
won their decorations together, were my great friends; they were

inseparable from each other.   Famous cricketers both, they joined together.   The three of us landed side by side in Holland and Bill Griffith and Hugh Bartlett shared the same slit trench.

Major Dickie Dale, D.F.C. and Bar, I have mentioned.   His courage was also legendary and we all owed a great deal to him.

R.S.M. Briodey, M.B.E., was an outstanding man.   It was he who put the spirit into the regiment in the early Depot days. His personality was the spark and I say that the regiment knew none better than he.

*   *   *

I have mentioned many names in this book.   Obviously it is impossible to remark on all who were there.   Let it be said that all those I have mentioned—*and* those whom I have not—contributed alike to this story, a story of achievement which has the following figures to support its claims.

The numbers of officers and N.C.O.s who took part in the exploits of the Glider Pilot Regiment were as follows:

Officers	409
Staff-Sergeants and Sergeants ...	2,893
Making a total of	3,302 of all ranks
The casualties showed:	
Killed	551
Wounded	200
Prisoner-of-War	550
Total	1,301 casualties

The following were the numbers of awards given for gallantry in the field and otherwise:

D.S.O. 3	American Star 3
C.G.M. 1	Polish Cross 2
D.C.M. 7	Croix de Guerre ... 4
M.C. 24	A.F.C. 2
M.M. 31	A.F.M. 6
D.F.C. 26	M.B.E. 9
D.F.M. 52	B.E.M. 2

A total of 172.

R

In Salisbury Cathedral there is a memorial window: two 20-ft. lights. This was unveiled by Field Marshal Lord Alanbrook, and is a memorial to 551 officers and N.C.O.s who made the supreme sacrifice. In the Memorial Chapel lies a book of the Roll of Honour. Upon its covers are three badges: The Army Air Corps, The Glider Pilot Regiment and the Royal Air Force. In this book the names of all those who gave their lives are written. Fittingly, there are also the names of the Royal Air Force pilots who were killed in action fighting with the Glider Pilot Regiment on the Rhine. Surely this is the final endorsement of the perfection of the inter-Service co-operation which had been created by these men. Indeed when I asked that the glider pilots might stay upon the airfields and live, laugh and drink with the Royal Air Force, little did I realize that I should have added finally "and fight and die as comrades in arms on the ground". Yet this was so.

At the foot of the window are these words: words which I have had printed at the top of my Battalion and Final Regimental Orders during the war.

> See that ye hold fast the heritage that we leave you.
> Yea, and teach your children that never in the coming
> centuries may their hearts fail or their hands grow weak.

These words were taken from a pageant play, *Drake,* by Louis N. Parker. To me, they represent the whole spirit of what was and will always be The Glider Pilot Regiment.

Appendix II

GERMAN WAR DIARY

SS Panzer Grenadier Depot and Reserve Bn. 16

The Battle at ARNHEM
18 Sep. 1944 – 7 Oct. 1944

Dear Krafft,

SINCERE THANKS FOR YOUR BIRTHDAY WISHES,

Heil Hitler!

Congratulations on the
Arnhem Operation.
Sincere Greetings to you
and your men.

(Signed) H. HIMMLER,
Leader of the SS,
Home Secretary.

HQ in the Field. October 1944.

Part of the 16 Bn under the command of Sturmbandfuhrer KRAFFT, was taken from positions on the coast and brought under von TETTAU'S command as Divisional Reserve in the OOSTERBEEK area. It consisted of HQ and HQ united, Def P1, Trench Mortar, A tk, Flak, Flamethrower and hy Mortar sections, and 2 and 4 coys. A total strength of 12 officers, 65 NCOs and 229 OR. Its operational orders were : —

(a) to recce its own sector along the WAAL with relation to its duties as divisional reserve and take the necessary steps for employment. (b) To prepare for and attack airborne landings. (c) To defend the bridges and ferries over the R. RHINE at ARNHEM and to prepare them ready for demolition.

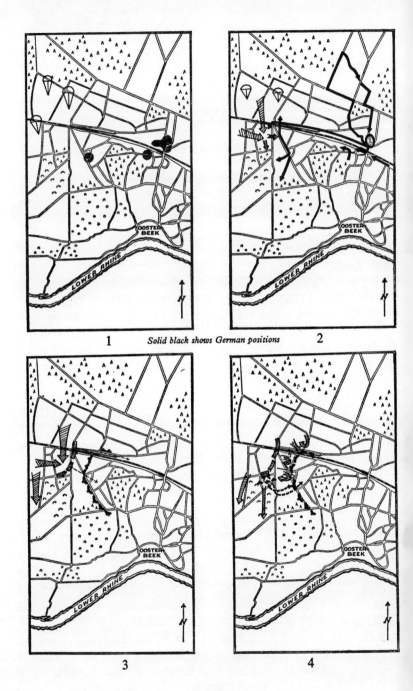

1   *Solid black shows German positions*   2

3   4

The 6th Airborne Division, near Wesel, March, 1945. The troops are pinned down by snipers in the farmhouse in the background.

Airborne troops in action at Arnhem.

Wrecked glider and jeep at Hammelkiln railway station, 1945.

A picture taken from the cockpit of one of the gliders during the journey to the east of the Rhine, March, 1945.

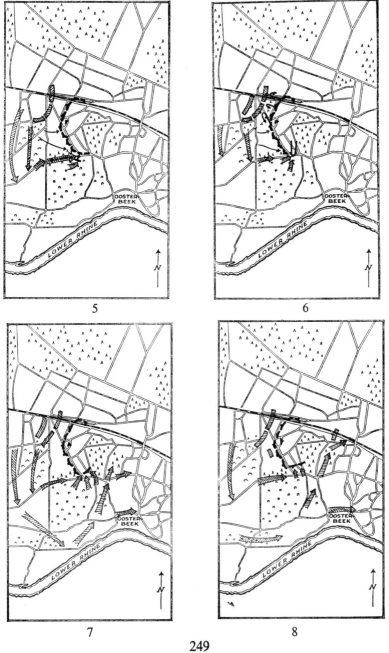

5

6

7

8

249

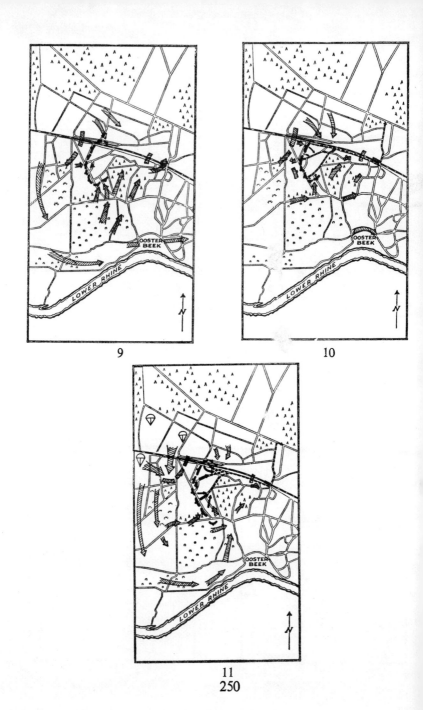

9

10

11

17 Sep. 44
1130 hrs.

About this time, a terrific air bombardment begins on the ARNHEM—DEELEN—WOLFHEZE area.

Observers report the arrival of gliders and paratroops over a large area while the air bombardment is still continuing (Map 1).

(*Note.* It was later recorded that these landings took place some 2–3 kilometres WEST of the Bus sector in the WOLFHEZE area.)

(a) The Bn has orders to attack enemy air landings without delay.

(b) The Bn is in immediate readiness for such action in the vicinity of the DZ. (2 Coy is the nearest unit).

(c) Other units near are the Defence Forces, Army Group. Battle HQ and Army Group B, whose assistance we can probably not depend upon.

(d) 2 SS Panzer Corps lies in the area to the EAST and NE of ARNHEM, but the greatest part of it is said to be on its way to GERMANY. Therefore, we do not know if we can have assistance from this formation.

(e) Thus, the Bn has practically no support and must rely on itself in the imminent battle.

(f) Now that the number of gliders already down has been noted, we consider that the minimum force to be reckoned with is some 3–4,000 strong.

What is the enemy's intention?

(a) To isolate or destroy the Army Group B HQ, whose arrival in OOSTERBEEK is certainly not unknown to him?

To accomplish this, however, he must surround OOSTER-BEEK, but his landings to the NW of the village do not give definite grounds for assuming this to be the case.

(b) To take possession of the aerodrome at DEELEN where the HQ for all DUTCH and WEST GERMAN COMMAND is located?

The bombardment of the aerodrome previously carried out gives weight to this assumption. But if this is his real objective, why didn't he pick a DZ closer, especially as the surrounding district is very suitable for airborne landings?

(c) To advance on ARNHEM, occupy the town and take the RHINE bridges, thus forming a bridgehead for the Allied land forces now advancing through BELGIUM towards NIJMEGEN?

This is the most probable of his intentions, especially as there are more pointers in its favour than for the other two.

It must be taken for certain that the enemy knows what he is doing and the situation of his own battle formation. Which, naturally, makes our job of defence more difficult.

(*Note.* As was discovered later, either this was not the case, or the enemy did not consider that the slight German forces opposing him would offer such stubborn resistance.)

A further difficulty for us is the attitude of the civilian population. They will surely side with the enemy and will be particularly dangerous on the appearance of the enemy in the Bns rear.

(*Note.* As a matter of fact we did have trouble with Dutch terrorists about 2–300 metres from the Bns original defence position. They were suitably dealt with!)

Several possible approaches to Arnhem are open to the enemy from his excellently chosen DZ.

(a) He can go SOUTH towards the RHINE and travel along the river or NORTH to the EDE-ARNHEM rd.

It is most probable that he will follow either of these courses, since he doubtless wants to take both the rly br at OOSTER-BEEK and the rd br at ARNHEM, before we can bring up reinforcements. He will also lose precious time and will not be able to bring up his hy weapons along the RHINE.

(b) The thick woodlands between his DZ and OOSTERBEEK and extensive parkland between there and ARNHEM afford good cover for a rapid advance. Also the WAGENINGEN-ARNHEM rd makes it possible for his motorized and hy weapons to follow up quickly.

(c) A no less favourable way is along the deep rly cutting between OOSTERBEEK and ARNHEM. It provides a quick entry into the centre of the town, and immediate possession of the station provides a good stepping-off place for further objectives. Our only hope of frustrating the enemy's intention, is either to divert him from his drive to ARNHEM or delay him until our own forces can be brought up.

The scheme with most chance of success for us is to have a delaying body of troops facing the WEST and concentrated on the weakest point of the enemy's line. In any case, in the woodlands between the EDE-ARNHEM rly and the WAGENHINGEN-ARNHEM rd. to the WEST of OOSTERBEEK.

In this way the enemy's advance on OOSTERBEEK and ARNHEM can be blocked.

He would then, therefore, be forced either to fight his way through the defence line or lose precious time carrying out a northerly or southerly flanking movement.

We know from experience, that the only way to draw the teeth of an airborne landing with an inferior force, is to drive right into it. From a tactical point of view it would be wrong to play a purely defensive rôle and let the enemy gather his forces unmolested.

2 Coy's position is so favourable that it can be sent into the attack straight away with some hope of success. The other units, being so far away would first have to be brought up, thus losing any surprise that is so necessary. They are, therefore, serving a much better purpose forming a defence line and backing up 2 Coy.

It would be to our advantage also, if we could be certain that all our officers and men had a good knowledge of the terrain.

To conclude, it is still doubtful whether it is better to bring up our rear units, viz., HQ and 4 Coy on foot or by trucks. Of course, the only way of bringing up the heavier weapons—A tk, Flak, Trench Mortars, Flame Throwers and Hy Mortars, which are about 3–4 Kms from DZ—is to bring them up by truck.

4 Coy has the choice of two routes to get into position, one about 6–800 m shorter than the other. The disadvantage of the short route is that it is unsuitable for vehicles. On the other hand, even though the vehicles will RV from their dispersal points, the coy can be brought up sooner by them than by marching, and

irrespective of what the enemy may do, 4 Coy can follow up quicker to harass him, with the extra mobility.

1. 2 Coy will go into attack.

2. 4 and 9 Coys will form a defence line to block the enemy going to ARNHEM.

3. HQ will prepare further measures to succeed this first one.

To execute the CO's plan the following messages are sent out: —

1. To 2 coy, Hotel WOLFHEZE 1500m from the enemy
  "Attack immediately. Send accurate intelligence of enemy's positions."

2. To Bn HQ and 4 Coy
  "Proceed independently in vehicles to Hotel WOLFHEZE. Your orders await you there."

3. To 9 Coy in ARNHEM
  "Proceed to battle positions. Further orders await you there."

4. To Recce Tp MOELLERKE. (Str 1 NCO 3 OR)
  "Inform on rly in direction WOLFHEZE."
To Recce Tp HUEBER
  "Inform on NORTH of EDE-ARNHEM rd."

I wish to know: —

(a) Place of landing, strength and armament of enemy.

(b) Whether motorized.

(c) Eventual direction of advance.

(d) Messages will reach me on rd from here to Hotel WOLFHEZE.

(*Note*. The Recce Tp "M" was captured but escaped four days later. The Recce Tp "H" informed that the area was free of enemy.)

5. To Div von TETTAU.
  "Enemy landed NORTH and NW WOLFHEZE. Strength about two regts. This bn attacking."

6. To rear party.
"Stay where you are. Dig in. Prepare for defence. Keep in touch."

On the assumption that the enemy has landed WEST of 2 Coy's position, the OC orders the coy into attack without first making a recce.

(*Note*. Because of the height of the trees in the wood, the DZ has not been accurately pinpointed.)

To protect his right flank, OC 2 Coy brings the hy MG Sec into position NORTH of WOLFHEZE. From here, it can also cover the heath NORTH OF WOLFHEZE and keep control of it.

Due to inaccurate pinpointing of the enemy's DZ and thus inaccurate placing of the coy the hy MG section find themselves opposite to the DZ.

This favourable position enables the MGs to bring good fire to bear on troops just landed and still landing. They create great confusion and wreak great havoc.

(*Note*. The troops from about four gliders were completely wiped out and the gliders shot to pieces.)

The hy MG sec have been in action about 20 mins and are forced, by fear of encirclement, to vacate their position and rejoin their coy along the WOLFHEZE rd. (Map 2.)

Following message is sent out to all units under command of Bn. HQ.

1. Bulk of enemy in WOLFHEZE. Weaker forces advancing SOUTH in direction WAGENHINGEN-ARNHEM rd.

2. Bn preparing for defence EAST and SE WOLFHEZE in area between EDE-ARNHEM rly and WAGENINGEN-ARNHEM rd in order to prevent further enemy advance. Dig in.

3. Our own forces should link up with us at earliest this evening.

4. Fighting now taking place in WOLFHEZE, along EDE-ARNHEM rly, and along WAGENINGEN-ARNHEM rd in direction WAGENINGEN.

Task: report enemy approach, strength and armament.

5. *Course of FDL.*

In vicinity of rly, 500 metres EAST of WOLFHEZE sta, turning off to SSW along rd to street junction 300 metres WEST Hotel WOLFHEZE, sharp WEST of WOLFHEZE rd to UTRECHSAHE rd 300 WEST of rd junction.

ARNHEM-WAGENINGEN-WOLFHEZE rd junction incl.

6. *Precaution*

Depending on topography, do not form up more than 400 metres front of FDL so that our line becomes screened. If enemy press strongly, withdraw to FDL.

8. *Battle tactics*

(1) Coys will detach reserves to counter-attack any enemy break-through.

(2) Do not desist fighting until ordered.

(3) The enemy will be attacked continuously with shock tps and will be harassed in order to cover our real intentions.

9 Coy arrives at the HQ and remains for a time in reserve. Orders are then given for it to take up position in the rear of the defence line (to the EAST). (Map 3.)

Bn KRAFFT is defending $2\frac{1}{2}$ Km WEST of old posn. Strong recce opposition progress. Night attack intended. Not been in action yet. One prisoner. WOLFHEZE occupied. Enemy recce observed in direction of WAGENINGEN.

We are now in new defence positions. The enemy has recce'd on 4 Coy front and is attacking with two coy strength. Our advance defence beat him off and took prisoners.

An order is sent out to 9 Coy to send a pl of shock tps into position between 2 and 4 Coys. They push into the area SOUTH of WOLFHEZE to prevent further advance of the enemy from NORTH to SOUTH.

At the cost of a heroic platoon commander and his successor, they succeed in dealing the enemy a serious blow and delay the enemy advance to the WAGENINGEN-ARNHEM rd for a considerable time.

Division telephones the Bn: —

"Enemy airlandings at DRIEL, CULENBORG, ZALT-BOMMEL and NIJMEGEN. Attack independently."
The British break through the left flank of 4 Coy in the neighbourhood of Hotel WOLFHEZE. Our gallant soldiers, of 4 Coy, counter-attack and neutralize the enemy's pressure. (Map 4.)

A message comes in from 2 Coy to say that only slight forces are attacking on their front. But their weak left flank is threatened by a two coy force supported by hy infantry and A tk weapons in their positions on the cross-rds WOLFHEZE-OOSTERBEEK-WAGENINGEN-ARNHEM.

Gen. KUSSIN, GOC of ARNHEM district is here. He arrives from the WAGENINGEN-ARNHEM rd via the UTRECHT rd.

He is given the latest intelligence and agrees with the steps taken by the Bn and tells us that the higher command is 2 SS Panzer Corps.

He tells us that on the WAGENINGEN-ARNHEM rd WEST of ARNHEM, he had visited a sentry post manned by the sick, convalescent and odd details of the Bn. They had assured him that all was well.

The general calls on us for all endurance and leaves to return by the same route, but in view of the intelligence just received from 2 coy, the CO requests him to return along the rd by the rly. No, the general will not be put off.

A few minutes later we hear a burst of MG bullets and we have lost a gallant soldier and his three companions. He is surely the first of the German dead in the intense fighting now beginning.

The cross-rds held by 2 Coy are now lost to them, for the enemy increases his pressure, engaging the front as well as the flank, but he pays a heavy price. (Map 5.)

This message is sent to 2 and 9 Coys and OC mixed Mortar Pl:
"Enemy attacking left flank from WOLFHEZE. Cross-rds in enemy hands. Left flank of Bn threatened with encirclement. Reinforced 9 Coy attacking cross-rds. Re-taking cross-rds and preventing further advances along WAGENINGEN-ARNHEM rd.

"One by MG Sec of 2 Coy, Bn Mortar Pl, plus seven more mortars one Flak gun and two 3.7cm A tk guns are supporting attack. A fwd observer of Bn Mortar Pl is directing fire. Line connections to fire positions will be kept secure." (Map 6.)

A message from 4 Coy says that enemy has been beaten off but is concentrating for attack SOUTH and SE WOLFHEZE after his last recces.

Hy trench-mortar is instructed to fire HE and AP shells into this concentration. (Map 7.)

A message comes in from Div von TETTAU:

"A bn from the NORTH will go into attack at 2000 hrs."

We renew our bombardment of the cross-rds bringing our trench mortars to bear on it, but do not gain any ground. We suffer heavy casualties from a counter-attack by a heavily reinforced enemy and only just succeed in beating it back. But the efforts of our heroic soldiers force the enemy to relax his grip on the WAGENINGEN-ARNHEM road, which is so essential for his heavy weapons. Our efforts delay him and he now has to make for the R. RHINE, with small forces, moving in an arc to the SOUTH. But this movement, unhindered by any of our tps means that the enemy is encircling the left flank of the Bn.

We are now almost completely surrounded. There is a small corridor to the NE for the enemy, pushing to the NORTH in the Bn's rear, and he has reached the EDE-ARNHEM rly and cut us off from our supplies. (Map 8.)

At the same time, a stronger force of the enemy (about 3–400 men) is advancing EAST along the R. RHINE.

We have a pl guarding the RHINE ferries, under instructions from Div, and it checks the enemy so successfully that he does not capture the rd bridge at ARNHEM until 2200 hrs. (Map 9).

The ambulance, with wounded, has to go back to Battle HQ because the previously safe rd to OOSTERBEEK, along the rly, is now impossible.

WT message from 4 Coy:

"Coy now in slight contact with enemy. Battle noises in direction of WIEGAND pl."

The increasing enemy pressure on the whole Bn line from the WEST makes it apparent that he intends, under any circumstances, to wipe out the Bn and be in ARNHEM before dark.

We must delay them at all costs, even that of self-sacrifice. We must give the High Command time to put into effect efficient counter-measures to beat the enemy back and to relieve pressure on the Bn and prevent its otherwise certain annihilation.

What possibilities does the situation hold out for us?

(1) We cannot break out to the WEST or SOUTH because of the enemy's strong grip.

(2) We can move out through the undergrowth along the corridor still open to the NE. This attempt would very likely succeed as the enemy's line is thin here. But it would mean discarding and destroying all our heavy weapons and transport—an irreplaceable loss to the Bn. It would also result in lack of co-ordination between the units due to the necessity of dispersing them.

(3) Finally, we can break out to the EAST—the way we came. This plan is not too pleasant—it offers appreciably less chance of success as the enemy has completely blocked the line of retreat. However, it can be done, but with heavy losses.

So we have two alternatives. To take the sure way over the rly, and lose the vehicles and heavy weapons, or force a way through with the total strength of men and material.

The CO makes his decision: —

The Bn will hold its positions until dark and then, with the magnificent fighting spirit the troops have shown up to now, fight through to the EAST.

The enemy are still massing on the cross-rds and are throwing in everything in an attempt to wipe out the Bn. They advance along the WOLFHEZE rd to the NW.

The defending force on this sector, N.C.O.s and men, put up a gallant fight. They are helped by the Bn's heavy weapons, including five sections of trench mortars, and the hy mortars alone fire off 750 bombs. They succeed in their action and the Bn Cd can go ahead with the plan for the break-through.

"Heavy small-arms fire 1–2 km. behind our lines.
Coy attack NORTH of rly repulsed."

1. Bn encircled by enemy. Massed break-through intended after dark. (Map 10.)

2. Hold existing line under all circumstances until then.

4. After darkness, Bn will break-out along rd parallel to rly. "With the advent of darkness, the Bn will fight out the pocket over the EDE-ARNHEM rly NORTH in direction of SCHARS-BERGEN" "Do not count on attack until 2300 hours."

(*Note.* Actually this intended attack did not take place until midday 18 Sep.)

The pls begin, one by one, to retreat, unnoticed by the enemy.

The Bn is given the order to move. Two amn trucks hit at midday and still blazing, restrict the movement of the convoy, which only moves very slowly. The enemy in position in the woods and under the br at the OOSTERBEEK-HOOG rly sta (according to reports from escaped prisoners) attempts to deny the Bn the use of the rd with fire of varying strength. Our losses from enemy mortar fire are small.

We meet the battle gp "SPINDLER" from SS Pz Div "HOHEN-STAUFFEN" on the EDE-ARNHEM rd. They have just reached the battlefield and are now at our disposal.

Thus ended the first day of battle, of the SS Panzer Grenadier Ausbildungs and Reserve Bn 16, which was to be the opening phase to one of the Allies' most crushing defeats.

Before continuing with this diary, the editor takes the liberty of setting down and commenting on the opinions voiced by people of importance. He does so in order to justify the actual steps taken by the Bn CO.

According to these opinions, the CO, after appreciating the enemy's intention, viz., the setting-up of a bridgehead in ARNHEM, should have taken the Bn without delay, to defend the RHINE bridge in ARNHEM.

This would not only have been wrong in view of present-day knowledge of airborne actions, but would also have reversed the most elementary of tactical principles—attack is always the best defence.

Apart from this, a weak bn, merely composed of HQ and two

coys would never have succeeded in this plan in a positive sense because

1. The enemy would have got to ARNHEM in the shortest possible time and would not only have occupied it, but strongly fortified it with the aid of the Dutch terrorists.

The operational intentions of the British could not then have been frustrated, for any who fought against them when they were encircled at OOSTERBEEK, can well imagine how much more difficult it would have been to take an ARNHEM strongly held and fortified, particularly when it is realized what slight forces we had at our disposal.

2. Our own operation in NIJMEGEN, *started in part from the bridgehead SOUTH of ARNHEM,* could no longer have been carried out, once ARNHEM was in enemy hands, and this would have meant, quite possibly, that the Allied armd tps would have achieved the much desired link-up.

3. To keep open the bridge on the NORTH bank of the RHINE would probably have been impossible because of Dutch terrorists, fortified and entrenched in the houses on the NORTH bank of the river. The alternative to this would have been to concentrate the Bn on the bridge, which in the editor's opinion, offered no cover, and would have been a militarily impossible situation, and merely a question of time before the slight forces were outflanked and wiped out.

4. It has been remarked that enemy forces of similar strength held out for four days on the NORTH bank in front of the bridge. Yes, but look at the difference.

(a) Our own forces opposing the enemy here were only a fraction of the enemy's strength.

(b) The enemy had the heaviest A tk defence at his disposal.

(c) Air support in great strength was his for the asking.

(d) Last, but by no means least, he had the valuable assistance of the Dutch terrorists who, quite probably, had also prepared the houses on the NORTH bank for defence, before the landings.

5. On the other hand, the surprise attack put in by 2 Coy and the preparation of a defence line in the woodlands WEST of OOSTERBEEK gave great promise of success even with inferior forces.

The Bn mmst, therefore, still take the view that the suggested alternative (to march into and defend ARNHEM) could never have led to the success which followed the adopted plan.

Success is always the decisive tactic. In any case, the degree of success resulting from the plan carried out by the Bn is for the powers-that-be to decide. Even according to quite cautious estimation, the Bn has:

1. Inflicted the heaviest of losses on the enemy on 17 Sep, even at the expense of heavy losses itself. The enemy's losses were, in fact, ten to fifteen times as heavy as the Bns (see prisoners' statements in the Intelligence Report).

2. Held up the mass of the enemy for 7 hrs and delayed, thereby, the capture of ARNHEM.

3. By delaying him, given our High Command the opportunity of introducing timely and promising counter-measures, principally in respect of the capture of ARNHEM.

4. Thereby initiating the first steps to annihilating the BRITISH 1 Airborne Div, ENGLAND'S finest troops.

To conclude. Great importance must be attached to the action fought by the Bn especially in view of the decisive nature of the Battle of ARNHEM at that time. (One order from Div von TETTAU stated that the HIGH COMMAND "regard the battle as a decisive factor in the fate of the entire German people".)

Comments made in this, and those published in the German press should also be taken into account.

It may be interesting to surmise—with due regard to what has been said above—what would have happened if the Bn had not been employed as it was.

The above could also be the answer to this, since in an intelligence report from Div von TETTAU to WEST HOLLAND Command citing Bn KRAFFT as proof it is stated that " . . . it is wrong for a superior force to be attacked, as destruction of the enemy is out of the question".

The report is all the more astonishing when it is noted that the command to attack was given over the radio at 1620 hrs by Div to the Bn (long after the attack had begun!)

The contradiction of these two facts is obvious.

If this opinion, cited in the report, is correct, the lessons learnt from the handling of airborne troops (confirmed into tactical lessons) are wrong.

The editor's personal opinion is this : —

That while it is not the rule to attack far superior forces, there are occasions when this must be done. And in this present fight for existence by the German people, there are occasions occurring every day when only *a virile offensive spirit can lead to success.*

That is the opinion, often repeated, of our highest War Lord— the Führer—who called to account any officer who shuns an enemy far superior to himself, particularly in a critical situation.

Any commander who had led a Bn of first-class troops back to ARNHEM, even if it had been intended to occupy the town and hold the bridge, should have been summarily court-martialled. That is my opinion.

The situation at the end of Sunday 17 Sep 44 is shown on Map 11.

17 Sep

2245 hrs

Changes in command of the Bn are being made. The Bn is now under the command of SS Pz Div "HOHENSTAUFEN".

18 Sep 44
0200 hrs

2 Coy are now positioned on the WEST perimeter of ARNHEM and the rest of the Bn has arrived at the SCHAARSBERGEN sector and linked up with Bn JUNGHANS.

The rest of the day is spent replenishing stocks of munitions, fuel and rations and the preparation and cleaning of weapons and vehicles for further action. What little defensive action is carried out is inconclusive.

1500 hrs.

The enemy drops large reinforcements and supplies between now and 1640 hrs, in the WOLFHEZE area.

19 Sep 44
1200 hrs.

The first detail given to the new formation is to press from NORTH to SOUTH on a wide front and contact parts of the Div von TETTAU attacking from the WEST.

The first objective is the EDE–ARNHEM rd, the second, the edge of the wood 800m SOUTH of the rd. The EDE–ARNHEM rly is to be reached during the course of the attack.

1600 hrs.

Shortly after the attack begins, the enemy begins new landings and drops supplies. These landings take place on the left flank of the Battle-Gp where Bn KRAFFT is located, SOUTH of the EDE-ARNHEM rd.

4 and 9 Coy, therefore, cross the rd and inflict considerable losses again on the British. This is the only success Bn KRAFFT has as the salient across the rd is withdrawn due to concentric counter-attacks on both its flanks.

9 Coy commander, SS Obersturmfuhrer LEITERITZ, who dies a hero's death, has some very bad luck with his tactics, the coy suffering heavy casualties in consequence.

The Bn Flak Pl registers its first successes—one single-engined aircraft and one twin-engined.

2400 hrs

Our right flank contacts the left flank of Div von TETTAU, thus closing the pocket.

During the night a bn of the Battle Gp attacks the enemy and forces him to retreat SOUTH over the rly, so that the Battle Gp has only small pockets of enemy in the woodlands to mop up in the new attack at 0600 hrs.

20 Sep 44
0830 hrs

Units of Div von TETTAU have leap-frogged past us, so that now, being temporarily free of action, the Battle Gp can go to its new RV on the SCHWEIZER–HOHE sector to prepare for further enemy landings.

No sooner have we left to go to the RV when the enemy threaten to break out of the pocket to the NORTH. All previous orders are rescinded and the two Marine Regts are ordered in to close the gap.

The enemy put up a spirited defence, especially the snipers in the trees, so that the Marines cannot advance any farther.

The enemy now increases pressure on our right flank neighbour, threatening to break through to the EAST. It becomes necessary to withdraw one of the Marine Regts and send it into the attack at the threatened point together with 4 Coy.

4 Coy has to march to ARNHEM to close a gap at the ARNHEM rly sta.

21 Sep 44

During the night the Battle Gp is relieved and sent to ARNHEM. Here, at the request of the CO we take over our own units again.

The Battle Gp receives 500 Marines from the Reception Camp at ZWOLLE, to strengthen it for future tasks.

22 Sep 44

The increasing pressure on the pocket necessitates a defence line along the RHINE, in order to prevent a crossing by the relief force coming from NIJMEGEN. For this, SS PZ Div "HOHENSTAU-FEN" forms a Defence Gp "KRAFFT" under its direct command with orders to mop-up and defend the line of the RHINE.

The first job to be done is to strengthen and extend the right flank so as to close by fire the gap in the perimeter of the pocket, and prevent men and materials from making the crossing.

The hy mortar pl, formed by the bn, continues to have success in the hy fighting. They are able to fire off fifty bombs a day due to well-organized munitions supply. (Map 12.)

23 Sep 44

The day is without incident, intermittent fire by both sides. We bring up amn, captured weapons etc, and, in the light of experience gained on the DUTCH coast, prepare our defensive posns.

A Polish Bde, sent as a relieving or a re-inforcing force for the encircled British Airborne Div, lands SOUTH of the RHINE in DRIEL sector, three km SOUTH of OOSTERBEEK.

24 Sep 44
0815 hrs

To hasten the clearing up of the pocket, all hy weapons fire into it, including the heavy mortar pl and eight French mortars of Bn KRAFFT. Our subsequent attack, however, is not successful.

1630 hrs

Battle Gp HQ receives several direct hits in an air bombardment. Casualties, mostly among Signal personnel, are six dead and eighteen seriously wounded.

During the night the enemy gives us a five hrs hy bombardment in return for the pasting we gave him in the morning. Our casualties are slight.

25 Sep 44

One of our coys is loaned to the Battle Gp on our RIGHT for a further attack on the pocket. The concentrated British forces fight desperately and ferociously for every house and every posn. The attack has little success because our tps have little experience in house and wood-clearing.

Arty and mortar fire is exchanged during the night.

26 Sep 44

Up to about 0400 hrs the RIGHT flank of the Battle Gp receives a hy bombardment put up by the enemy to cover his withdrawal over the river. We realize this in time, and the well-prepared RIGHT flank goes into action. Under the fire of its hy weapons only two/three boatloads get across. Those who are left—15 offrs and 580 ORs are captured in a keen attack in the morning. More than 150 German soldiers and one female signaller are set free at the same time.

27 Sep 44

Now that the pocket is cleared, the 2nd Bn of the Battle Gp is re-formed and joins the Div von TETTAU, on our RIGHT. (Map 13).

28 Sep 44

Enemy arty fire lessens.

A gun at DRIEL, that has done us a lot of harm, is spotted and put out of action by trench mortars.

29 Sep 44

Enemy arty and mortar fire is experienced all day and night, becoming really hy on occasions. A LUFTWAFFE coy joins the Battle Gp but 2 offrs and 120 men are detached until 2400 hrs to a Battle Gp engaged in the brhead at ARNHEM.

Our hy mortars go into action.

30 Sep 44

Enemy arty fire on the EAST sector and mortar fire on the WEST sector.

About 1200 hrs there are signs of stronger enemy motorized movement in the DRIEL area.

1 Oct 44

More arty and mortar fire, heaviest in the morning.

All our hy weapons are directed on the Driel area between the rly and the village.

2 Oct 44

During the night of the 1/2 Oct fire from hy mortars and captured weapons was directed on to DRIEL.

Under orders from Div, two reserve coys each equipped with 6LMGs and 4 Hy MGs are to be held in readiness against any future landings. The CO of the Battle Gp is to have complete command of them.

3 Oct 44

Intermittent fire all day. All the hy weapons of Bn "KRAFFT" are to be used in support of an attack by assault tps tomorrow (4th).

1800 hrs

The assault tp detachment—NCOs and men of the 16 SS Pz Gren Bn are sent to the Battle Gp "von RAUTENFELD".

During the night, they cross the RHINE to the brhead, which is to be the SP.

4 Oct 44

They start at first light and adv in open order in an easterly direction SOUTH of WAGENINGEN.

5 Oct 44

The assault is supported by directed fire on the bns hy weapons. Due to having many and well-prepared OPs the bn was able to give continuous and accurate fire in support. The OPs were so well connected that the bn was able to give the higher HQs infm quickly, and an immediate exploitation was possible.

6 Oct 44

Enemy fire continues all day and at times reaches unprecedented ferocity. This is particularly so in the VERHUIS and areas either side of the rly (1000m SOUTH of the rly br).

At night this operation ends, posns are dug and barbed wire defences set up.

EPILOGUE

The relatively high losses sustained by the bn proves the toughness and fine offensive spirit of the offrs and men. Proof of this is the award of decorations to such a large proportion—decorations won for bravery and resolution.

An SS Heroes Cemetery was prepared by the bn in VELP near ARNHEM to give our honourable dead a worthy resting place.

In spite of the short time available, the bn, through diligent work, prepared it as a memorial and an exhaltation to all passers-by.

1. *OWN TROOPS*

(a) *Composition and Battle-value.*

The Bn Krafft had a fighting strength of 12 offrs, 65 NCOs and 223 ORs at the beginning, and was later increased to 13 offrs 73 NCOs and 349 ORs.

The Bn was mainly composed of half-trained 17 to 19-year-old personnel, 40 per cent of it graded not fit for action. The NCOs enthusiasm and determination can only be described as astounding. Even when the Bn was surrounded and fighting against hy odds, the morale was unshakeable. This was the more astonishing as most of them had not been blooded. A proof of the morale is that all who were taken prisoner subsequently escaped.

This high morale can be put down to two factors:

(i) Thorough training in the NCOs corps.

(ii) Training in world philosophy thoroughly imparted by 2/Lt RAULI, who unfortunately was killed in action. The following conclusions can be drawn from this:

(i) It is possible to fight hy battles with forces still under training.

(ii) They must, however, be well led and fully understand world philosophy.

(iii) Only a good standard of training and of world philosophy to-gether gives a high combat value to personnel.

(iv) Training in cover and camouflage, drilled in to the point of vexation, and thorough weapon training have helped appreciably towards strengthening morale.

(b) *Attached Personnel—Marines*

In the course of the battle, two bns of Marines were att to the bn to form the Battle Gp. As these bns were trained with respect to naval fighting, it is natural that they were not entirely suitable as inf, particularly in attack, but they did not lack keenness or courage. Particularly was this the case for one of the bns, which was from a reception camp and therefore not of the elite. As the too few offrs and NCOs were also not inf-trained, they must have found it most

s

difficult leading their men. Under these conditions, therefore, too much success could not be expected from these tps.

On 23 Sep 44, a further force of 500 men without offrs and almost without NCOs was sent to the Battle Gp as reinforcements. This meant that the Battle Gp had to form them into coys, increase their efficiency and distribute them for the coming defensive fight on the NORTH bank of the Rhine. In this the Battle Gp tried an experiment, with good results. That was to stiffen them with SS personnel, so that all coy, Pl and section commanders were SS. This led to some difficulties, but under the energetic guidance of these commanders, the marines soon learned enough of cover, camouflage and entrenching to make them useful in defence.

Here, too, a well-thought-out world philosophy was apparent and the men were grateful for the concern shown for them. This was really necessary, as they had been sent out to the front without greatcoats, blankets, or even the most necessary articles of equipment.

2. THE ENEMY

(a) Composition and Battle Value

The tps were about 25 years of age on the average, and the best type, mentally and physically. They all had had some five or six years service and most of them were veterans of NORTH AFRICA, SICILY, ITALY and NORMANDY. They were well-trained, particularly for independent fighting and of good combat value. Even so, they were no better than the best German tps.

All positive things said above about the tps apply even more so to the NCOs.

The offrs, graded up in rank according to age, were the finest of the whole British Army. Very well schooled, personally hard, persevering and brave, they made an outstanding impression.

(b) Tactics

The German and British tactics and battle management correspond somewhat, at least at bn stage, and therefore we could anticipate enemy moves to a certain extent. Through our recces, carried out immediately after the landings, we discovered enemy weaknesses at an early stage and were able to exploit them at once.

Some of the principal enemy weaknesses are: —

(i) He lacks the courageous and resolute advance.

(ii) When opposing tps are steadfast, he prefers to withdraw to his starting point instead of digging-in.

These points confirm previous experiences against the enemy.

His tree and ground snipers were used in great numbers and caused us many cas.

Quickly constructed positions differ from the German pattern— a hole about five or six feet deep and about one sq yd in area, with a parapet of several logs about 10cm thick used to increase the height and act as a rifle-rest. As these positions were usually in woods, they could not be seen from the air.

He employs hy inf weapons at strong points, in the same way as ourselves, and therefore is restricted to roads in spite of the cross-country capabilities of his vehs. The airborne forces did not bring any armour with them.

In house fighting the enemy was very skilled and had a great advantage over our tps, who, it must be remembered, were not all of our best type.

The enemy comd exploited, with great cleverness, our weakest points in order to get breathing space, and thereby delayed the mopping up of the pocket, in which, it can be said, the battle was fluid.

Prisoners stated that the British adhere to, and have always adhered to, the Geneva Conventions. They allowed our Red Cross flags to go unmolested.

Jeeps (German spelling Sceps) were brought in large numbers. These small vehs are a fast general-purpose type with a powerful tractive effort. They are converted to either carry radio equipment and LMGs or to carry stretcher cases.

Behaviour in Captivity

Extremely soldierly and disciplined.

NCOs seldom made statements and offrs practically none.

However the men, due to moral exhaustion from the rigours of the battle, did talk, but they either knew nothing or very little about the essential things.

Many of the prisoners showed great anxiety due to the erroneous idea that the Waffen SS shot all prisoners. A Fl/Lt GODMAN declared that whilst this was not officially advertised in England, it was generally understood.

Unfortunately the NCOs were not always separated from the men but the offrs always were.

The immediate searching of all prisoners yielded valuable infm, particularly for the higher cmds.

Treatment of Prisoners

The enemy treated our own prisoners quite well. The 150 of them were kept caged on a tennis court near OOSTERBEEK and were there exposed to our own hy fire. Food supply was short but so it was for the British as well—they were nearly starving.

Valuables like rings, watches, etc., were always taken away but papers were given back after examination.

The Britisher expects soldierly bearing and discipline even from his prisoners. There is one case where a Captain interrogating a German soldier knocked the cigarette from his hand and demanded a correct deportment from him.

The British Div Comd is said to have appeared on the tennis court one day and told the prisoners that if they did not show more soldierly bearing and discipline, he would have them all locked-up.

Searching of the prisoners was superficial. One German NCO kept a grenade concealed in his trousers pocket and escaped by killing his guard with it.

Method of Landings and pre-operation precautions.

The DZ was doubtless very well chosen in view of the objectives —to take ARNHEM and establish a brhead (see appreciation of the situation in the War Diary).

As the surface of the DZ was of strong turf and there were woods surrounding it, the tps could land well and get into cover in the shortest possible time. Nor could it be seen from several main rds.

This choice was to our advantage as well, for the enemy's intentions were quickly recognized and suitable counter-measures taken.

Several things were noticed on the landings. The gliders came in from the SOUTH and cast off just before reaching their LZ, on which they landed after one spiral, the time elapsing between cast-off and landing being two minutes. The tug planes went off to the WEST.

These landings went off according to plan, the gliders finishing up about 50 to 100 metres apart.

The Paratps jumped from an estimated height of 70 to 100 metres and were in a high degree of concentration. They took about as long a time as the gliders in landing.

Since the enemy landed in forces almost formed-up, there can be no talk of a so-called "assembly period".

The total landings took an hour because the planes came over in waves.

Time needed to assemble a bn on the ground, ready for action, would be about fifteen minutes.

About thirty men can be carried in a glider and, thanks to their good weapons, can go into defence immediately and be able to go into the attack after a few minutes. The 4th and 9th Coys experienced this on 19 Sep.

The tail part of the glider swings open to the side and the vehs towing the hy weapons leave by running down rails or a ramp. These weapons, like the A tk gun, etc., are ready to go into action straight away.

It can be learnt from this that it is vitally important to attack the enemy immediately with any forces available, not with any hope of destroying him but to disturb and disrupt his preparations for battle. It is not possible to destroy overwhelming airborne forces with slight forces, but one can pin him down to secure time to prepare counter-measures.

The gliders are most vulnerable between casting-off and landing.

The British tps had been taken from their transit camps to different districts in England and had travelled at night to an aerodrome somewhere near London. Very few people, therefore, knew from where they had taken off. An offr prisoner gave us the first indication, for he had in his pocket a London paper of 17 Sep.

Offrs and NCOs certainly seem to have been accurately briefed as to the imminent operation, for a large number of accurate maps were captured. These were of the DZ E Holland and W Germany, particularly the RUHR area.

It is reasonable to presume that the ARNHEM operation had been practised previously but this cannot be proved.

Pre-landing Intelligence

The British Intelligence Service had prepared absolutely fully, accurately and in detail for the operation.

All data necessary for the occupation of ARNHEM was found— military, police, industrial and party offices. Heads of services, their representatives, and such details as their telephone numbers were recorded.

The following was known about our Bn:

Name, address and telephone number of the coys. All the barracks, with accurate estimates of numbers of personnel, state of training, quality of personnel, etc. This information, however, dated from the previous May.

Infm was given about supply dumps, tank positions and prisoners (the main prison between ARNHEM and OOSTERBEEK was opened by the British and the prisoners released).

An accurate plan of ARNHEM was found, complete with street names.

On the maps all flak positions were indicated, even on the aerodromes. The following point is interesting:

On the 8 Sep 44 the Bn took up positions in OOSTERBEEK and on the 9th moved out to the northern perimeter of the town. Two days later the 2cm flak pl was brought here. Maps found not only indicated this position but had it printed on. This particular flak pl, a serious menace to airborne landings, was attacked by armed Dutch terrorists during the two nights preceding the landings.

Political Convictions.

Not much infm on political convictions has been gleaned but it is known that, in England, when the truth conflicts with the military powers, the truth is withheld. In this respect, chalked inscriptions on the gliders are interesting: —

"We are the Al Capone Gang"

"Up the Reds"

"Up with the frauleins' skirts"

How far this is connected with the political convictions of the tps themselves or whether it is due to Bolshevist or American influences is not known.

Mistakes in Tactical Handling

The adversary only made one big mistake, and that not only thwarted his own intentions but exposed him to destruction.

In the opinion of the writer, if the enemy had pushed straight on to ARNHEM after having surrounded the Bn instead of trying to wipe it out, he would have succeeded in capturing the town. The Dutch terrorists were waiting there for him and were fully prepared to render him assistance.

Defence against Gliders.

For a long time standing orders of the German Army have been that "enemy aircraft will be attacked with all inf weapons". How much more important is this in the case of gliders, being a larger and slower target. It has been found on examination, that nearly every shot gets home. The gliders were holed by countless hits and the bloodstains inside showed that the enemy had suffered quite appreciable cas in the air.

Reaction of Dutch Civilians

Like the civilians of France and Belgium, the Dutch could not await the appearance of the "Liberators" with enough patience. In OOSTERBEEK, the British tps were received with flags, flowers, drinks and open arms. The Dutch terrorists, armed in part with German weapons and wearing the colours of the House of Orange, reinforced the British to an appreciable degree, their chief task being to create confusion and disturbance and to work towards the capture of ARNHEM. In OOSTERBEEK they went into action simultaneously with the landings.

General.

On the night 3/4 Sep 44, Bn HQ and two coys were moved into positions on the WAAL, the other four coys remaining on the coast for the time being. The difficulties arising from this—going into action well under str—can now be realized. If it had been at full str, the encircling movement round the LEFT flank would probably have been averted with better prospects of destroying the enemy. The enemy adv along the Rhine would have been stopped as well.

Thus, a rigid and resolute cmd on both fronts was impossible, and to what extent this was tactically necessary to higher cmd cannot be said here.

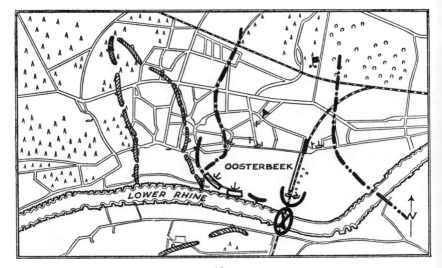

12

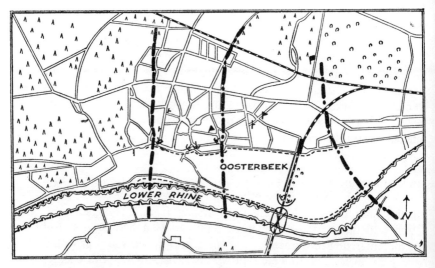

13

INDEX